EXPLORATIONS IN LOCAL AND REGIONAL HISTORY

Centre for Regional and Local History, University of Hertfordshire
and
Centre for English Local History, University of Leicester

SERIES EDITORS: NIGEL GOOSE AND CHRISTOPHER DYER

Previous titles in this series

Volume 1: *Landscapes Decoded: the origins and development of Cambridgeshire's medieval fields*
by SUSAN OOSTHUIZEN
(ISBN 978-1-902806-58-7)

Volume 2: *The Self-Contained Village? the social history of rural communities, 1250–1900*
edited by CHRISTOPHER DYER
(ISBN 978-1-902806-59-4)

Volume 3: *Deserted Villages Revisited*
edited by CHRISTOPHER DYER AND RICHARD JONES
(ISBN 978-1-905313-79-2)

THORPS IN A
CHANGING LANDSCAPE

BY PAUL CULLEN, RICHARD JONES
AND DAVID N. PARSONS

UNIVERSITY OF HERTFORDSHIRE PRESS

Explorations in Local and Regional History

Volume 4

First published in Great Britain in 2011 by
University of Hertfordshire Press
College Lane
Hatfield
Hertfordshire
AL10 9AB

British Library Cataloguing in Publication Data
A catalogue record for this book is available from the British Library

ISBN 978-1-902806-82-2

Design by Geoff Green Book Design, CB24 4RA
Printed in Great Britain by Hobbs the Printers Ltd, SO40 3WX

Contents

Figures

Tables

Abbreviations

ASC	*Anglo-Saxon Chronicle*
Cameron, Dict. LIN	K. Cameron, *Dictionary of Lincolnshire place-names* (Nottingham, 1998)
CDEPN	V. Watts, *Cambridge dictionary of English place-names* (Cambridge, 2004)
DB	Domesday Book (Phillimore)
DEPN	E. Ekwall, *The concise Oxford dictionary of English place-names* (1936; 4th edn, Oxford, 1960)
EHR	*English Historical Review*
EPNE	A.H. Smith, *English place-name elements*, 2 vols (Cambridge, 1956)
EPNS	English Place-Name Society
GDB	Great Domesday Book
HER	Historic Environment Register
JEPNS	*Journal of the English Place-Name Society*
Lat	Latin
LDB	Little Domesday Book
MSRG	Medieval Settlement Research Group
ODan	Old Danish
OE	Old English
OED	J. Simpson (ed.), *The Oxford English dictionary*, 3rd edn, online at www.dictionary.oed.com
OEG	A. Campbell, *Old English grammar* (Oxford, 1959)
OFr	Old French
OGer	Old German
ON	Old Norse
OS	Ordnance Survey
pers.n.	personal name
RCHME	Royal Commission on Historical Monuments (England)

S	P.H. Sawyer, *Anglo-Saxon Charters* (London, 1968)
SMA	*South Midlands Archaeology*
SMR	Sites and Monuments Record
SPNLY	G. Fellows-Jensen, *Scandinavian personal names in Lincolnshire and Yorkshire* (Copenhagen, 1968)
SPNN	J. Insley, *Scandinavian personal names in Norfolk* (Uppsala, 1994)
SSNEM	G. Fellows-Jensen, *Scandinavian settlement names in the East Midlands* (Copenhagen, 1978)
SSNY	G. Fellows-Jensen, *Scandinavian settlement names in Yorkshire* (Copenhagen, 1972)
TLAHS	*Transactions of the Leicestershire Archaeological and History Society*
TRE	Tempore regis Edwardi
VEPN	D.N. Parsons *et al.*, *The vocabulary of English place-names*, in progress (Nottingham, 1997–)

Abbreviations for EPNS volumes

EPNS BED & HNT	A. Mawer and F.M. Stenton, *The place-names of Bedfordshire and Huntingdonshire*, EPNS vol. 3 (Cambridge, 1926)
EPNS BRK	M. Gelling, *The place-names of Berkshire*, 3 parts, EPNS vols 49–51 (Cambridge, 1973–6)
EPNS BUC	A. Mawer and F.M. Stenton, *The place-names of Buckinghamshire*, EPNS vol. 2 (Cambridge, 1925)
EPNS CAM	P.H. Reaney,*The place-names of Cambridgeshire and the Isle of Ely*, EPNS vol. 19 (Cambridge, 1943)
EPNS CUM	A.M. Armstrong, A. Mawer, F.M. Stenton and B. Dickins, *The place-names of Cumberland*, 3 parts, EPNS vols 20–22 (Cambridge, 1950–2)
EPNS DEV	J.E.B. Gover, A. Mawer and F.M. Stenton, *The place-names of Devon*, 2 parts, EPNS vols 8 and 9 (Cambridge, 1931 and 1932)
EPNS DOR	A.D. Mills, *The place-names of Dorset*, 4 parts, EPNS vols 52–3, 59–60 (Nottingham, 1977–89)
EPNS DRB	K. Cameron, *The place-names of Derbyshire*, 3 parts, EPNS vols 27–29 (Cambridge, 1959)
EPNS DUR	V. Watts, *The place-names of County Durham*, EPNS vol. 83 (Nottingham, 2007)
EPNS ESX	P.H. Reaney, *The place-names of Essex*, EPNS vol. 12 (Cambridge, 1935)
EPNS GLO	A.H. Smith, *The place-names of Gloucestershire*, 4 parts, EPNS vols 38–41 (Cambridge, 1964–5)
EPNS HRT	J.E.B. Gover, A. Mawer and F.M. Stenton, *The place-names of*

	Hertfordshire, EPNS vol. 15 (Cambridge, 1938)
EPNS LEI	B. Cox, *The place-names of Leicestershire*, 3 parts, EPNS vols 75, 78, 81 (Nottingham, 1998–2009)
EPNS LIN	K. Cameron with J. Field and J. Insley, *The place-names of Lincolnshire*, 7 parts, EPNS vols 58, 64–65, 66, 71, 73, 77, 85 (Nottingham, 1985–2010)
EPNS NFK	K.I. Sandred and B. Lindström, with B. Cornford and P. Rutledge, *The place-names of Norfolk*, 3 parts, EPNS vols 61, 72, 79 (Nottingham, 1989–2002)
EPNS NTH	J.E.B. Gover and F.M. Stenton, *The place-names of Northamptonshire*, EPNS vol. 10 (Cambridge, 1933)
EPNS NTT	J.E.B. Gover, A. Mawer and F.M. Stenton, *The place-names of Nottinghamshire*, EPNS vol. 17 (Cambridge, 1940)
EPNS OXF	M. Gelling, based on material collected by D.M. Stenton, *The place-names of Oxfordshire*, 2 parts, EPNS vols 23, 24 (Cambridge, 1953 and 1954)
EPNS RUT	B. Cox, *The place-names of Rutland*, EPNS vols 67–69 (Nottingham, 1994)
EPNS SUR	J.E.B. Gover, A. Mawer and F.M. Stenton, with A. Bonner, *The place-names of Surrey*, EPNS vol. 11 (Cambridge, 1934)
EPNS WAR	J.E.B. Gover, A. Mawer and F.M. Stenton, with F.T.S. Houghton, *The place-names of Warwickshire*, EPNS vol. 13 (Cambridge, 1936)
EPNS WLT	J.E.B. Gover, A. Mawer and F.M. Stenton, *The place-names of Wiltshire*, EPNS vol. 16 (Cambridge, 1939)
EPNS WML	A.H. Smith, *The place-names of Westmorland*, 2 parts, EPNS vols 42, 43 (Cambridge, 1967)
EPNS WOR	J.E.B. Gover, A. Mawer and F.M. Stenton with F.T.S. Houghton, *The place-names of Worcestershire*, EPNS vol. 4 (Cambridge, 1927)
EPNS YOE	A.H. Smith, *The place-names of the East Riding of Yorkshire and York*, EPNS vol. 14 (Cambridge, 1937)
EPNS YON	A.H. Smith, *The place-names of the North Riding of Yorkshire*, EPNS vol. 5 (Cambridge, 1928)
EPNS YOW	A.H. Smith, *The place-names of the West Riding of Yorkshire*, 8 parts, EPNS vols 30–37 (Cambridge, 1961–3)

County abbreviations

BED	Bedfordshire
BRK	Berkshire

BUC	Buckinghamshire
CAM	Cambridgeshire
CHE	Cheshire
CMB	Cumberland
CRN	Cornwall
DEV	Devon
DRB	Derbyshire
DOR	Dorset
DRH	Durham
ESS	Essex
GLO	Gloucestershire
HER	Herefordshire
HMP	Hampshire
HNT	Huntingdonshire
HRT	Hertfordshire
KNT	Kent
LEI	Leicestershire
LIN	Lincolnshire
LNC	Lancashire
MDX	Middlesex
NFK	Norfolk
NTB	Northumberland
NTH	Northamptonshire
NTT	Nottinghamshire
OXF	Oxfordshire
RUT	Rutland
SFK	Suffolk
SHR	Shropshire
SOM	Somerset
SSX	Sussex
STF	Staffordshire
SUR	Surrey
WAR	Warwickshire
WLT	Wiltshire
WML	Westmorland
WOR	Worcestershire
YOE	Yorkshire East Riding
YON	Yorkshire North Riding
YOW	Yorkshire West Riding

Series Editors' Preface

The series of *Explorations in Local and Regional History* is a continuation and development of the 'Occasional Papers' of the University of Leicester's Department of English Local History, a series started by Herbert Finberg in 1952. This succeeding series is published by the University of Hertfordshire Press, which has a strong profile in English local and regional history. The idea for the new series came from Harold Fox, who, with Nigel Goose, served as series editor in its first two years.

Explorations in Local and Regional History has three distinctive characteristics. First, the series is prepared to publish work on novel themes, to tackle fresh subjects – perhaps even unusual ones. We hope that it serves to open up new approaches, prompt the analysis of new sources or types of source, and foster new methodologies. This is not to suggest that more traditional scholarship in local and regional history are unrepresented, for it may well be distinctive in terms of its quality, and we also seek to offer an outlet for work of distinction that might be difficult to place elsewhere.

This brings us to the second feature of the series, which is the intention to publish mid-length studies, generally within the range of 40,000 to 60,000 words. Such studies are hard to place with existing publishers, for while there are current series that cater for mid-length overviews of particular historiographical topics or themes, there is none of which we are aware that offers similar outlets for original research. *Explorations*, therefore, intends to fill the publishing vacuum between research articles and full-length books (the latter, incidentally, might well be eligible for inclusion in the existing University of Hertfordshire Press series, *Studies in Regional and Local History*).

Third, while we expect this series to be required reading for both academics and students, it is also our intention to ensure that it is of interest and relevance to local historians operating outside an institutional framework. To this end we ensure that each volume is set at a price that individuals, and not only university libraries, can generally afford. Local and regional history is a subject taught at many levels, from schools to universities. Books, magazines, television and radio all testify to the vitality of research and writing outside universities, as well as to the sustained growth of popular interest. It is hoped that *Explorations in Local and Regional History* will make a contribution to the continued flourishing of our subject. We will ensure that books in the series are accessible to a wide readership, that they avoid technical language and jargon, and that they will usually be illustrated.

This preface, finally, serves as a call for proposals, and authors who are studying local themes in relation to particular places (rural or urban), regions, counties or provinces, whether their subject matter comprises social groups (or other groups), landscapes, interactions and movements between places, microhistory or total history should consider publication with this series. The editors can be consulted informally at the addresses given below, while a formal proposal form is available from the University of Hertfordshire Press at uhpress@herts.ac.uk.

Nigel Goose
Centre for Regional and Local History
Department of Humanities
University of Hertfordshire
College Lane
Hatfield AL10 9AB
N.Goose@herts.ac.uk

Christopher Dyer
Centre for English Local History
Marc Fitch Historical Institute
5 Salisbury Road
Leicester LEI 7QR
cd50@le.ac.uk

Preface and Acknowledgements

Looking back, it seems so obvious that if you look at a group of places sharing a core name, think of them as a family having something in common which binds them together, and interrogate the evidence they provide from a variety of perspectives, insights into their origins and development should follow. Indeed, so simple is this idea that it seems extraordinary that no full-length studies of this kind have preceded that which is presented here. It would be wonderful to claim that we understood the need for a new approach to the subject of early medieval rural settlement. And it would be wonderful too to be able to claim that we knew, as we embarked upon this research, that it would result in a total re-evaluation not only of the settlements that form the focus of this book but also some of the fundamental processes which have played such a large part in the creation of the English rural landscape we see today. None of this could be further from the truth.

This collaboration began as three separate invitations to speak about the *thorps* and *throps* found in England at the Second International Torp Conference held in Malmö in April 2007. In a spirit of national collegiality, and fearing that our contributions might contradict each other, the three of us got together to discuss the various approaches we proposed to take. At this stage our objectives were far from ambitious. We would review the linguistic, archaeological and topographical evidence for *thorps* and *throps* for an international audience; and we would seek to identify the strengths and weaknesses of the widely held view that *thorps* were minor settlements, late arrivals in the English landscape, and dependent in some way on more central places. We went our separate ways promising to keep each other informed of our progress and share any flashes of inspiration that we might have. To our surprise these not only came fast but complemented each other. Out of subsequent discussions emerged the hypothesis that is set out in this book, ideas first tried out in what became a joint presentation at Malmö.

Our thanks, then, go to Peder Gammeltoft, whose invitation it was that first prompted this investigation. The kind reception that our ideas received at that conference encouraged us to take things further. Since then, we have had the opportunity to present our thoughts on other occasions: to the English Place-Name Society, at the University of Leicester Medieval Seminar Series, to the AHRC-funded Sense of Place in Anglo-Saxon England workshops and to local groups such as the Countesthorpe Local History Society and Melton Mowbray Historical Society. Looming over each airing of our ideas was the fear that our house of cards would be exposed for what it was and knocked over. This has not happened, although we are happy to acknowledge that the constructive criticism we received on these occasions has helped us to ground some of our wilder flights of fancy. We must express our grateful thanks to Harold Fox for the interest he showed in this project, the encouragement he gave to pursue it further and his approval of its publication in this series which he helped to establish. As a historian, historical geographer and place-name scholar, Harold approved of our approach, and this has meant much to us, for we all knew him well. We are sure that he would have had much to say about our hypothesis and it is extremely sad that his untimely death has deprived us of his insightful comments and criticism. The *Explorations* series is intended to act as an outlet for novel ideas and new approaches, and we have endeavoured to write this book in the spirit that Harold Fox and Nigel Goose expected for the series. Finally, we must thank the present editors of this series, Nigel Goose and Christopher Dyer, as well as the University of Hertfordshire Press, for the patience that they have shown as we dallied over its completion and for the improvements to the text that they have suggested.

The Aurelius Trust generously provided a grant to cover the costs of reproducing the maps and photographs in this volume.

Paul Cullen
Richard Jones
David N. Parsons

1

Introducing thorps

Thorps – in some areas *throps* – are familiar elements in the named landscape of much of England. In many instances they announce themselves to visitors and passers-by proudly and without disguise: Althorp NTH, the focus of national attention in 1997; or Mablethorpe LIN, seaside destination for land-locked Midlanders and inspiration for Tennyson's eponymous poem (Figure 1.1). Elsewhere they lie hidden from view behind a variety of spellings, only to be discovered by those who enquire within: Cock-a-Troop Cottages WLT; Eastrip SOM; Droop DOR; Burdrop OXF; Thrupp, Hatherop and Puckrup GLO.

Unlike places taking other commonly encountered generic name elements, such as -hām or -tūn, -worth or -burh, -lēah or -feld, thorps and *throps* are synonymous with the English countryside. When seen on road signs, they invariably point towards villages, hamlets or individual farms. Today only Scunthorpe LIN is a

Figure 1.1 Postcard of the beach and dunes at Mablethorpe LIN.

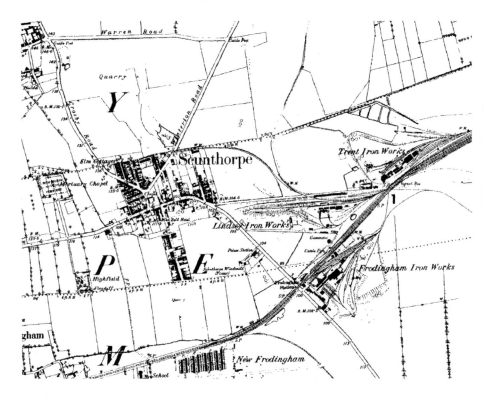

Figure 1.2 The early stages of urbanisation at Scunthorpe captured on the first edition OS map, 1889–90.

town of any size, having grown from a small village with the establishment of its iron foundry and the coming of the railway, a process captured by the first edition Ordnance Survey map (Figure 1.2). No other *thorp* or *throp* can compete in size with, say, a Birmingham WAR or a Taunton SOM, a Tamworth WAR or a Market Harborough NTH, a Burnley LAN or a Mansfield NTT. Even places taking the Old Norse term -bȳ, with which the *thorps* are most often associated, can boast in their midst towns such as Derby DRB, Grimsby LIN and Corby NTH.

By contrast, names such as Ringlethorpe LEI, Scagglethorpe YON, Algarthorpe DRB and Buslingthorpe LIN conjure up images of small, quiet, bucolic places, an impression rarely betrayed if the traveller turns off the major routes and down rural back lanes to visit them. It is unsurprising, then, to find that poets have found inspiration in their peaceful surroundings. *Thorps* have come to symbolise a bygone age, the lost rural idyll.

> Yes, I remember Adlestrop –
> The name, because one afternoon
> Of heat the express-train drew up there

Unwontedly. It was late June.
The steam hissed. Someone cleared his throat.
No one left and no one came
On the bare platform. What I saw
Was Adlestrop – only the name.
And willows, willow-herb, and grass,
And meadowsweet, and haycocks dry,
No whit less still and lonely fair
Than the high cloudlets in the sky.
And for that minute a blackbird sang
Close by, and round him, mistier,
Farther and farther, all the birds
Of Oxfordshire and Gloucestershire.[1]

The thorp heartland lies north and east of the line of Watling Street, now the A5, and comprises the north-east Midland counties of Leicestershire, Nottinghamshire, Derbyshire, Lincolnshire and north-east Northamptonshire (Figure 1.3). These were the Five Boroughs of the Danelaw, where Scandinavian influence in place-naming is most clear. Some sense of their density in the medieval landscape can be gauged from sources such as the Leicestershire Survey, compiled c.1130: in the small administrative unit of Seal Hundred, no more than a few square miles in extent, we find no fewer than four thorps – Boothorpe, Donisthorpe, Oakthorpe and Osgathorpe.[2] Thorps are and were thick on the ground in Yorkshire and Norfolk too. In these various settings the words of another of Tennyson's poems find resonance:

By thirty hills I hurry down
Or slip between the ridges
By twenty thorps, a little town
And half a hundred bridges[3]

Although conspicuous by their near-total absence in Cambridgeshire, outlying thorps are found in Northumberland and Cumbria, and some even spill over south and west of Watling Street – but this is really throp (rather than thorp) country, and

---

1   A.G. Thomas, The collected poems of Edward Thomas (Oxford, 1978), pp. 71–3. A landscape historian might point out that in 1917, when the poem was first published, Adlestrop station was located on the borders of Worcestershire and Gloucestershire. The nearest Oxfordshire bird was one mile away and inaudible!

2   C.F. Slade, The Leicestershire Survey c. AD 1130: a new edition, Department of English Local History Occasional Papers 7 (Leicester, 1956), p. 19.

3   Alfred, Lord Tennyson, 'The Brook', in Maud and other poems (London, 1869), p. 118.

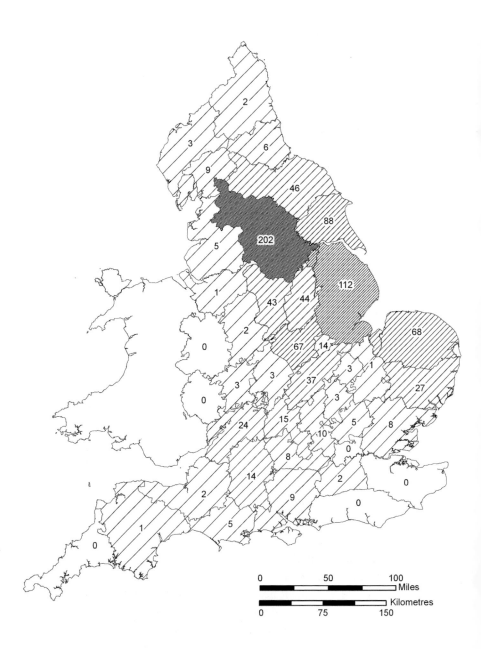

Figure 1.3 Density of *thorps* and *throps* mapped by historic county.

certainly becomes so the further one leaves the Roman road and the Danelaw behind. There are notable concentrations of such names in Oxfordshire, Gloucestershire and Wiltshire, while surrounding counties such as Dorset, Hampshire, Herefordshire, Worcestershire and Warwickshire have their own smattering of *throp* names too. Isolated on the south-western edge of their distribution is a single example in south Devon.

This book is about these places. It will challenge the current consensus that *thorps* have always been marginal settlements in the English countryside. What is presented develops existing work by integrating linguistic, archaeological and topographical approaches and, for the first time, treats both the *thorps* of the Danelaw and the *throps* of the south together. Particular attention will be paid to the relationship between the *thorps* and the *throps*. Do similar name-types represent two distinct and unconnected groups of settlements operating in different ways within the pre-Conquest landscape? Or are they so closely interrelated that they belong together and represent a single settlement phenomenon? We will show that it is possible to suggest a context for the creation of these place-names which locates them – in both time and space – in a rapidly developing English landscape. Far from being simple by-products of these events, we will propose that these apparently unassuming places may have played an integral and active part in the changes that revolutionised agricultural practice across a large belt of the country between c.850 and 1250.

Histories and approaches

There is much of interest to be extracted from the later histories of the *thorps* and *throps*, in their contrasting fates or continuing tenacity to exist within the English countryside in the face of social and economic change. And it is often in the better-recorded periods that clues to their undocumented origins – the principal concern of this book – may be found. Consequently, what can be gleaned of the form and function of *thorps* and *throps* in the later medieval period is a critical starting point for any retrogressive analysis which seeks to elucidate their beginnings. Nor should we ignore their post-medieval histories. As a group of settlements, *thorps* and *throps* have tended, over the last 500 or so years, to share a narrow set of common experiences. Some have simply been consumed by growing towns and cities: Shelthorpe and Thorpe Acre LEI, engulfed by the expansion of Loughborough, are just two examples. This is nothing new, however; Clementhorpe YOE was described in a coroner's inquest of 1377 as *in suburbia Ebor'* (York) (Figure 1.4).[4] Proximity to urban centres has also led some *thorps* to grow rapidly during the twentieth century, as these once-rural places have become dormitories for their larger neighbours. Such has been the experience of Countesthorpe, just south of Leicester. By contrast, many others, particularly those located away from the major centres of population and industry, have just not

4   C. Gross (ed.), *Select cases from the coroner's rolls, AD 1265–1413*, Selden Society 9 (London, 1896), p. 120.

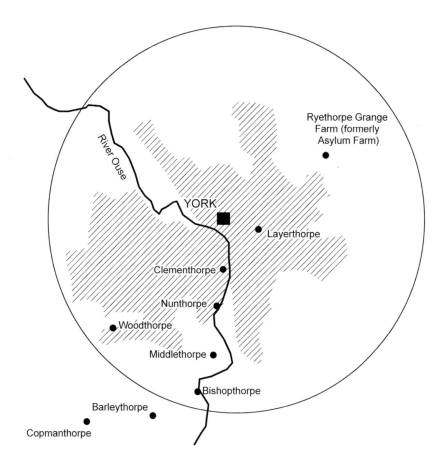

Figure 1.4 The location of *thorps* in the vicinity of York. The extent of modern urban spread is indicated by the hatched shading. The circle represents a three-mile radius from York minster.

grown since the end of the Middle Ages, although their housing stock will invariably have been replaced and improved. Yet others have atrophied, shrinking in population and size to be represented by a lone farm or small collection of buildings where once a whole village stood. And a surprisingly large number have disappeared altogether.

Late medieval and parliamentary enclosure accounted for many of these losses. The observations made by the local curate of Gainsthorpe LIN in 1697 that the village had 'been eaten up with time, poverty and pasturage' could be applied to many others sharing similar names. Robert Thoroton's description of the fate of Thorpe-in-the-Glebe NTT could equally find more general validity:

> inclosing the lordship, as it doth in all places where the soil is anything good in this
> county for certain, hath so ruined and depopulated the town, that in my time there

Figure 1.5 Althorp House NTH, seen from the edge of the deer park.

was not a house left inhabited in this notable lordship (except some part of the hall, Mr. Armstrong's house) but a shepherd only kept to sell ale in the church[5]

The cause of the demise of other *thorps* and *throps* lay with other important post-medieval and early modern landscape developments. A good number were cleared to make way for the country seats of the gentry: Williamstrip GLO and Althorp NTH might serve to typify a much wider trend (Figure 1.5).[6] At Thorpe Malsor NTH, one half of the village was removed in the eighteenth century as a result of emparkment.[7] In the same county the entire village of Thorpe Achurch

5 Quoted in A. Cameron and C. O'Brien, 'The deserted mediaeval village of Thorpe-in-the-Glebe, Nottinghamshire', *Transactions of the Thoroton Society*, 85 (1981), p. 56.

6 K.J. Allison *et al.*, *The deserted villages of Northamptonshire*, Department of English Local History Occasional Papers 18 (Leicester, 1966), p. 34: in 1505 Althorp manor was said to contain 80 acres of arable, 200 acres of woodland, 400 acres of pasture and 60 acres of woodland. There were no tenants. The manor was sold to the Spenser family in 1508 and by 1547 they were grazing a flock of 1200 sheep on this land.

7 C.C. Taylor, *Village and farmstead* (London, 1983), p. 211.

was razed to the ground in 1830 in advance of agricultural improvements, and new housing was built by the beneficence of the lord of the manor.[8] The reasons behind other changes which radically affected the plans of *thorps* and *throps* are more difficult to establish; between 1810 and 1884, for instance, the three streets of Rothersthorpe NTH were silently reduced to two, documents providing no clues as to why the community chose, or was compelled, to take this course of action.[9]

Such examples remind us that the plans of all villages and hamlets might change dramatically over time and that *thorps* and *throps* are not immune to the processes involved. Some later layouts will preserve elements of their original design, but equally – and more usually – most of the evidence for the earliest phases of these places will tend to be obscured by later developments. In this respect, settlement plans derived from the survey of earthworks preserved on deserted medieval *thorp* and *throp* sites are extremely useful. But they too only take us back halfway to the origins of these places and might also mislead. We are left to reconstruct the original shape and size of *thorps* and *throps* through the careful combination of both above- and below-ground archaeology, informed wherever possible by documentary sources which help to establish population size, economic function and social organisation. For our purposes, information contained within pre-Conquest charters, and Domesday Book in particular, is key to our analysis. Over and beyond the physical form of these places, such sources help to suggest chronologies for settlement foundation, or at least to establish in each case a *terminus ante quem*, times before which individual *thorps* and *throps* had taken root in the landscape. And they also help us to locate these places both in the physical landscape and within the less visible and changing landscapes of administrative and tenurial units into which the English countryside was organised. They point us to particular structures associated with these settlements – churches, mills and the like – which begin to throw light on their probable position within broader settlement hierarchies. They offer a means of assessing the status of their inhabitants and the social and economic activities which helped to support the communities they housed.

Interdisciplinarity is central to the success of any investigation of the remote beginnings of a rural settlement. In applying approaches and methods drawn from historical geography, history and archaeology to the problem of *thorps* and *throps*, we are attempting nothing new. But what has drawn us to these places in the first instance is the fact that they have something in common. Their names define the scope of this study and we are concerned with understanding what these names can tell us about these places. As will be seen, linguistic analysis is

8   *Ibid.*, p. 211.
9   *Ibid.*, pp. 213, 218.

given due and appropriate prominence in this book. In linking the study of place-names so closely with the physical evidence for the settlements themselves, the methodological basis of this book does represent a new departure for the study of early medieval, indeed medieval, settlement history.

Treating groups of names together is a method of procedure much used by place-name scholars, but it is not one familiar to landscape historians and archaeologists,[10] who have tended to seek out defined areas for study, often drawn to the types of rural settlement they contain. This is because the questions they have sought to address – such as the process of nucleation, or the relationship between nucleated and dispersed settlement patterns, or the desertion of medieval villages – are most appropriately explored in these local and regional settings.[11] Undoubtedly the assessment of place-name evidence has been an important plank in many of these studies, but the presence or absence of particular place-name forms has never been used as a primary factor in choosing areas for study. If the place-names that these areas contain have later been found to be informative then so much the better, but their analysis has always remained a secondary preoccupation. In place-name studies, by contrast, the investigation of complete subsets of names finds a prominent position in the literature alongside continuing regional, county and linguistic surveys.[12] It is an approach that has been used to great effect, most notably by Margaret Gelling in the study of toponyms, those names which refer to aspects of the surrounding physical landscape. Using field observations, she showed how names in -hōh refer to a particular type of heel or projecting piece of raised ground; that names in -ofer and -ufer are indicative of a 'flat-topped ridge with a convex shoulder'; and that names in -ōra refer to a bank,

10 There have been some recent pioneering surveys which have begun to adopt this approach, such as R. Faith, 'Worthys and enclosures', *MSRG Annual Report*, 21 (2006), pp. 9–14; M. Gardiner, 'Hythes, small ports, and other landing places in later medieval England', in J. Blair (ed.), *Waterways and canal-building in medieval England* (Oxford, 2007), pp. 85–110; S. Semple, 'Defining the OE *hearg*: a preliminary archaeological and topographic examination of *hearg* place names and their hinterlands', *Early Medieval Europe*, 15/4 (2007), pp. 364–85; S. Draper, 'Old English *wīc* and *walh*: Britons and Saxons in post-Roman Wiltshire', *Landscape History*, 24 (2002), pp. 27–44; J. English, 'Worths in a landscape context', *Landscape History*, 24 (2002), pp. 45–52.

11 For example, S. Parry, *Raunds area survey: an archaeological study of the landscape of Raunds, Northamptonshire* (Oxford, 2006); R. Jones and M. Page, *Medieval villages in an English landscape: beginnings and ends* (Macclesfield, 2006).

12 For example, K. Bailey, 'Some observations on *gē*, *gau* and *go*', JEPNS, 31 (1998–9), pp. 63–76; C. Hough, 'Chilton and other place-names from Old English *cild*', JEPNS, 30 (2003–4), pp. 65–83; A. Cole, 'The use of *Netel* in place-names', JEPNS, 35 (2002–3), pp. 49–58; A. Cole, 'Ersc: distribution and use of this Old English place-name', JEPNS, 32 (1999–2000), pp. 27–40; M. Gelling, 'Some meanings of *stōw*', in S.M. Pearce (ed.), *The early church in Western Britain and Ireland: studies presented to C.A. Ralegh Radford*, BAR British Series 102 (Oxford, 1982), pp. 187–96; K.I Sandred, *English place-names in -stead* (Uppsala, 1963); V. Watts, 'Some place-name distributions', JEPNS, 32 (1999–2000), pp. 53–72.

shelf or level hilltop. Similarly, the characteristic profile of a *cumb*, a 'short, broad valley, usually bowl- or trough-shaped with three fairly steeply rising sides', could be contrasted with the more gently sloped, wide, sweeping outline of a *denu*-type valley.[13] Advances have also been made by exploring habitative names (of which *thorps* and *throps* are examples) as groups, but this approach continues to lag behind the progress made in our understanding of toponyms.[14]

The specificity of the range of early medieval place-names which take their cue from the physical landscape reveals those who coined them to have been keen observers of the detail of topography and the environment; and it shows them using identifiable features in the landscape to differentiate one place from another. We might suspect that similar precision lay behind the habitative names too. The term *-ceaster*, for instance, was applied to walled Roman towns, and names in *-minster* must refer to a particular kind of ecclesiastical establishment, although the precise meaning of the term is still much debated. Such examples clearly demonstrate that aspects of the built environment could be used to define a particular place. The use of different terms for enclosures, such as *-loc* and *-worth*, might imply a visual difference between so-named features that allowed them to be distinguished. And it might have been the small size of places in *-cot*, a name which is usually taken to denote 'cottage or mean dwelling', which earned them their name. But there are indications that settlement facets other than form could also influence the choice of name. We might think of more intangible realities such as function: thus specialised farming activities, perhaps dairying, are associated with places in *-wīc*, and trading functions with places in *-port*. Armed with such examples, we are left to wonder whether in fact it was how a *-loc* or a *-worth* was used, and not how it looked, that allowed one to be separated from the other. The status and social structure of a particular community might also play its part in the naming process. Names such as Kingston (OE *cyning*, 'king'), Preston (OE *prēost*, 'priest'), Charlton (OE *ceorl*, 'peasant') and Walton (OE *walh*, 'Briton/foreigner/slave') – to slide down the ranks of Anglo-Saxon society and beyond – are largely unambiguous cases in point. This raises the question of whether it was the dependent status of the occupants of *-cots*, and not principally the size or meanness of the dwellings, which earned them their designation. In other instances, it may have been a combination of physical appearance, function and status. Perhaps place-names in *-burh* were not just fortified places, nor just

13   M. Gelling and A. Cole, *The landscape of place-names* (Stamford, 2000), pp. 103–9, 113–22, 186–90, 199–203, 203–10.

14   For example, R. Coates, 'New light on old wicks: the progeny of Latin *vicus*', *Nomina*, 22 (1999), pp. 75–116; L. Abrams and D.N. Parsons, 'Place-names and the history of Scandinavian settlement in England', in J. Hines *et al.* (eds), *Land, sea and home*, Society for Medieval Archaeology Monograph 20 (Leeds, 2004), pp. 379–431, largely on *bȳ*.

thegnly residences, nor simply estate centres, but rather at one and the same time all three. If any of these characteristics was absent, they could not be described by this name.[15]

The role of form, function and status in the naming of places remains poorly understood, a situation which will only be redressed by further studies of the kind offered here, focusing on particular name groups. But this discussion has, at least, led us to the most difficult of all names, the generic habitative names, names such as those in -tūn or -hām and, of course, *thorp* and *throp*. These provide no clues as to what may have lain behind them. They do not appear to refer to anything visually distinctive, or say anything about the make-up of the communities who lived within them, or reveal anything of the activities that might have taken place in and around them. And yet we must assume that as distinguishing labels these terms were meaningful to those who coined them and those who, in turn, used them through the critical early years, guaranteeing their perpetuation. Indeed, there is little in the corpus of English place-names to suggest that names were generated at random or applied without considerable thought. Place-name elements were not ready-to-wear clothing, picked off a rack of alternatives, to be worn by any nameless settlement. They were tailored and fitted. They were a uniform, attesting to membership of a particular family of places sharing something in common. And this forces us to ask just what was it that linked together *thorps* and *throps* and meant that they belonged to this exclusive club and no other? Put simply, what was a *thorp* or a *throp*? This is the question this book seeks to answer by combining the historical and archaeological evidence for settlement activity in these places with the information deriving from the place-names themselves.

The study of thorps

This book focuses on the *thorps* and *throps* of England. But, of course, these forms of place-name have a far wider geographic distribution. Names in -torp can be found today in great numbers in Denmark, where over 3,000 of an estimated 7,000 still survive, and they occur with frequency in Sweden, Norway and the Netherlands.[16] They are present in lesser numbers in northern Germany, Finland (where around 800 have been recorded),[17] Iceland and France.[18] The element -torp

15 S. Draper, 'The significance of Old English *burh* in Anglo-Saxon England', *Anglo-Saxon Studies in Archaeology and History*, 15 (2008), pp. 240–53.

16 M. Lerche Nielsen, 'Sognekriteriets betydning for vurderingen af *torp*-navnenes alder', in P. Gammeltoft and B. Jørgensen (eds), *Nordiske torp-navne* (Uppsala, 2003), pp. 177–202.

17 S. Sigmundsson, '*þorp* på Island', in Gammeltoft and Jørgensen (eds), *Nordiske torp-navne*, pp. 223–9.

18 R. Lepelley, *Dictionnaire étymologique des noms de communes de Normandie* (Condé-sur-Noireau, 1993) records 28 place-names in -torp in Normandy.

lies behind Danish settlement names in -*rup*, -*strup*, -*trup* and -*drup*; in Germany it appears as -*dorp*, -*dorf* and -*dörp*;[19] and in the Netherlands it is the root of *Terpen* names. Consequently, the study of *thorp* names is an international concern. It is a lively field of enquiry, warranting major conferences devoted exclusively to the subject and producing an ever-growing body of literature.[20]

What European studies have shown is that *thorps* tend to be small, often dependent, low-status and outlying places. This is true across their whole distribution. Beyond this, however, they appear to share little in common. It has been suggested, for example, that *thorps* in Denmark have their origins in a period of settlement expansion and landscape colonisation beginning in the last quarter of the tenth century and concluding before 1100.[21] In Sweden, the establishment of *thorp* places often appears to lie in social, administrative and territorial reorganisation in the thirteenth and fourteenth centuries.[22] *Thorps* in Finland are an eighteenth- and nineteenth-century phenomenon, part of the cultural package introduced after Swedish settlement.[23] In Denmark association has been made between *thorps* and certain soil types, suggesting that these were primarily places engaged in agriculture,[24] while the earliest recorded example of a *thorp* in the region of South Schleswig – the name *Sliesthorp*, which appears in the Frankish Annals from the ninth century – is linked to a trading station.[25] In Iceland, *thorps* might occupy coastal locations and be involved in maritime activities.[26]

The observation that medieval *thorps* were characteristically small had already been made by the end of the nineteenth century. In a survey of the Danish king Waldemar's land tax rolls, Johannes Steenstrup showed that places in -*torp* and -*inge* on the island of Falster were, on the whole, always smaller than settlements in -*lev* and -*bȳ*.[27] These conclusions clearly influenced the thinking of early

---

19 W. Laur, 'Torp-navne i Sydslesvig og sprogskiftet', in Gammeltoft and Jørgensen (eds), *Nordiske torp-navne*, pp. 167–76.

20 P. Dam *et al.* (eds), *Torp: som ortnamn och bebyggelse*, Konferensrapport, Tvärvetenskaplig torp-konferens Malmö, 25–27 April 2007 (Lund, 2009).

21 T. Thurston, 'The knowable, the doable, and the undiscussed: tradition, submission and the "becoming" of rural landscapes in Denmark's Iron Age', *Antiquity*, 73 (1999), pp. 661–71 at 665.

22 M. Widgren, 'Is landscape history possible? Or, how can we study the desertion of farms?', in P. Ucko and R. Layton (eds), *The archaeology and anthropology of landscape: shaping your landscape* (London, 1998), pp. 94–103.

23 G. Harling-Kranck, 'Namn på -torp och torpnamn i Finland', in Gammeltoft and Jørgensen (eds), *Nordiske torp-navne*, pp. 79–94.

24 L. Hedemand *et al.*, 'De danske torp-landsbyers jordbundsforhold', in Gammeltoft and Jørgensen (eds), *Nordiske torp-navne*, pp. 95–108.

25 Laur, 'Torp-navne'.

26 Sigmundsson, '*þorp* på Island', pp. 203–22.

27 W. Westergaard, 'Danish history and Danish historians', *The Journal of Modern History*, 24/2 (1952), pp. 167–80.

scholars of English place-names, such as Eilert Ekwall and Frank Stenton, the latter of whom was familiar both with Steenstrup's continental work and his study of the Danelaw. In 1924, Ekwall argued that:

> some names in -thorp [in England] are no doubt English, but the great frequency of names in -thorp in the Danelaw, as compared with other English counties shows that there the majority of thorpes must be Scandinavian. Dan[ish] Thorp means 'a hamlet, a daughter settlement from an older village'. This is no doubt the meaning also of the element in Scandinavian place-names in England.[28]

Examining the occurrence of thorps and throps in different English counties, Allen Mawer suggested that:

> there were two centres of distribution of the suffix, so to speak, one in the South Midlands, the other in Scand[inavian] England and ... that, with the exception of a few examples in We[stmorland], the suffix in Scandinavian England must be of Danish rather than Norse origin. The two-fold origin of this suffix is confirmed by its form. In the first group of counties, it is very rarely found in the form thorp at all ... In the other group it is rare to get anything except a thorp-form...[29]

The distinction between thorps and throps based on their spellings was thus established early in the literature.

Subtle differences were also noted in their meanings. OE throp was noted in early documents as glossing terms such as tūn, compitum (a cross-roads), fundus (estate) and villa (farm), and in one instance thing-stōw (a place of assembly).[30] Given these alternatives, early scholars proposed its translation as '"village" or "hamlet", though medieval usage suggests that in names of late origin it was generally used of some smaller form of settlement'.[31] Old Scandinavian thorp, they offered, 'denotes a group of homesteads, perhaps also a farm or croft, but as the word in England seems to be of Danish origin rather than Norse we should perhaps look rather to the meaning of ODan thorp "smaller village due to colonisation from a larger one"'.[32] By the mid-1930s opinion was moving away from the idea that thorp might refer to a village. Ekwall, in his dictionary, expressed doubt regarding the precise meaning of OE thorp or throp. He offered the advice

---

28 E. Ekwall, 'The Scandinavian element', in A. Mawer and F.M. Stenton, (eds) Introduction to the survey of English place-names, EPNS 1, part 1 (Cambridge, 1924, 2nd edn, 1933), pp. 55–92 at 57–8.

29 A. Mawer, The chief elements used in English place-names, EPNS 1, part 2 (Cambridge, 1924), p. 59.

30 See Appendix 1 for a detailed discussion of these glosses and a rejection of several of the senses cited here.

31 Mawer, Chief elements, p. 59.

32 Ibid. Note that Mawer uses 'Norse' here to denote Norwegian or West Norse. More modern scholarship tends to generalise 'Old Norse' for the old Scandinavian language as a whole, which is our usual practice in this book.

that '[i]t was certainly used in the sense "farm", possibly in the sense "hamlet"', but that '[t]here is no reason to suppose that it meant "village".'[33] As an example, he suggested that '[t]he name Thrupp cannot well mean simply "village". A name such as "the village" is not distinctive enough.'[34] As for the Scandinavian cognate, Ekwall was more clear. Drawing on its meaning in both Denmark and Sweden, where it was used to denote a farm or new settlement, later a croft, he suggested that

> the original meaning of *þorp* was 'newly reclaimed land, new settlement'. It should not be rendered by 'village', but rather by 'farm'. In origin, the Danelaw *thorps* were evidently as a rule outlying, dependent farms belonging to a village.[35]

More detailed discussion of *thorp* and *throp* had to wait until the publication of the two volumes of *English Place-Name Elements* by Albert Smith in 1956.[36] Additional early senses were offered. Gothic *thaurp* 'a field' was identified as a cognate, while Primitive Germanic **thurpa-* was associated with Latin *turba* 'a tumult, a mob, a crowd'. The latter was linked to a meaning 'village', and supported by the fact that in Old High German the term *dorf* could mean 'a gathering of people'. Smith identified Germany as the early centre of a place-name element already well established by the fifth and sixth centuries. From here it spread into southern Denmark, where it had become common by the Viking period. It continued its northerly advance into Sweden, and ultimately, but in a more limited way, to Norway and Iceland. Smith argued that it entered England with an early wave of Anglo-Saxon settlers coming from the Germanic homelands. His case rested on the observation that *throp* as a productive element in place-naming had a restricted geographical distribution outside the Danelaw.[37] He argued that it was absent from Kent and Sussex because the earliest Anglo-Saxon settlers of these parts had come from a region in which *thorp/throp* was not used – that is, Jutland; and that it was absent from Devon and Cornwall because the element had ceased to be productive by the time of the Anglo-Saxon conquest of this region, somewhere around the early eighth century AD.

Smith therefore established a model in which English *throps* were early Anglo-Saxon settlements and Danelaw *thorps* represented Scandinavian settlements of a later period. However, aspects of chronology have remained matters for debate. In the 1970s, for instance, Niels Lund suggested that OE *throp* may have lain behind

---

33 E. Ekwall, *The concise Oxford dictionary of English place-names* (1936; Oxford, 2nd edn, 1947), pp. 446–7.

34 *Ibid.*, p. xv.

35 *Ibid.*, pp. 446–7.

36 EPNE, 2, pp. 214–16.

37 *Ibid.*, pp. 215–16. This argument is examined in detail further below, pp. 70–5.

the majority of *thorps* in the Danelaw,[38] a possibility accepted in part by Gillian Fellows-Jensen.[39] Yet she also observed that *throps* were often later recorded than the Danelaw *thorps*, which prompted her to suggest that the English names 'may be younger as a class' and to float the idea that some of the *throp*-names may have arisen under the influence of Danish *thorp* as a loan word.[40]

A key contribution to the debate was offered in the late 1960s and 1970s by Kenneth Cameron, who studied the *thorps* of the East Midlands in their landscape context.[41] His conclusions continue to influence how these places have come to be viewed within broader settlement patterns. Places taking either OE or ON generic elements, he argued, were not distributed evenly across the East Midlands, but rather tended to appear in defined concentrations. OE elements such as -*tūn* and -*hām* appeared to cluster on the best, most fertile soils, such as the alluvial deposits and gravel terraces found within the major river valleys. This group also included the Grimston-type place-names (ON pers.n + *tūn*), places which it has been suggested had earlier Anglo-Saxon origins and names that were replaced by Scandinavian settlers. By contrast, settlements taking Old Norse -*bȳ* occupied less optimal sites, but still managed to find positions along the valleys of tributary streams, often sitting on small patches of better-draining glacial sands and gravels to be found within the heavier, more ubiquitous, glacial boulder clays. The latter were the 'less favourable' geologies, characteristic of the watersheds and remote from both the major and minor watercourses, that were occupied by the *thorps*.

For Cameron this suggested a settlement ranking linked to the chronology of foundation, an idea influenced by the notion of physical determinism: good geologies would be the first to be occupied and the poorest would be the last. From this emerged his suggestion that the association of different name forms with particular geologies attested to successive waves of land colonisation. Settlements in -*tūn* represented the earliest phase, taking root in a landscape of low population where prime sites were still available; places in -*bȳ* marked a second wave of colonisation following Danish settlement; and those in -*thorp*

---

38 N. Lund, 'Thorp-names', in P.H. Sawyer (ed.), *Medieval settlement: continuity and change* (London, 1976), pp. 223–5 (see below, pp. 61, 75–81).

39 G. Fellows-Jensen, 'Place-names in -*þorp*: in retrospect and in turmoil', *Nomina*, 15 (1991–2), pp. 35–51.

40 Fellows-Jensen, 'Place-names in -*þorp*'; G. Fellows-Jensen, 'Torp-navne i Norfolk i sammenligning med torp-navne i andre dele af Danelagen', in Gammeltoft and Jørgensen (eds), *Nordiske torp-navne*, pp. 47–59 at 49.

41 K. Cameron, *Scandinavian settlement in the territory of the Five Boroughs: the place-name evidence*, inaugural lecture (Nottingham, 1966); K. Cameron, 'Scandinavian settlement in the territory of the Five Boroughs: the place-name evidence, part II, place-names in Thorp', in K. Cameron (ed.), *Place-name evidence for the Anglo-Saxon invasion and Scandinavian settlements* (Nottingham, 1975), pp. 139–56.

Figure 1.6 Lanes named after and leading to Woolsthorpe LIN and Easthorpe, near Bottesford LEI.

formed a final movement into those areas least attractive to the early medieval farmer, areas developed only as the countryside filled up and further land had to be brought into cultivation. Thus forced to take up these marginal locations, *thorps* remained small and vulnerable to economic vagaries and depopulation, and were as a consequence always more prone to abandonment and loss than the earlier, larger and better-placed *tūns* and *bȳs*.

Cameron's work has carried such authority since its publication that the idea that *thorps* were small, dependent settlements, late arrivals, marginally located and socially and economically disadvantaged places has been accepted by all subsequent scholars. In this book we subject this hypothesis to critical scrutiny, armed with considerably more data and technological tools than Cameron himself had access to. We can, we think, question some of his conclusions, but it is a mark of his scholarship and deductive reasoning that his model is difficult to demolish entirely. Few historical 'truths' survive much more than thirty years, and in proposing a new hypothesis, one which seeks to incorporate both *thorps* and *throps* for the first time, we are very aware that the lifespan of our model is unlikely to be as long as that which preceded it. Certainly, the flaws in our arguments will be more easily seen and exploited by others than those which we have had to seek out and prize apart to arrive at our conclusions. Areas of conjecture will be obvious where no evidence is currently available to prove or disprove our interpretations. Such deficiencies should perhaps have been taken as reasons to keep our counsel. But the evidence that we have been able to bring together – acknowledging that this could always be augmented – appears to point in such intriguing directions, and seemingly has such wide implications, that we have decided to take the risk of putting it in this book. We hope, at the very least, that it will stimulate others to explore these fascinating places themselves, to question our findings, and to develop their own ideas based on their further discoveries.

2

Establishing the corpus

The following chapters seek to establish what has been learned, and what might be learned, from a study of the groups of places named with *thorp* and *throp*. It is customary to treat the place-name material in two groups: the *thorps* of Danelaw England and the *throps* of the 'English' part of the country.[1] This convention is followed here in Chapters 3 and 4. In this chapter, the focus is on defining the corpus itself, defining these groups and setting dating limits.

Numbers and dates

For the present study we have collected a corpus of some 896 place-names in *thorp* from 35 of England's 41 historic counties (Table 2.1). This 896 is a gross figure, including everything from ancient parishes to medieval and modern field-names. Overwhelmingly the element appears in the earlier records of a name as a generic – that is to say, either on its own as a simplex place-name, as 'Thorpe', or as the second element in a compound name, as 'Southorpe'.[2] When it appears as a qualifier, the first element in a compound, it usually simply repeats a known nearby place-name: thus Thorpe Grange, Thorpe Head, Thorpe Hill and Thorpe Wood are all found in Thorpe Underwood YOW (itself a simplex *Thorp* in the twelfth century).[3] Naturally, such repetitions have been omitted. There remain a small number of qualifiers, however, that may point to *thorps* which have not survived as generics. A clear instance comes in Wheathamstead HRT, where *Thropfeld* and *Thropmulle* appear among medieval minor names: evidently there was

---

1   Note that we often generalise the whole group of *thorps* and *throps* as *thorps*: this is discussed further below.
2   A rather large number of *thorp*-names show alternation between simplex and compound forms, or between different qualifying elements. These features are discussed further below.
3   EPNS YOW, 5, pp. 5–7. Note that, as in the case of Thorpe Underwood, the later addition of a distinguishing affix to an originally simplex name is a very common phenomenon.

a *Throp* in the parish, although it is not recorded in its own right.[4] Some 25 other cases of qualifiers which may record lost *thorps* have been included in the gross total, and appear on Figure 2.1, which aims to show the overall distribution of *thorp* in England at any date.[5]

Our interest in this work is the earlier medieval period, when *thorp*-names and the settlements that bore them first came into being. It would therefore seem sensible to restrict the corpus to names that belong to that period, but place-name evidence is not so straightforward. The recording of early place-names and the survival of the records depend on various factors. It is well known, for instance, that Domesday Book is not the complete catalogue of eleventh-century settlements that it may appear to be, and the omissions are often exactly the kind of small, dependent units which *thorps* are believed in origin to have been.[6] Other medieval records, too, are inevitably more or less partial, and settlements are in general more likely to appear if they thrive and grow than if they start small and remain so. Under these circumstances, places can go unmarked for hundreds of years before they first enter the surviving written record. There is thus an argument for considerable leeway in the delimitation of the corpus.

On the other hand, the inclusion of late-recorded names clearly poses problems for maintaining a chronological perspective. While some *thorp*-names no doubt slipped through the net only to be recorded many years after their coining, other names probably arose in the later medieval or modern periods. In some areas *thorp* appears to have remained particularly productive: the West Riding of Yorkshire and the neighbouring north-eastern part of Derbyshire, for instance, evidence high proportions of *thorp*-names first recorded after 1500, which tends to suggest that the element continued to be applied here to new farms and settlements at late dates (Figures 2.2 and 2.3).[7] Such survival, while

---

4 EPNS HRT, p. 260.

5 One other type of deliberate omission should be mentioned: names which are adjudged to be 'manorial' – that is, transferred as surnames from elsewhere. A number of these are identified in Essex in particular. A clear example is Instep's Farm in White Colne (EPNS ESX, p. 384), which is *Ingaldestorp* 1230, *Ingoldestorp* 1254, and so on, but all six forms recorded before 1350 are found as surnames: the family almost certainly came from Ingoldisthorpe NFK. Less certain are Thorpe's Farm in Felsted (EPNS ESX, p. 424), cf. *Walter de Thorp* 1291, and Thorpe's Wood in Thaxted (EPNS ESX, p. 498), cf. *William de Thorp* 1285. Here, where there are single early forms to go on, the *thorps* could well be small lost settlements in the parishes, but without further evidence we have followed the decisions of the place-name collections on this question.

6 P.H. Sawyer (ed.), *Medieval settlement: continuity and change* (London, 1976), pp. 1–7; SSNY, pp. 2–3; D. Roffe, 'Place-naming in Domesday Book: settlements, estates, and communities', *Nomina*, 14 (1990–1), pp. 47–60.

7 The figures are set out above in Table 2.1. It should be noted that the uneven coverage of the country by place-name surveys renders comparisons on this point awkward: YOE and YON, for instance, probably register low numbers of late-recorded names because the earlier EPNS surveys

Table 2.1
Numbers of *thorps* and *throps* by historic counties, with dates of first reference.
The totals in the fourth and fifth columns are cumulative.

County	Total thorps	1086 or earlier	1300 or earlier	1500 or earlier
Bedfordshire	3	0	2	2
Berkshire	8	0	3	5
Buckinghamshire	10	1	6	8
Cambridgeshire	1	0	1	1
Cheshire	1	0	0	0
Cornwall	0	0	0	0
Cumberland	3	0	1	2
Derbyshire	43	3	17	24
Devon	1	0	0	1
Dorset	5	0	3	3
Durham	6	1	5	6
Essex	8	4	6	7
Gloucestershire	24	4	14	17
Hampshire	9	1	9	9
Herefordshire	0	0	0	0
Hertfordshire	5	0	1	5
Huntingdonshire	3	0	2	2
Kent	0	0	0	0
Lancashire	5	0	5	5
Leicestershire	67	23	48	57
Lincolnshire	112	67	106	112
Middlesex	0	0	0	0
Norfolk	68	44	59	60
Northamptonshire	37	19	34	35
Northumberland	2	0	2	2
Nottinghamshire	44	19	36	40
Oxfordshire	15	5	9	14
Rutland	14	5	12	12
Shropshire	0	0	0	0
Somerset	2	1	1	2
Staffordshire	2	1	1	2
Suffolk	27	13	20	20
Surrey	2	1	1	2
Sussex	0	0	0	0
Warwickshire	3	0	3	3
Westmorland	9	0	6	8
Wiltshire	14	0	9	13
Worcestershire	3	1	3	3
Yorkshire East Riding	88	70	86	87
Yorkshire North Riding	46	41	45	46
Yorkshire West Riding	202	41	101	123
unassigned	4	2	3	4
Totals	896	367	660	742

7 *cont.*

were not concerned to note them. Yet there is clearly a significant difference between DRB and
YOW, on the one hand, and LIN, LEI and RUT on the other; in the latter counties, recent and
ongoing surveys are not picking up new late-recorded thorp-names in anything like the numbers
found further north and west.

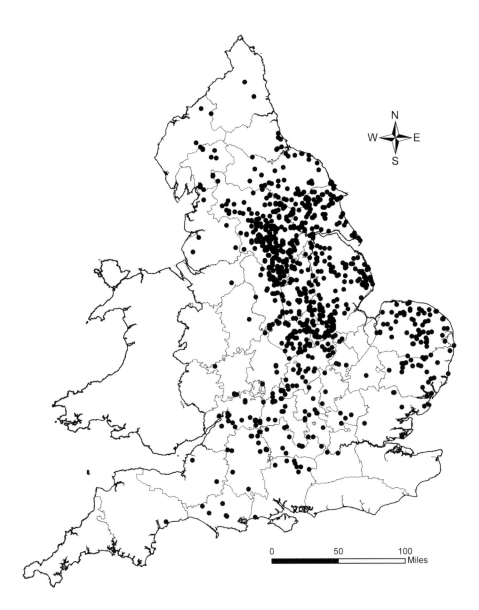

Figure 2.1 Total distribution of *thorps* and *throps* of all periods.

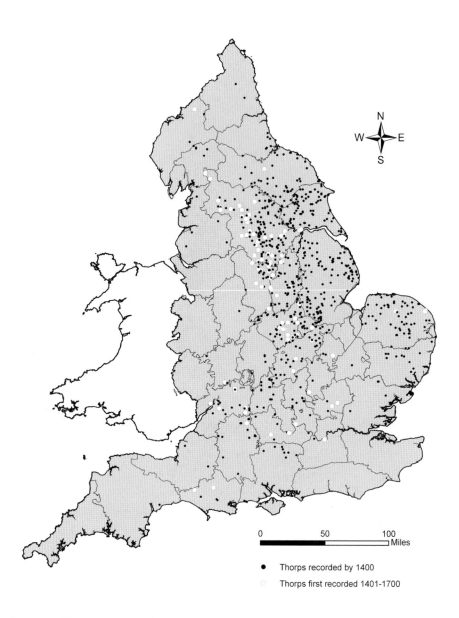

Figure 2.2 The geography of *thorp*-name coinage based on first documented mention of the place-name in the period 1401–1700. The map appears to show that the name enjoyed a late currency particularly in the Yorkshire West Riding and Leicestershire, with other examples in many other counties.

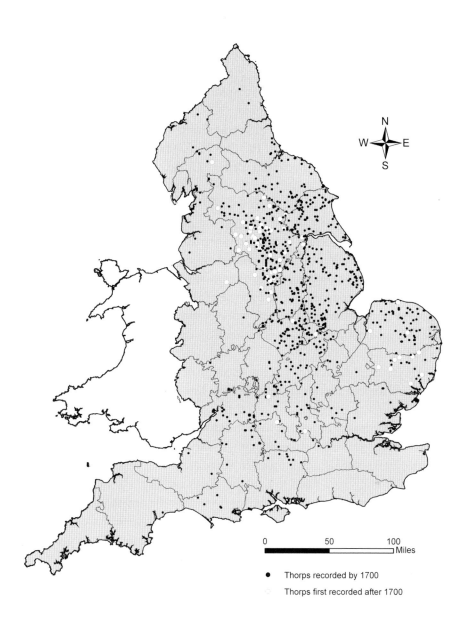

Figure 2.3 The geography of *thorp*-name coinage based on first documented mention of the place-name in the period 1700–present. This map shows that the use of *thorp* as a place-name element was particularly widespread in the Yorkshire West Riding.

interesting in itself, is not necessarily helpful for the study of early medieval usage: in particular, it is possible – perhaps likely – that any specialised early sense of the term was lost or modified in later centuries. Although variation in usage is possible over any period and any geographical spread, it is clearly advisable to set some chronological limits on this study.

Previous scholars have put different limits on their material. Kenneth Cameron, in studying the *thorps* of the East Midlands, restricted himself solely to those found in Domesday Book and earlier.[8] Gillian Fellows-Jensen also initially concentrated on names recorded by 1086 when she published her study of Scandinavian settlement-names in Yorkshire.[9] When she came to work on the East Midlands, however, she cast the net wider to allow the inclusion of a group of twelfth-century land surveys in her primary material, taking her nominal cut-off point to *c.*1150; in addition, she included an appendix of names first recorded between *c.*1150 and 1500 because of the possibility that some of these were old settlements that happened not to have been recorded early.[10] In her subsequent articles on *thorp* Fellows-Jensen has worked with a corpus of material from the whole of England found in sources earlier than 1500: this comprises 576 names in *thorp* and 54 in *throp*.[11]

There is no right and wrong in the selection of a date: it is a question of 'feel' as much as of logical argument. Drawing the line at Domesday Book is evidently defensible for a study of the origins of the settlement-type, but it is quite certain that it excludes many names that were in existence by 1086 and were overlooked by that record. There is also an argument, as we shall see, that the 'thorp phase' of early medieval settlement continued in some areas well beyond the late eleventh century. Certainly it is notable that the *throps* of 'English' England would be reduced to an unworkably small number if we drew the line so early. On the other hand, 1500 feels generous. Guided in part by archaeology, we have set the upper limit of our study of the historical and archaeological phenomenon represented by the names at *c.*1250, and with this in mind, given that the recording of names inevitably lags behind the establishment of settlements, we have chosen to make 1300 the cut-off date for our primary place-name statistics (Figure 2.4; Appendix 2). However, since we have collected fuller material, we naturally draw attention to later examples where they seem to be significant or interesting, or where they seem to offer a challenge to the indications of the earlier group.

8   Cameron, 'Scandinavian settlement, part II', p. 148, n. 6.
9   SSNY, p. 2. She also admitted a few examples that almost certainly existed but were omitted by Domesday Book: *eadem*, p. 3.
10 SSNEM, pp. 5–6, 98.
11 Fellows-Jensen, 'Place-names in -*þorp*', pp. 35–51 at 40; Fellows-Jensen, 'Torp-navne i Norfolk', pp. 47–9.

Table 2.2

Number of *thorps* by date of first record collated by century. The graph shows a peak in the eleventh century, largely accounted for by the appearance of large numbers of *thorps* for the first time in Domesday Book (1086), but it also shows that large numbers also first appear in the twelfth and thirteenth centuries.

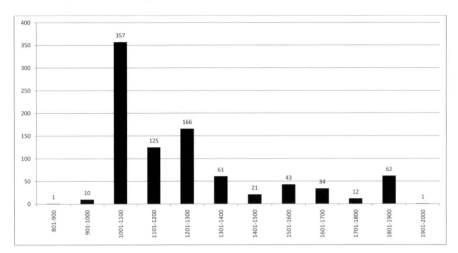

Our complete material, broken down by date of first record, is shown in Table 2.2. Where we cover the same ground, our figures are closely similar to Cameron's and to Fellows-Jensen's earlier categories (to 1086 in Yorkshire and to *c.*1150 in the East Midlands).[12] By 1500 we tend to have more examples than Fellows-Jensen, both in the East Midlands subset and in the countrywide survey.[13] To some extent this reflects a difference in practice: Fellows-Jensen identifies a category of name 'where *þorp* seems to be used of a division of settlement', which she excludes.[14] In our opinion this is a very uncertain category, and one that – should it exist – poses considerable problems of identification.

Fellows-Jensen gives two particular instances of the 'division of a settlement' usage. The first is the pairing of *Benyfeld Netherthorp* and *Upthorp* in Benefield parish NTH. This is certainly a peculiar case, but it does not seem to us to have been

12 Cameron's corpus was 109 names: our equivalent figure is 117 for the counties he treated, DRB, NTT, LEI, LIN and RUT. In Yorkshire, Fellows-Jensen's total was 155 names, including 4 later-recorded instances; our equivalent, strictly to 1086, is 152. In the East Midlands Fellows-Jensen's corpus to *c.*1150 was 145: our equivalent total (not listed in Table 2.1) would be 146. Minor discrepancies like these are in part due to the occasional re-identification of early, especially Domesday, forms, and in part due to different judgements over the dating of documents.

13 In the East Midlands she includes 102 additional thorp-names recorded between *c.*1150 and 1500 (SSNEM, p. 99); our equivalent with the same criteria would be 133. For the whole country her 576 *thorps* and 54 *throps* give a combined total of 630, as opposed to our 742 recorded by 1500. It is not clear precisely where Fellows-Jensen draws the Danelaw dividing lines in her material: by our reckoning (for which see below), by this date, we have 641 names in the Danelaw and 100 outside it.

14 SSNEM, p. 98.

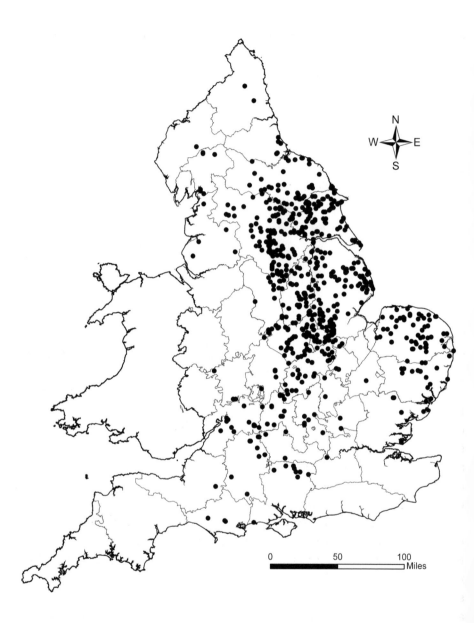

Figure 2.4 The total distribution of *thorps* first recorded by 1300 (based on the list provided in Appendix 2, below pp. 163–202).

satisfactorily interpreted. Benefield is a well-attested settlement-name for which many eleventh- to fourteenth-century forms are recorded by EPNS NTH.[15] In the fifteenth century a single example of the form *Benyfeld Netherthorp* is noted with the editors' comment: 'i.e. "lower village" in contrast to *Upthorpe* now Upper Benefield'. This *Upthorp* is recorded frequently as a settlement-name in its own right in the thirteenth and fourteenth centuries (e.g. *Upthorp* c.1220, *Upthrop al. Upthorp* 1325),[16] and the editors add a form *Benefeild Overthorpe* from 1641, explaining that this 'upper village' lies above Benefield. This pattern of spellings surely indicates not that *Netherthorp* and *Upthorp/Overthorpe* originated as names for divisions of one village but that *Upthorp* was a minor settlement originally established outside Benefield. It looks as if the main village grew to encompass the outlier, and that at this point a transfer of name would become tempting: if the higher part of the expanded settlement was *Upthorp* then the lower could be termed, as a one-off, *Netherthorp*. It seems to us clear that in this case the two instances of *thorp* can be readily distinguished – *Upthorp* looks like an old minor settlement, a perfectly good *thorp*; *Netherthorp* was a later play on the earlier name. There are no grounds here to omit Upthorp, at least, from the corpus. And it is doubtful whether this instance of *Netherthorp* goes far towards ascribing to *thorp* a generalised sense of 'division of a settlement'.

    The second particular example given by Fellows-Jensen is the group of minor names *le Esthorp*, *le Medilthorpe* and *le Westhorp* in Kirby Bellars LEI. Here there is no commentary on the names in the source to which she refers,[17] and interpretation is speculative. Fellows-Jensen infers that different parts of Kirby Bellars were known as 'East-', 'Middle-' and 'West-thorp', but an alternative explanation is presumably possible: that these *thorp*-names denoted three minor outlying settlements within the township. Fellows-Jensen goes on to list a further group of minor names 'mostly in Lei[cestershire], which cannot be located exactly and which probably only ever referred to parts of a settlement': these include various instances of *Netherthorp*, *Northorp* and *Westhorp*, together with a few simplex names such as *Thorp* in Croxton Kerrial and *Thorp on le toftis* in Belgrave. Again, there seems to us little solid reason for these omissions, especially because – as Fellows-Jensen herself accepts – simplex names and directional qualifiers such as *nether* and *north* are markedly characteristic of the *thorps* as a whole (see below, pp. 45, 63, 66). If we were to exclude these names as 'probably only ever referr[ing] to parts of a

---

15 EPNS NTH, p. 211.

16 EPNS NTH, p. 212.

17 B. Cox, 'The place-names of Leicestershire and Rutland', PhD thesis (Nottingham, 1971), p. 290; the material is now published (with some earlier forms: the names are recorded between the thirteenth and fifteenth centuries) in EPNS LEI, 3, pp. 89–93.

settlement', we might have our doubts about very many more that are similarly constituted. In fact, however, it seems sensible to be wary of the alleged application to parts of a settlement. [18] Indeed, in at least one case here, *Thorp on le toftis*, we have further information to counter the idea. Cox notes that this *thorp* is 'a lost farmstead described in 1278 as a tillage'.[19] The possibility that the other names mentioned here are similarly lost medieval settlements seems to us likely enough. We shall come back to the *thorps* apparently dotted among the common fields of medieval Leicestershire (see below, pp. 148–51); for the moment we certainly do not want to exclude such examples on any grounds other than, in some cases, a relatively late date of record.

Boundaries

The next issue that arises is the division of Danelaw from English names. For the most part this is, of course, straightforward: *thorps* in Yorkshire, Lincolnshire and Norfolk lie in the historical Danelaw, territory that came under the political control of Scandinavian invaders for an extended period in the ninth and tenth centuries; *throps* in Gloucestershire, Hampshire and Dorset lie outside it. That is not to say that some *thorps* in the east and north may not have been established by an Anglo-Saxon population before the Danes ever arrived, nor that some *throps* in the south-west Midlands may not represent linguistic drift from the Norse-influenced speech of the Danelaw. But before we delve into the potential complexities of chronological layers and shifting linguistic influence, it is sensible simply to draw a coherent line that divides the total corpus into two, so that we can examine the broad characteristics of one region as compared with the other.

Although the division is generally clear, there are some problems at the margins. It might be hoped that we could always simply distinguish the name-groups by their spellings, Scandinavian *thorps* versus English *throps*. Unfortunately, as we discuss in the next section, this is not workable in the way that early scholars proposed. Instead it is preferable to try to fix a line on historical grounds, albeit that this involves its own difficulties. The only early description of the Danelaw boundary, the late-ninth-century agreement between King Alfred and the Danish

---

18   Clear evidence for the use of medieval habitative terms in this way is found in the types *Northiby*, 'north in the *bȳ*', and *Suthinton*, 'south in the *tūn*', but with *thorp* there seems to be no sign of such forms distinguished by the prepositions *i* or *in*. (These types, incidentally, are clearly original bynames or surnames, not place-names.) See P.H. Reaney, *The origin of English surnames* (London, 1967), pp. 52–3; K. Cameron, 'Bynames of location in Lincolnshire subsidy rolls', *Nottingham Medieval Studies*, 32 (1988), pp. 156–64.

19   EPNS LEI, 3, pp. 52–3. Cf. *OED* tillage, sense 2, 'Tilled or ploughed land; land under crops as distinct from pasturage'.

leader Guthrum, is limited in its extent and probably misleading in some of its details.[20] It provides no guidance on what to do with names in Durham and Northumberland, for instance, and it places all of Essex in the Danelaw when other evidence strongly suggests that only the far north-east of the county, Colchester and its hinterland, was in Scandinavian hands for any length of time.[21]

We have taken pragmatic decisions to delimit the effective Danelaw in these cases. The Durham *thorps* may well be associated with Scandinavian influence, for Victor Watts showed that their distribution – in a group near the coast, between the Tees and the Wear – correlates well with some other types of Norse-influenced name, particularly the so-called 'Grimston-hybrids'.[22] Thus, although they lie beyond the middle Tees valley region which may be the only part of the county that received dense early Scandinavian settlement, there is still some reason to consider them Norse-inspired, as Watts certainly did.[23] In contrast, the two apparent instances of *throp* in Northumberland, Throphill and Thropton, are much further north and beyond any grouping of unambiguous Scandinavian place-names, and we count these with our English group, which otherwise belongs entirely south or south-west of the Danelaw counties.

In the case of Essex we accept the historical indications that probably only the Colchester region belonged to the Danelaw. In terms of *thorp* place-names, this has the effect of assigning Thorpe-le-Soken to the Scandinavian group and the county's six other locatable instances to the English. It may be noted that much the same conclusion is drawn by P.H. Reaney in EPNS ESX,[24] and is implied also by A.H. Smith's map of English *throps*, which is reproduced here as Figure 2.5: unlike us, Smith was happy both to plot the instances as he does and to draw in the conventional Alfred–Guthrum line.[25]

---

20 A translated text is conveniently available in S. Keynes and M. Lapidge, *Alfred the Great* (Harmondsworth, 1983), pp. 171–2, with commentary pp. 311–13. Doubts about details and/or the length of time that the treaty held in this form are expressed by D.N. Dumville, *Wessex and England from Alfred to Edgar* (Woodbridge, 1992), pp. 1–23 and R.H.C. Davis, 'Alfred and Guthrum's frontier', EHR, 97 (1982), pp. 803–10.

21 Dumville, *Wessex and England*, pp. 3–12; cf. Keynes and Lapidge, *Alfred*, p. 289, n. 29.

22 V. Watts, 'Scandinavian settlement-names in County Durham', *Nomina*, 12 (1988–9), pp. 17–63 at 19–26.

23 *Ibid.*, p. 57.

24 EPNS ESX, p. 569. Reaney makes some appeal to the formal argument that occasional *throp* forms point to an English origin. We are not comfortable with this (see further below), and Reaney anyway has to concede that there are exceptions.

25 The text of EPNE suggests that in fact Smith was, quite reasonably, unsure what to do with Essex examples: he mentions Gestingthorpe under both *thorp* 'if it is Scandinavian' and *þrop* 'if it is English'; he also includes Easthorpe, without comment, under both headwords (EPNE, 2, pp. 209, 211, 215, 216).

Figure 2.5 A.H. Smith's map of *throps* (redrawn here), showing the traditional line of division established by the treaty of Alfred and Guthrum in the late ninth century. While the majority of *throps* lie to the south and west of this line, Smith does not account for those which he identifies, particularly in Essex and the Yorkshire West Riding, that lie north and west of this political boundary.

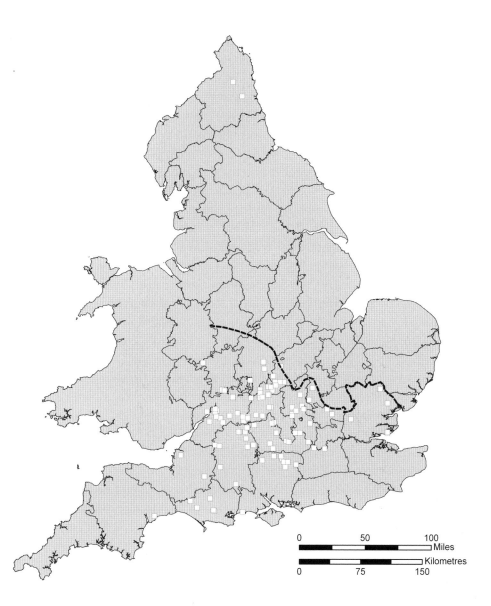

Figure 2.6 The new division of Danelaw and 'English' *throps* showing the modified Alfred–Guthrum line now incorporating the greater part of Essex. The map also shows further examples of *throps* in counties such as Dorset unrecognised by Smith, and the removal of some of his probable *throps* in Essex and Yorkshire West Riding, now reassigned as *thorps*.

Finally, it should be acknowledged that even where the Alfred–Guthrum line is clear, and appears broadly significant, it was not necessarily firm and impenetrable. A scatter of distinctive bȳ-names just to the west of Watling Street in the Midlands, for instance, suggests that Scandinavian influence did not simply break off at that boundary.[26] However, since the distribution of thorps and throps continues south-westwards from Northamptonshire through Oxfordshire and deep into West Saxon territory, it is not easy in this case to say exactly where direct Scandinavian influence stops. For consistency, and to avoid a jumble of ad hoc arguments, we have decided in our calculations absolutely to respect the Alfred–Guthrum boundary, except in the special case of Essex. Thus we pick up the line where the river Lea leaves the Essex boundary; thence to the source of the Lea; then north in a straight line to Bedford; then up the Ouse to Watling Street at Stony Stratford; and then along Watling Street as far as its line can be traced (Figure 2.6).[27]

In the 'border counties' this has the following effects: in Hertfordshire the only pre-1300 name lies on the 'English' side of the line;[28] in Bedfordshire the parish of Souldrop is north of the Ouse, in Danelaw territory, while the minor Thrup End in Lidlington lies to the western, English, side of a line from the source of the Lea to Bedford; in Buckinghamshire the parish of Castle Thorpe is found in a narrow strip of the county that lies north of the Ouse while the remaining 5 thorps in the county are on the English side; in Northamptonshire there are 26 pre-1300 thorps on the Danelaw side of Watling Street and 8 on the English; in Warwickshire, which is just cut by Watling Street, the 3 thorps all fall on the English side; in Staffordshire the single thorp lies on the Danelaw side.[29] There is no doubt that this categorisation is artificial, but some pragmatic solution to the problems of drawing the line is required. Having said all this, it should be noted that the numbers of thorps in the border counties, Northamptonshire aside, are low and will not have much effect on comparative statistics.

26 See, for example, the map in SSNEM, p. 251.
27 These are essentially the terms of the Alfred–Guthrum boundary (above, n. 20), save for the beginning, which runs 'Up the Thames, and then up the Lea', and the end, where the document does not specify what happens to the boundary having arrived at Watling Street.
28 Three further names first recorded in the fourteenth and fifteenth centuries fall on the English side, one (le Throp 1441 in Hertingfordbury) lies on the Danelaw side of the Lea.
29 D. Horovitz, The place-names of Staffordshire (Brewood, 2005), pp. 271–2 and 407, notes two more possible thorps in Staffordshire, although they are both first recorded after 1300 and neither is securely located. The site of Gerardsthorpe 1342 may have been under Blithfield Reservoir (c. SK 0723), while Neuthorp 1413 may have been near Hamstall Ridware (c. SK 1019), although Horovitz concedes that this second instance may in fact not even fall within Staffordshire. Both of the suggested locations would be, like the parish-name Thorpe Constantine, on the Danelaw side of the line.

Thorp and throp

It might seem that the simplest means of distinguishing Anglo-Saxon and Danish names would be by the forms of the words. Linguists habitually cite Old English *throp* and Old Norse *thorp* because these are the predominant forms found in manuscript records of the languages. And it is a distinction that often seems to be reflected in the spellings of names in England: places in Dorset and Gloucestershire are called Throop and Southrop, places in Lincolnshire and Norfolk are Thorpe and Gunthorpe. Yet, while there is a degree of truth in it, the formal argument proves a very slippery one. Problems arise partly because we do not know enough about the form of the word in early English usage, and partly because the records that we have are inevitably later in date than the coining of the names.

The various cognates in Germanic languages indicate that *thorp-* is the ancestral form, and that it is Old English *throp* which is out of line. In fact, *throp* exhibits a well-known type of linguistic change called metathesis, a change by which 'a consonant moves from immediately before a vowel to immediately after it, or the reverse'.[30] Metathesis is particularly common where the consonant is r, and it is often sporadic, occurring in some dialects or registers of a language but not others; examples in Old English of words recorded both with and without it include *gærs* and *græs* 'grass', and *wrenna* and *wærna* 'wren'. The sporadic nature of the sound-change makes arguments based upon it weak. Since our knowledge of this Old English word is extremely restricted – it can be argued that the textual record comes down to two instances of *throp* against one of *thorp*[31] – it is perfectly possible that the unmetathesised *thorp* was always the usual form across much of eastern and northern England. Indeed, it is striking that the parish of Thorpe in Surrey is *Torp* in Domesday Book and *Thorp* or *Thorpe* in the majority of medieval documents, including a number of post-Conquest copies of Anglo-Saxon charters, some of which may accurately reflect pre-Conquest content.[32] Moreover, when the

---

30 *OEG* § 459.
31 Outside place-names, the total OE corpus comprises five instances of *throp* in glosses, four of which descend from a common source (see Appendix 1); there is then one vernacular text with the form *þa þorpes*, although since the document in its surviving form is both post-Conquest and relates to places near Peterborough, within the historical Danelaw, it is possible that this *thorp* derives directly from the Norse word. See further below, p. 39.
32 EPNS SUR, p. 134. The editors collected a single *throp* form from 1272. The list of Anglo-Saxon charters given by EPNS SUR is incomplete: the place-name is found in S 353, 420, 752, 1035, 1093, 1094 and 1165. These are all charters from the Chertsey archive, and none survives in a copy earlier than the thirteenth century. Most are considered to be dubious, if not blatant forgeries, but for the possibility of an underlying authentic pedigree for Thorpe see below, pp. 69–70.

spelling *throp* occurs in records of a Danelaw place-name, it is often implausible to suggest that this betrays the influence of native Anglo-Saxon usage. Sixteenth-century spellings appear to indicate that metathesis often took place in Yorkshire *thorps* at that date, which looks like the independent onset of a change that might be considered latent.[33] When we are faced with occasional thirteenth- and fourteenth-century Yorkshire *throp*-forms, therefore, it must be possible that these reflect earlier tendencies towards the same sporadic change,[34] rather than that they are necessarily indicative of native, non-Scandinavian survival.[35]

Having said this, there are reasonably coherent patterns of attestation in the 'border-counties' discussed above. To the north-west, the Staffordshire and Warwickshire names are consistently *thorp* (even though the former are one side of the historical Danelaw line and the latter the other). In the south-east the Essex names are all exclusively or predominantly *thorp*, save one lost field-name for which the recorded spellings are mixed. In between, in Hertfordshire, Bedfordshire and Buckinghamshire, the names are mostly in *throp* rather than *thorp*, whichever side of the line they fall.[36] This leaves, in the middle of the country, Northamptonshire, where the distribution is striking. On the Danelaw side of Watling Street 24 pre-1300 names always or usually evidence spellings which indicate unmetathesised *thorp*, 2 have thoroughly mixed forms, and none are predominantly in *throp*. On the other side of the road, there are 5 names with mixed spellings plus 1 predominantly in *thorp* and 2 predominantly in *throp*.

The pattern of these forms merits further examination elsewhere, but it is at once clear that they may well have some relationship to the Danelaw and its Scandinavian settlers. The Northamptonshire distribution suggests this in particular, with many *thorps* and no *throps* on the Danelaw side of the historical boundary, and more *throps* than *thorps* on the other. The other counties, it might be noted, gently challenge the historical line: in Warwickshire and Essex *thorp* could represent Scandinavian 'incursion' into English territory; in Hertfordshire,

---

33 Thus, for example, the forms for Gelsthorpe, Coneythorpe and Cowthorpe in the West Riding (EPNS *YOW*, 5, pp. 10, 14, 22): all are well recorded as *t(h)orp(e)* in the medieval period, but commonly become *t(h)rop(pe)* from the sixteenth century onwards. Metathesis in the modern pronunciation is recorded for Gelsthorpe and Cowthorpe.

34 Examples include *Painestrop* 1263 EPNS *YOE*, p. 131; *Yarpestrop* m.13th EPNS *YON*, p. 46; *Aylsithrop* 1350 EPNS *YOW*, 1, p. 282. The last example contains an OE pers.n. < *Æthelsige*, but there is no clear correlation with English first elements here: the other examples appear to contain Continental Germanic and ON pers.ns respectively.

35 Two names in the West Riding of Yorkshire have been identified as instances of English *throp* somehow kept apart from the prevailing dialectal *thorp*, but there are uncertainties in their interpretation: see further below, p. 81, n. 68.

36 The only instance in these counties which has no *throp*-forms is *Westthorpe* in Puttenham HRT, which is recorded just the once, in 1312: it is on the 'English' side of the boundary.

Bedfordshire and Buckinghamshire the English *throp* creeps into the Danelaw.

A major difficulty in using this as evidence for the ultimate 'ethnicity' of the names, however, is the dating of the spellings. If – for argument's sake – most of the relevant settlements were established by *c*.950, then 95 per cent of the names in these border counties are first recorded over 130 years later; and even for most of the handful found in pre-Conquest records there could still be a lag of several generations.[37] It is quite possible that there may have been variation between metathesised and unmetathesised forms during the many unrecorded decades.[38] In particular, it is a commonplace that the dialects of eastern and northern England were substantially influenced during the later Anglo-Saxon and early post-Conquest periods by Old Norse language, and that this influence was felt as much in the form and pronunciation of native words as in the introduction of Norse loans.[39] *Thorp* was clearly the dominant Scandinavian form, and it evidently became the dominant form in most of the Danelaw. In so far as *throp* was in native use here it would, in areas of strong Scandinavian linguistic influence, almost inevitably give way to *thorp* over the generations.[40] The isogloss through Northamptonshire is a fascinating one, but it is probably better interpreted as an indicator of the limits of Scandinavian-influenced Middle English dialect than as a straightforward guide to the linguistic origins of the original name-givers.

37 Early instances include Gestingthorpe ESX, found in a pre-Conquest manuscript as *æt Gyrstlinga þorpe* 975×1016 (S 1487), and Longthorpe NTH, *æt Þeorp* in a twelfth-century composite copy of documents dating from around the 980s (S 1448a; cf. S.E. Kelly (ed.), *Charters of Peterborough Abbey* (Oxford, 2009), no. 30, p. 332). See also the following note.

38 Noteworthy is what may be the earliest recorded instance, Thrupp in Norton NTH, which is probably the *æt Þrope* of Æthelgifu's will (S 1497), recently re-dated by Crick to 956×1002 (J. Crick, *Charters of St Albans* (Oxford, 2007), no. 7 and pp. 92–4, where it is suggested that the document may have been first drawn up early in this period, although the surviving single sheet is a copy of the late tenth or early eleventh century). The spellings for this place, which is adjacent to Watling Street on the 'English' side, are very variable: it is unmetathesised *Torp* in Domesday Book, *Thorp* in a twelfth-century record, and then commonly both *T(h)rop* and *Thorp* from the thirteenth century onwards (EPNS NTH, pp. 27–8).

39 See, for example, M. Townend, *Language and history in Viking age England: linguistic relations between speakers of Old Norse and Old English*, Studies in the Early Middle Ages 6 (Turnhout, 2002); T. Styles, 'Scandinavian elements in English place-names: some semantic problems', in J. Graham-Campbell, R. Hall, J. Jesch and D.N. Parsons (eds), *Vikings and the Danelaw: select papers from the proceedings of the thirteenth Viking congress* (Oxford, 2001), pp. 289–98.

40 A familiar parallel is found in the place-names Charlton and Carlton. These names are generally believed all to derive from Old English *ceorla-tūn* 'farm/estate of the peasants' (i.e. genitive plural), but Carlton, which is very regular in 'Scandinavian England', points to pervasive influence on pronunciation, perhaps by the formal substitution of ON *karl* for OE *ceorl*. Compare Charlton, in Newbottle, with East Carlton, in Northampton, on the English and Danelaw sides of Northamptonshire respectively. See H.P.R. Finberg, 'Charltons and Carltons', in idem, *Lucerna* (London, 1964), pp. 144–60; VEPN, 3, pp. 19–23.

In sum, then, the argument is that the presence or absence of metathesis in the recorded forms of names is more directly a reflection of Middle English dialect than of the language of pre-Conquest namers, and that anyway we know too little of the distribution of the metathesised variant in pre-Scandinavian England. Similar conclusions were reached by Niels Lund ('metathesis is no reliable guide for distinguishing OE from ODan instances of *thorp*'),[41] and by Gillian Fellows-Jensen ('the formal distinction between *þrop* and *þorp* is not a satisfactory criterion for distinguishing between English names and Danish ones').[42] This is the consensus view: form cannot simply be considered diagnostic of linguistic origin. Having said that, there is no doubt that *thorp* is the hugely prevalent form in the Danelaw, while *throp* is usual in the English counties to the south and west. It is therefore often convenient for us to generalise as 'Danelaw *thorps*' and 'English *throps*' and this is how they will be treated in the following two chapters. It should perhaps also be reiterated that, partly to avoid wearisome repetition of 'thorps and throps', we often use *thorps* to include the entire class of names, as in the title of the book.

---

41 Lund, 'Thorp-names', pp. 223–5, at 224.
42 Fellows-Jensen, 'Place-names in -*þorp*', p. 36.

3

Danelaw thorps

Our analysis of the Danelaw *thorps* begins with the evidence provided by the place-names themselves. We have found it sensible to divide our discussion into three sections, dealing first with what these names might tell us about the size and status of *thorps*, secondly with the kinds of qualifiers that were used to differentiate or distinguish individual *thorps*, and finally with what the linguistic evidence might tell us about the dating of these place-names and the settlements with which they were associated.

Size and status

Analysis of the Danelaw *thorps* emphasises that they were in origin small settlements dependent on larger estate centres. This is familiar ground for all those who have previously studied the name-group, and we do not intend to labour the point here. Four factors which point in this direction are discussed below, with a summary of the arguments and statistics presented by others, compared – where appropriate – with results from the present survey.

Direct evidence for the early dependence of thorps

In a few cases there are early records to suggest that *thorps* are dependent on, or in some way secondary or subservient to, other places. In Domesday Book, for instance, Littlethorpe YOW was a berewick ('outlying farm/estate') of Ripon, and the two berewicks of Bridlington YOE were Hilderthorpe and Wilsthorpe.[1] In Lincolnshire the survey records that Claythorpe, Dexthorpe, Trusthorpe,

---

1   GDB fols 303v and 299v (for Littlethorpe see DB Yorks, 1, 2W15; for Hilderthorpe and Wilsthorpe see DB Yorks, 1, 1Y11). Important work remains to be done, for those parts of the Domesday survey which indicate distinctions between manors and berewicks, in analysing the correlation with place-name types.

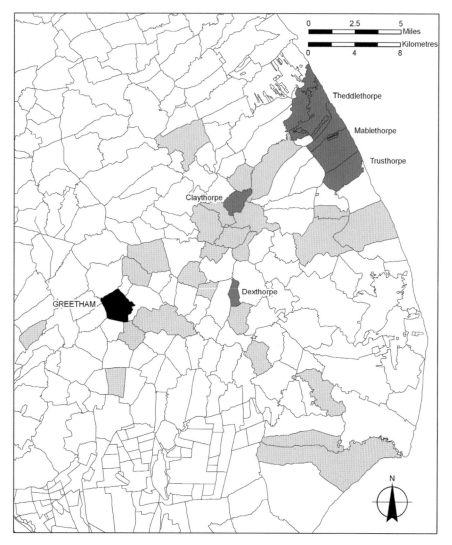

Figure 3.1 The manor of Greetham LIN in Domesday Book. This manor is mapped against nineteenth-century ecclesiastical parishes. The head manor is identified in black, *thorp* holdings in dark grey, and other holdings in light grey.

Mablethorpe and Theddlethorpe all lay in the jurisdiction of Earl Hugh's manor of Greetham (Figure 3.1).[2] In an early-twelfth-century document, which perhaps has an earlier basis, the *appendices* of Peterborough are translated as *þa þorpes*: the estates so categorised included *Dodesthorp*, now Dogsthorpe NTH, beside three non-thorp place-names, *Æstfeld*, *Ege* and *Pastun*.[3] At the end of the twelfth century a lost Thorp in Suffolk was similarly a pertinence of Pakenham (*Torp que est pertinencia de Pakeham*).[4]

Another example that has been cited under this heading is Ashwellthorpe NRF, which is probably to be identified with the *Thorp* from which eight acres of land were conveyed to Ashwell by the terms of a mid-eleventh-century will.[5] This transfer may indeed be indicative of dependency, though the relationship between the places is not clearly indicated by the document. In this example there is overlap with a category discussed below in the section 'Place-name evidence', in which a parish-name is affixed to an earlier simplex *Thorp* (see pp. 44–5).

Later tenurial and ecclesiastical records can also indicate earlier dependency. In some northern counties, in particular, the medieval arrangement of parishes, townships and chapelries gives an idea of earlier settlement hierarchy. In a much-studied part of the Yorkshire Wolds, for instance, this kind of evidence has suggested that Mowthorpe was dependent on Kirby Grindalythe, that Painsthorpe was dependent on Kirby Underdale and that Raisthorpe and Towthorpe were dependent on Wharram Percy.[6] The pattern is much the same in Lincolnshire. The later medieval manorial chapels at Southorpe, Elsthorpe, Grimsthorpe and Scottlethorpe all looked to Edenham. Hawthorpe was a chapelry of Irnham; Counthorpe was originally dependent on Castle Bytham; and similar linkages can be seen at Casthorpe from Barnsby, Woolsthorpe from Colsterworth, Laythorpe from Kirby, and Birthorpe from Stow by Threekingham.[7] In Leicestershire, only

2   DB Lincs, 13.3; 13.5; 13.7–8.

3   The OE text was copied into a version of the *Anglo-Saxon Chronicle* under the year 963: see S. Irvine (ed.), *The Anglo-Saxon Chronicle: a collaborative edition*, 7 MS. E (Cambridge, 2004), pp. xc–xcvi, 57; also edited by Kelly, *Peterborough*, no. 16A. The English paraphrases a Latin document, itself fabricated early in the twelfth century: this Latin 'original', or a text very closely related to it, is S 787, edited by Kelly, *Peterborough*, no. 16. Latin *cum suis appendiciis* is rendered *ealle þa porpes þe ðærto lin*. Note that in yet another version of the text (S 69; Kelly, *Peterborough*, no. 1A) the number of *appendiciis* has grown to ten, three of which are thorp-names.

4   R.H.C. Davis (ed.), *The Kalendar of Abbot Samson of Bury St Edmunds and related documents* (London, 1954), p. 10.

5   S 1516. The suggestion is made in EPNE, 2, p. 209.

6   J.G. Hurst, 'The Wharram Research Project: results to 1983', *Medieval Archaeology*, 28 (1984), pp. 77–111, at 91; Fellows-Jensen, 'Torp-navne i Norfolk', pp. 51–4.

7   D. Owen, 'Chapelries and rural settlement: an examination of some of the Kesteven evidence', in Sawyer (ed.), *Medieval settlement*, pp. 66–71.

Table 3.1

Leicestershire *thorps* with chapels dependent on
another church.

Thorp	Dependent upon
Alsthorpe	Burley
Barleythorpe	Oakham
Belmesthorpe	Ryhall?
Countesthorpe	Blaby
Edmondthorpe	Wymondham?
Elmsthorpe	Burwell?
Gunthorpe	Wardley
Hothorpe	Theddingworth
Keythorpe	Tugby
Lubbesthorpe	Aylestone
Osgathorpe	Whitwick
Othorpe	Slawston
Skelthorpe	Loughborough
Thorpe Acre	Dishley?
Thorpe by Water	Barrowden
Thorpe Parva	Cosby
Thorpe Satchville	Twyford
Ullesthorpe	Claybrooke
Wilsthorpe	Greatford

6 of the 25 *thorps* had parish churches – the remaining 19 (76 per cent) had chapels dependent upon another place (Table 3.1). Again, there is overlap here with another category of evidence, that of the significance of parish status, discussed in the section below.

Smith notes an ecclesiastical group which appears to show the idea of dependency still operative in names coined relatively late: Priesthorpe in Calverley YOW was probably a possession of Kirkstall Abbey, while Priest Thorpe in Bingley YOW probably belonged to Drax Abbey, both of which monasteries were post-Conquest foundations.[8] Comparable is Monksthorpe LIN, said to been held by Bardney Abbey, presumably after its post-Conquest refoundation;[9] *Prestethorpe* in Whitby YON, and held by Whitby Abbey, would be similar.[10] In some instances (for example, Chapelthorpe YOW, Canonthorpe YOW) the French origin of the qualifiers reinforces the post-Conquest flavour of these names. Whether the nature of the dependency in this type is directly equivalent to that found in the secular names is not clear, however.

---

8   EPNE, 2, p. 209; cf. EPNS YOW, 7, p. 49 n. 3. It is notable that the relationships are less certainly expressed under the individual discussions of the names: 'The allusion may be to the monks of Kirkstall who possessed lands in the neighbourhood' (EPNS YOW, 3, p. 225); 'The reference is doubtless to the possession of property here by the monks of Drax Abbey' (EPNS YOW, 4, p. 164).

9   Cameron, *Dictionary of Lincolnshire place-names* (Nottingham, 1998), p. 89.

10   EPNS YON, p. 117.

Table 3.2

Percentage of *thorps* and other name elements in the Danelaw recorded before 1500 and now lost. The graph shows how prone to loss *thorp*-places appear to be, while survival rates for *ing(a)ham* and *tūn* settlements appear much higher.

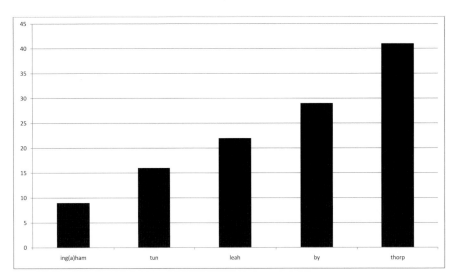

Measurable evidence

Places named *Thorp* or *-thorp* often survive as small settlements or single farms, sometimes as villages, but almost never as towns. Many that are recorded in early documentation later disappear. These observations support the contention that *thorps* were in origin small and, quite probably therefore, dependent. Fellows-Jensen has attempted to quantify survival rates: she calculates that 46 per cent of her Danelaw *thorps* first recorded before 1500 (264 out of 576) are now completely lost or are represented by little more than a single farmstead.[11] This is clearly a high proportion, although it is not easy to find countrywide comparative figures for other place-name elements. In the area of the East Midlands, however, Fellows-Jensen carried through a detailed survey of various name-types, the results of which are shown in Table 3.2. In this sample *thorp*-names are at least twice as likely to represent small or deserted settlements as the place-names of undisputed OE origin chosen for comparison.[12]

11 Fellows-Jensen, 'Place-names in *-þorp*', p. 49.
12 Fellows-Jensen earlier offered figures for Yorkshire which hint at a similar pattern, although she examined only wholly and partially Scandinavian-named places. The figures for *thorps* and *býs* are higher than in the East Midlands – 57% and 34% respectively – but the *thorps* are again much the most liable of her name-categories to shrink or disappear (SSNY, p. 235). Watts ('Scandinavian settlement-names', p. 53) offers figures for County Durham: although the numbers are very small, *thorps* interestingly come top of his list too as places prone to loss.

Table 3.3

Percentage of *thorps* and other name elements in the Danelaw recorded before 1500 that became parish centres. Here the pattern seen in Table 3.2 is reversed: *thorps* seem to have developed far less frequently than places of other name types into parish centres.

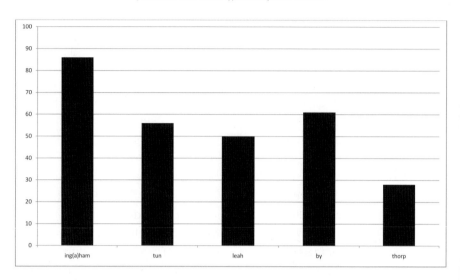

On the other side of the coin, it is observed that although some *thorps* did become parishes – centres of local (ecclesiastical) administration – this is relatively rare: other name-elements have a much higher success rate in this respect. Again, Fellows-Jensen provided the fullest comparative figures in her work on the East Midlands (Table 3.3). In this region she calculated that 28 per cent of *thorp*-named settlements were medieval parishes, not an insignificant total, but considerably lower than those for the other generics studied, which all reached at least 50 per cent.[13] For the whole corpus of Danelaw *thorp*-names Fellows-Jensen has since calculated a figure of 18 per cent with parish status.[14]

One further measurable indicator of the size and status of name-groups that has been examined by Fellows-Jensen is the recorded level of assessment for taxation in the Domesday Book of 1086. Her statistics for the complete Danelaw corpus show that, although there are a handful of highly valued *thorps* (assessed at over ten carucates), most are of relatively little value (assessed at below four carucates).[15] Once more, a great deal of comparative work for other place-name

13 Again, she provided some comparable figures for Yorkshire, where just 7% of the *thorps* were parishes, as opposed to 21% of *bȳs* (SSNY, p. 227). In Durham none of the *thorps* became parishes, although two are townships (Watts, 'Scandinavian settlement-names', p. 51).

14 Fellows-Jensen, 'Place-names in *-þorp*', p. 49.

15 Fellows-Jensen, 'Place-names in *-þorp*', p. 48, gives figures for *thorps* named in Domesday Book as follows: 85 assessed at 2 carucates or fewer, 60 between 2 and 3, 59 between 3 and 4, 30 between

generics in Domesday remains to be done, but for the East Midlands Fellows-Jensen has shown that the assessments, although varying hugely from county to county, consistently show *thorps* as less valuable than *bȳs*, *tūns* and *hāms*.[16] In Yorkshire *thorps* are again clearly the lowest-rated of the name-groups studied (although in the West Riding they are closely comparable with the *bȳs*).[17]

The general implications of all these statistics are clear: *thorps* are much more likely to appear – if they survive at all – as small settlements or single farms than as parishes or villages, and their relatively small size and lack of status can be traced back at least as far as the pages of Domesday Book. It would be most desirable to see more detailed analyses region by region and involving a wider range of place-name elements.[18] We have not attempted to present figures of our own in the various categories covered here, however, for various reasons. Study of a wide range of elements across the whole country opens up a new area of work which is potentially huge. It will be best undertaken by historians familiar with a range of medieval complexities, such as the land tenure of the different regions or the intricacies of establishing the earliest recoverable parish structure.[19] Likewise, there are many fine judgements to be made in deciding, for instance, when a settlement is 'shrunken' and when it is not.[20] These are skilled and labour-intensive fields of work that we cannot take on thoroughly now: Fellows-Jensen's figures are clearly carefully arrived at, and are more than adequate for present purposes.

The demonstrable relative 'smallness' of the *thorps* as a group is presumably to be interpreted as indicative of their original diminutive size. How far it also reflects the date(s) at which they were established is a question that will be discussed further below.

---

15 *cont.*
 4 and 5, 62 above 5 carucates, of which 11 are above 10; in addition 32 *thorps* are named but not independently assessed (itself a significant group). According to these numbers, 49% of assessed *thorps* were rated below 3 carucates, 69% below 4 carucates.

16 SSNEM, pp. 337–9.

17 SSNY, pp. 223–4.

18 It would be particularly interesting to compare *thorps* in this respect with other name-types thought to be indicative of dependent settlements, such as *bere-wīc*, *bere-tūn* and *stoc*.

19 On the problems of the latter, see SSNY, pp. 225–6 and especially SSNEM, pp. 349–53. F.A. Youngs, *Guide to the local administrative units of England*, 2 vols (London, 1979 and 1991), goes some way towards easing the burden.

20 Watts, 'Scandinavian settlement', pp. 52–4, takes from the work of Brian Roberts 'three categories of unsuccessful settlement: shrunken, deserted, and possibly deserted': the last of these in particular, which accounts for three of the five *thorps* in his corpus, hints at the problems here in drawing sharp lines to create statistics.

Place-name evidence

The form of names in thorp gives further indications of the original size and nature of the settlements. One of the most striking features of the group is the number of simplex *Thorps*; that is to say, names in which the term is not – in its early records – compounded with another distinguishing element, as, for example, 'Ulfs-thorp' or 'High-thorp'. Such simplex names, it is argued, are a symptom of restricted importance: places called 'Thorp' or 'the thorp' have a very local significance; they are not generally the building blocks of a larger territory in which different thorps would need to be distinguished. Certainly the contrast here with many other habitative generics is very marked – in EPNE Smith gives no instances of *tūn*, *hām* or *bȳ* as simplex place-names – whereas, tellingly, it is not an uncommon feature of other elements where small size and/or dependency are apparently factors, such as *stoc*, *wīc*, and *worth*.

The various calculations for the number of simplex thorps have given similar results. Cameron's East Midland corpus to 1086 gave him 21 per cent (23 of 109) which were simplex at first record.[21] For the whole Danelaw, in names recorded by 1500, Fellows-Jensen gives a total for simplexes of 23 per cent (132 of 576).[22] Our calculations, for Danelaw names recorded by 1300, are very similar: 132 of 582, giving a percentage identical to Fellows-Jensen's of 23 per cent. To these we would be inclined to add a further fourteen names which, although they are compounds at first record, are subsequently sometimes or often recorded with simplex forms. An example is Edmondthorpe LEI: *Edmerestorp* 1086, *Torp* 1094 1123, *Thorp* c.1130, *Edmeretorp* 1183 and so on.[23] These 'unstable simplexes' are a marked characteristic of the group: many of the names first found as simplexes are later recorded sometimes with a qualifier and sometimes without. Thus, for instance, Thorpe in the Fallows LIN: *Torp* 1086, *Turuluestorp* c.1115, *Torp* c.1175, *Thorelthorp* 1254.[24] In such runs of spellings one gets the impression that it is sometimes just chance as to which type is first recorded. In any case, it is clear that a good proportion of the corpus of thorp-names – a full quarter by our reckoning if the unstable instances are included – are found in simplex form at an early date.

Other characteristic types of thorp-name also seem to be indicative of their original status. There are some early instances – and many later – which combine

---

21   Cameron, 'Scandinavian settlement, part II', p. 141.

22   Fellows-Jensen, 'Place-names in -*þorp*', p. 41.

23   EPNS LEI, 2, pp. 297–8. This name, rather unusually, goes on also to have spellings of the type *Thorp Edmer* 1290, in which it could be said that the qualifier of the conventional compound has become separated and added as an affix to the simplex!

24   Cameron, *Lincolnshire place-names*, p. 126.

thorp with the name of a parish.[25] Examples include Burnham Thorpe NRF, which is unusually found as early as Domesday Book, and Wilby Thorpe NTH, first recorded, more typically, in the thirteenth century.[26] These can be added to the evidence for minor dependent *thorps* which sit within a structure of more significant estates.

Similar, it seems, are the many 'directional' *thorps*, in which the element is qualified by a compass-point or another locational term, such as 'up', 'down' or 'middle'. Examples include Easthorpe YOE, Austhorpe YOW (with ON *austr*, the equivalent of OE *ēast*), Westhorpe SFK and Netherthorpe in Staveley DRB. By our calculations there are some 41 (of 582: 7 per cent) of these in the pre-1300 Danelaw corpus; Fellows-Jensen offered a rather lower 26 (of 576: 5 per cent) in her pre-1500 collection.[27] Such names can often be taken to imply a relationship to the estate centre, although sometimes they may rather relate to one another, perhaps still within one larger estate, although not necessarily so.[28] Again, there is also a further category of 'unstable' directional names, in which a name first recorded as a simplex or with another qualifier is later qualified by a directional term. An example is Thorpe Hall in Selby YOW, which is recorded as *Thorpe* in the twelfth century and *Westhorp'*, as well as *Thorp' Seleby*, in the thirteenth: such instances are not included in the statistics quoted above.

25 Although these are telling examples, they are not statistically impressive: we have only some nine found before 1300. It should be noted, however, that this is the number of names in which a place-name (usually the parish-name) appears as qualifier in the first record of the name: there are a good number of other examples in which the place-name qualifier is added to an earlier simplex at a relatively early date. We have not made a systematic count of these.

26 This fact is not noted in the standard place-name dictionaries (DEPN, CDEPN), where the earliest form cited for Burnham Thorpe is from 1199, but *Bruneham torp* appears on both folios 169r and 262r of LDB (DB Norfolk, 8, 105; 38, 2). There seems to be a Norfolk phenomenon here. Cleythorpe is not noted by the dictionaries at all, despite appearing in Domesday Book (*Cleietorpa* LDB fol. 232r; DB Norfolk, 21, 14); presumably it takes its name from the adjoining [Cockley] Cley, well attested as a simplex from Domesday onwards. A further Norfolk example may be Morningthorpe, which is both simplex *Torp* and *Maringatorp* in Domesday Book (fols 212r and 150v; DB Norfolk, 14, 40; 4, 56): it is argued by DEPN, p. 469, and CDEPN, p. 422, that the *Maringa-* perhaps represents a lost local place-name *Mering (< *Mǣringas).

27 As we have seen (pp. 25–8), this is a type of name that she chooses to reject in some later records, which evidently affects the statistics here.

28 Inter-relationship does not seem to have been commonly proposed for the Danelaw examples, but see the discussion of 'English' instances below, p. 63 and n. 5. It is true that Fellows-Jensen ('Place-names in -*þorp*', p. 45) does suggest that Easthorpe and Westhorpe in NTT refer to one another, but she cites EPNS NTT, p. 176, where it is simply observed that the two hamlets lay to the east and west of Southwell, presumably with the implication that they were named in relation to Southwell rather than to each other.

Date of first record

It is often considered symptomatic of their status that *thorp*-names are first recorded at relatively late dates. Fellows-Jensen observes that 39 per cent (224 of 576) of the names in her Danelaw corpus are first found in records later than the Domesday Book;[29] our equivalent figure for the pre-1300 material is actually slightly higher, at 41 per cent (237 of 582). The implications of these figures are not straightforward, of course. There are two potential explanations for them – that *thorp*-names were being coined into the twelfth and thirteenth centuries, or that older *thorp*-names denoted places of very low status that fell beneath the notice of the Domesday surveyors. Probably, to judge in part by analysis of the qualifiers (which we take up in more detail in the following section), the truth is some combination of the two. But in both cases, the places named were predominantly small, for an abundance of evidence shows that late names did not, as a rule, replace established eleventh-century names for significant places in England after the Norman Conquest.

Qualifiers

Analysis of the qualifiers in compound place-names promises to offer information about the settlements' origins and early use. In the previous section some inferences have been drawn about, for instance, the size and status of *thorps* from their combination with directional qualifiers. In this section some other groups of qualifiers in the corpus of Danelaw *thorps* will be identified and examined.

Personal names

Much the most common type of qualifier among the Danelaw *thorps* is the personal name. By our reckoning, at least 207 pre-1300 *thorps* are compounded with personal names at their first record: this represents 36 per cent of the total, or 46 per cent of the compound names (that is, excluding the original simplexes). And these are minimum figures. Although the personal names are often obvious (for example, ON *Thorgrímr* in Thornthorpe YOE (*Torgrimestorp* 1086)), in many other cases it is very difficult to decide whether a qualifier is a personal name or another word: a simple instance is *Laysingthorpe* LIN, which contains ON *leysingi* 'freedman', or the same word used, as it often was, as the proper name of the man.[30] If we include all the examples that we have marked as uncertain, our total

---

29 Fellows-Jensen, 'Place-names in *-þorp*', p. 45.
30 SSNEM, p. 129; SPNLY, pp. 186–7. Numerous uncertain instances come up in discussions below: pp. 55–7.

Table 3.4

Minimum percentage of personal names found among compounded *thorp* place-names in those counties with more than 15 such compounds.

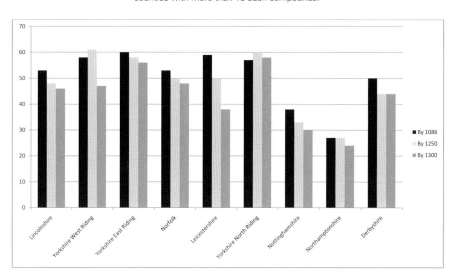

rises to 273 names: 47 per cent of the whole corpus, 61 per cent of the compounds.

Even then, however, our approach to the thorny question of what can safely be identified as a personal name and what cannot has been generally minimalist. Other scholars have made different judgements. Cameron adopted a maximalist approach, identifying 71 personal name qualifiers among his corpus of 109 early recorded names in the north-east Midlands.[31] This equates to 65 per cent of his total corpus, or a huge 83 per cent of the compounds. Fellows-Jensen, examining broadly the same material (with somewhat wider geographical and chronological limits) calculated that personal names accounted for 60 per cent of the compounds.[32] In Yorkshire, when she worked rather more like Cameron, she had found that the equivalent figure was 75 per cent.[33] Some of the principles that have informed these differing philological decisions have been discussed elsewhere in connection with *bȳ*-names,[34] but the upshot is, with the *thorps* as with the *bȳs*, and for all of our differing figures, that personal names make up a very significant proportion of the qualifiers. Place-names like Yaddlethorpe LIN, Sculthorpe NFK and Rogerthorpe YOW point to the close association of individuals called Ēadwulf, Skúli and Roger with the *thorp*-settlements, a type of

---

31 Cameron, 'Scandinavian settlement, part II', p. 141.
32 SSNEM, pp. 92–7. In the corpus to *c*.1150 she has 67 pers.ns in 112 compounds.
33 SSNY, pp. 46–53. She counts 85 pers.ns in 114 compounds.
34 Abrams and Parsons, 'Place-names', pp. 379–431 at 395–7.

association that is found in around half, if not more, of the compound *thorp*-names in the Danelaw.

Closer examination of our figures suggests that personal name qualifiers are not evenly distributed. Table 3.4 shows the minimum percentages of personal names among compound *thorps* in those counties with more than 15 such compounds. It indicates that, in general, personal names are most common in Yorkshire *thorps* and least common in those of Northamptonshire; the Midland counties and Norfolk, off to the east, come fairly neatly in between: there is something of a coherent geographical pattern here.[35]

There is also a chronological pattern to be detected. In every county bar one (the North Riding of Yorkshire) there is a drop in the percentage of personal names found in *thorp*-compounds recorded by 1300 compared with the percentage found in those recorded by 1086. In most cases there are traces of a gentle decline over the centuries, while in two counties there is a rather dramatic fall in the second half of the thirteenth century. In Leicestershire, 13 of 25 compounds recorded by 1250 seem clearly to contain personal names, while, of a further 11 that appear in the record by 1300, only one is certainly of this type. At this date the directional qualifiers mentioned above (p. 45) become predominant, which may help to account for the shift. In the West Riding of Yorkshire the percentage fall is sharper still: from 31 of the 51 compounds found by 1250, to 36 of the 76 recorded by 1300. Here there are also a few directional qualifiers to reckon with among the later-recorded examples, but in addition there is a greater range of nouns and adjectives, including three Milnthorpes ('mill') and two Woodthorpes, to consider.

These patterns of attestation are perhaps illusory: there is clearly a need for caution when absolute numbers of personal names are so hard to quantify. On the other hand, there is little reason to suspect that our linguistic judgement has varied by county or date of record, and the resultant patterns are geographically and chronologically coherent.[36] We shall give these questions further attention in due course (pp. 153–4), but for now we note that personal name qualifiers are particularly common in the north, and that in general they are everywhere rather more common the earlier the records examined.

There remains one other obvious question to ask of the personal name qualifiers, for many of them can be assigned to a particular language or cultural

---

35 An interesting anomaly is thrown up by Rutland, where at least eight and perhaps nine of the ten compound *thorps* have personal name qualifiers.

36 Few comparable figures can be drawn from the other published investigations, but for the East Midlands Fellows-Jensen also records a drop in the proportion of pers.n. qualifiers, from 60% by c.1150 to 55% by 1500 (SSNEM, pp. 92, 99, the quoted figures adjusted to omit simplexes).

Table 3.5
Thorp personal-name qualifiers divided by language/cultural background found in place-names attested by 1300 and 1086.

County	Minimum personal-name thorps by 1300	Total confidently ascribed to language	ON	OE	Post-Conquest
Derbyshire	7	7	4 (57%)	0	3 (43%)
Leicestershire	14	13	5 (38%)	6 (46%)	2 (15%)
Lincolnshire	40	32	24 (75%)	7 (22%)	1 (3%)
Norfolk	22	18	15 (83%)	2 (11%)	1 (6%)
Northamptonshire	5	4	3 (75%)	1 (25%)	0
Nottinghamshire	9	5	2 (40%)	2 (40%)	1 (20%)
Rutland	8	6	4 (67%)	2 (33%)	0
Suffolk	5	5	4 (80%)	1 (20%)	0
Yorkshire East Riding	41	31	29 (94%)	1 (3%)	1 (3%)
Yorkshire North Riding	18	12	10 (83%)	2 (17%)	0
Yorkshire West Riding	36	31	15 (48%)	10 (32%)	6 (19%)
Total	205	164	115 (70%)	34 (21%)	15 (9%)

County	Minimum personal-name thorps by 1086	Total confidently ascribed to language	ON	OE	Post-Conquest
Derbyshire	1	1	0	0	1 (100%)
Leicestershire	10	9	3 (33%)	5 (56%)	1 (11%)
Lincolnshire	28	20	15 (75%)	4 (20%)	1 (5%)
Norfolk	17	14	12 (86%)	1 (7%)	1 (7%)
Northamptonshire	4	3	2 (67%)	1 (33%)	0
Nottinghamshire	6	3	1 (33%)	2 (67%)	0
Rutland	4	4	2 (50%)	2 (50%)	0
Suffolk	3	3	3 (100%)	0	0
Yorkshire East Riding	35	26	25 (96%)	1 (4%)	0
Yorkshire North Riding	16	10	9 (90%)	1 (10%)	0
Yorkshire West Riding	14	12	8 (67%)	3 (25%)	1 (8%)
Total	138	105	80 (76%)	20 (19%)	5 (5%)

background. There are three main groups: Old English (*Godrīc*, *Wulfstān* or *Wine*, for example), Old Norse (*Úlfketill*, *Gamall* or *Gunni*, for example), and the rather heterogeneous 'Norman' or 'Continental' group of names that were, in general, introduced to England in and after 1066 (*Hubert*, *Jourdain* and *Willelm*, for example). It is naturally of interest to learn how the qualifiers in the *thorp* names divide along these lines, and an indication is given in Table 3.5.

The relative proportions quoted for Danelaw names recorded by 1300 – 70 per cent Old Norse, 21 per cent Old English and 9 per cent Continental – are closely comparable with Fellows-Jensen's calculations on her pre-1500 corpus: she gives 67 per cent Old Norse, 20 per cent Old English and 13 per cent Continental. Such figures, with over three times as many identifiable Norse names as English ones, are clearly of importance in considering the issue of the degree to which the *thorp*-names of the Danelaw are Scandinavian, and again we shall return to this point later (pp. 59–61, 153).

Before looking into the figures a little more closely, however, it is appropriate, once again, to draw attention to some of the difficulties involved in arriving at them. Just as it is often hard to be sure whether a qualifier is a personal name or some other word, so, when we think we have identified a personal name, it is often hard to assign it to one language or another. Because Old English, Old Norse and the Continental Germanic dialects which contributed to the Normans' name-stock are related languages, with shared naming-practices, a good number of name-forms are ambiguous. Thus OE *Sigemund*, ON *Sigmundr* and OGer (Frankish) *Sigimund* can all give us *Simund* in medieval English records.[37] Naturally we have not counted such cases: indeed, we have set the bar high in only allowing instances for which no reasonable alternative comes to mind; and in so doing we have not counted a good number of names which recent commentators have accepted as probably Scandinavian when there is some chance of an English equivalent.[38] In this way ours are again minimum figures, over-cautious if anything. This goes some way towards explaining apparent inconsistencies with some of the figures produced by others: it is notable, for instance, that we ascribe a total of only 164 pre-1300 names to particular languages, while Fellows-Jensen has almost exactly a hundred more in her pre-1500 corpus – the difference is not all due to the (relatively few) *thorps* first recorded in the fourteenth and fifteenth centuries.

Again, our cautious analysis has at least the virtue of being equally applied across the country, so that when patterns emerge from the data there is no obvious reason to doubt them. And it is encouraging that the geographical and chronological patterns that do emerge are, very broadly, supported by the results of the earlier investigators. These patterns are, first, that Yorkshire, especially its East and North Ridings, boasts a higher proportion of Scandinavian personal names than the Midlands; and, secondly, that this distribution was more marked

---

37 SPNN, p. 330; the example (an extreme one, admittedly) is further complicated by confusion in medieval records, and probably usage, with the etymologically unconnected biblical name *Simon*. For further discussion of ambiguities, and brief definition of the 'Continental' names introduced to England by the Normans, see D.N. Parsons, 'Anna, Dot, Thorir ...: counting Domesday personal names', *Nomina*, 25 (2001–2), p. 39.

38 An example would be Bagthorpe NFK, for which SPNN, pp. 93–4, and CDEPN, p. 32, accept an ON *Bakki* or *Bak*; but, as DEPN, p. 23, observes, OE *Bacca* is attested, and cannot be formally excluded here. Cf. Parsons, 'Anna, Dot, Thorir' pp. 29–52 at 37.

in 1086 than in 1300.[39] Once more, the West Riding of Yorkshire shows a particularly sharp change between those dates, falling from 67 per cent Old Norse at Domesday Book to 48 per cent by 1300, with concomitant rises in both Old English and Continental names. In the other parts of Yorkshire the shift is less dramatic, but in the same direction: in the East Riding from 96 per cent to 94 per cent, in the North Riding from 90 per cent to 83 per cent. In the East Midlands, on the other hand, percentages of ON personal names either remain the same (Lincolnshire 75 per cent), or they tend to rise (as Leicestershire from 33 per cent to 38 per cent, Nottinghamshire 33 per cent to 40 per cent, Northamptonshire 67 per cent to 75 per cent, Rutland 50 per cent to 67 per cent), although in the counties that record a rise the absolute numbers are small and perhaps not too significant.[40] Yet the trend appears clear, and sets this region apart from Yorkshire, and also from East Anglia, because Norfolk is among the most Norse counties by this measure (86 per cent by 1086, 83 per cent by 1300); Suffolk is no doubt statistically invalid, but it might be noted that all three of its personal name qualifiers recorded by 1086 are identifiably Old Norse, four out of five by 1300.

Other qualifiers

Personal names are not the only qualifiers: many compound *thorp*-names involve a noun or an adjective as the first element. We have already mentioned the largest category, the directional terms, and some classification of the remainder is given below. Following on from the end of the last section, however, it is convenient to begin with their distribution by language.

Once again, it is necessary to preface the figures with a brief discussion of the nature of the material. In particular, the considerable inherited similarities between Old English and Old Norse make confident attributions to one language or the other more difficult, if anything, than with the personal names. Thus, of the four compass points, three are identical when filtered through the medieval English record (OE *north*/ON *northr*, OE *west*/ON *vestr*, OE *sūth*/ON *súthr*); only 'east' (OE *ēast*, ON *austr*) allows a distinction to be made. 'Up' and 'nether' are likewise ambiguous, although 'middle' (OE *middel*, ON *methal*) is not. The number of

39 Taken together the three Ridings of Yorkshire show, according to our figures, 88% ON pers.ns in 1086; SSNY, p. 46, had 85%. For the combined East Midland counties our equivalent figure is 58%, Fellows-Jensen's – to c.1150 – is 56% (SSNEM, p. 92). Cameron's figure for the East Midlands is much higher, at 77%, but this is explicable because he is not only predisposed to accept pers.n. explanations (see above, p. 47), but also to accept ON interpretations (cf. Abrams and Parsons, 'Place-names', p. 395); the fact that, despite his preferences, Cameron's East Midlands total is some 10% lower than our figures for Yorkshire, tends to encourage us to believe that there is a real phenomenon here.

40 Clearly the case of Derbyshire, 0% to 57%, belongs here.

Table 3.6
Non-personal-name compounds found with *thorp* divided by language/cultural background
found in place-names attested by 1300.

County	Non-personal-name compounds thorps by 1300	Total confidently ascribed to language	ON	OE	Post-Conquest
Derbyshire	9	4	0	4 (100%)	0
Leicestershire	21	5	0	5 (100%)	0
Lincolnshire	49	18	9 (50%)	9 (50%)	0
Norfolk	16	3	0	3 (100%)	0
Northamptonshire	12	6	0	6 (100%)	0
Nottinghamshire	21	11	5 (45%)	6 (55%)	0
Yorkshire East Riding	32	13	10 (77%)	3 (23%)	0
Yorkshire North Riding	13	9	5 (56%)	4 (44%)	0
Yorkshire West Riding	37	27	10 (37%)	15 (56%)	2 (7%)
Total (including other Danelaw counties)	228	104	41 (39%)	59 (57%)	4 (4%)

names in which the first element can be satisfactorily identified and also confidently assigned to one language is not, therefore, very high. On the other hand, we have included here the (relatively few) names which we have marked as being possible, but uncertain, personal names, but which we can nevertheless ascribe to a language – an example is the *Laysingthorpe* quoted above, which contains a term that is distinctively Old Norse, whether it be a common noun or a name.

The figures produced by this exercise are shown in Table 3.6. Once more there is a clear chronological dimension here. By 1300, of 104 compounds in which the first element can be assigned confidently to one language, 59 (57 per cent) are Old English, 41 (39 per cent) are Old Norse and 4 (4 per cent) are French. Two centuries earlier, admittedly with a markedly smaller sample, the ranking of English and Norse is reversed: 26 (57 per cent) are Old Norse and 20 (43 per cent) are Old English. When broken down by county, the figures also show similarities with those we have seen before: Yorkshire is particularly Norse, especially the North and East Ridings, while the West Riding shows the most marked change between 1086 and 1300, with its ON percentage falling from 50 per cent to 37 per cent. Each of the other counties which has more than one or two examples by 1086 also shows a fall in the percentage of 'Norseness' between these dates, save for the East Riding, which records a slight rise.

These figures, then, show some intriguing similarities with and points of difference from those derived from the personal names. The overall proportions of identifiable ON nouns and adjectives – 57 per cent by 1086, 39 per cent by 1300 – are much lower than those of ON personal names – 76 per cent by 1086, 70 per cent by 1300. Yet some of the general trends over time and in distribution are comparable: Norse is most common in the north, but generally declines over the centuries as English and, to a lesser extent, post-Conquest linguistic influences penetrated into this region. These are not surprising conclusions: what they might suggest about the origins and nature of Danelaw *thorps* will be discussed below (p. 60 and n. 84).

It remains here to note some of the types found among the nominal and adjectival qualifiers in the pre-1300 Danelaw *thorp*-names. Some names are descriptive of the local ground and vegetation, as for example Grassthorpe NTT, Fenthorpe LIN, Willingthorpe LIN (OE *wilign* 'willow'), Besthorpe NTT, Beesthorpe NTT and Beasthorpe LIN (OE *bēos* 'bent-grass'),[41] Staythorpe NTT (ON *storr* 'sedge'),[42] Londonthorpe LIN (ON *lund* 'grove'), Wothorpe NTH (OE *writh* 'shoot, bush, thicket'), Birthorpe LIN (ON *birki* 'birch'), Hollingthorpe YOW (OE *holegn* 'holly') and five instances of Woodthorpe in Derbyshire and the West Riding of Yorkshire.[43] Given that these are agricultural, probably arable, settlements (see below, pp. 117–37), the recurrent references to grass are interesting. If *bēos* is correctly equated with OE *beonet* 'bent', a term applied to various reedy or rush-like grasses (and the instances of Bes-, Bees- and Beasthorpe are all sited in wet, low-lying areas) then the association with fen and willow may well be significant: these would all be indicative of farms on poorly drained land.[44] Often, however, features in names like these may be open to various interpretations: Willingthorpe could be a boggy plot overgrown with willows, for instance, or it could be a neat, prosperous arable unit the homestead of which was marked by a prominent willow. In the case of the recurrent Woodthorpe there is perhaps reason to suppose a special application, rather than that the settlements were frequently marked by nearby woods. It has been suggested that as Woodhouse 'denoted a hamlet established by the clearing of woodland', so a Woodthorpe would be similar.[45]

41 Besthorpe NFK may be a fourth instance: recurrent medial -*e*- in the spellings suggests to Fellows-Jensen a derived *bēose* 'bent-grass-place' (rather than 'bent wood' as she glosses it at 'Scandinavian settlement names in East Anglia: some problems', *Nomina*, 22 (1999), pp. 52–3); to others it has suggested an alternative derivation from an ON pers.n. Bøsi (thus DEPN, p. 40, and also CDEPN, p. 53, explicitly denying *bēos*). See also below, p. 66.

42 If not a pers.n. Stari: sedge is preferred by SSNEM, p. 117, and CDEPN, p. 573.

43 Further instances, where *wudu* 'wood' is substituted at an early date for another qualifier, are known from LIN and LEI. There is also a Domesday *Widetorp* NTH which may contain the variant OE *widu* 'wood' (SSNEM, p. 108, s.n. Dowthorpe).

44 On *bēos* and *beonet* see VEPN, 1, pp. 83–5. For the sites of the places see SSNEM, pp. 103, 123. Staythorpe NTT is also said to stand on a bed of river gravel, an appropriate site for sedge (SSNEM, p. 117).

45 EPNS DRB, 1, p. 166; 2, p. 337. Certainly the name Woodhouse is characteristic of parts of DRB and YOW (together with NTT), and it is striking that the three early DRB Woodthorpes are all found in Scarsdale Hundred, in the north-east of the county, bordering YOW.

Other qualifiers denote people, presumably owners or occupiers. There are Danes in Danthorpe YOE, Frisians in Friesthorpe LIN and merchants (ON *kaupmenn*) in Copmanthorpe YOW. There is a significant group in royal ownership, incorporating OE *cyne-* 'royal' and *cyning* 'king', or its ON equivalent *konungr*: they include Kingthorpe LIN, Kingthorpe YON, Kingsthorpe NTH, Coneythorpe YOW and Coneysthorpe YON. Related may be Ellenthorpe YON, which appears to refer to *æthelingas* 'princes'. At the other end of the social scale there is Threlthorp DRH, with ON *þræll* 'slave'. There are also three instances of Boythorpe, apparently with the word 'boy', the origin and early application of which are elusive.[46] Nonetheless, other names may be comparable: Knapthorpe NTT seems to involve OE *cnapa* 'boy, youth',[47] and *Sevenetorp* YON possibly contains the genitive plural of ON *sveinn*, of similar meaning;[48] Banthorpe LIN could contain the plural of OE/ON *b(e)arn* 'child';[49] and for the suggestion that a word for 'boy' may be found in instances of Caythorpe see below, p. 65.

The group denoting ecclesiastical ownership has been noted above: to the priests, monks, chapel and canon mentioned there can be added bishops in Biscathorpe LIN (a holding of the bishop of Durham in Domesday Book) and Bishopthorpe YOW, although this was a simplex name at the time of Domesday Book: the place was acquired by the archbishop of York c.1225 and the name *Biscupthorp* appears in 1275.[50]

With regard to adjectives, the directional type has been discussed above. There is then one 'good' *thorp* (Godtorp LEI) and one 'foul or filthy' (Fulthorpe DRH); there are two 'new' ones, Newthorpe NTT (recorded in 1086) and Newthorpe YOW (first recorded c.1020), and one 'old', a thirteenth-century Nottinghamshire field-name *Aldethorpp*;[51] in addition, there are two 'wild' *thorps* in the West Riding of Yorkshire.

Two recurring compounds seem to have caught the imagination and exceeded ordinary patterns of usage: both Gawthorpe/Gowthorpe, with ON *gaukr* 'cuckoo' (at least 12 instances, 8 of them pre-1300), and Pockthorpe, with OE *pūca* 'evil spirit, goblin' (at least 8 instances, most of them in Norfolk, 3 of them pre-1300), have been discussed by Fellows-Jensen, who concluded that both may be derogatory compounds denoting insignificant places, and/or that in each case

---

46 VEPN, 1, p. 122. To the examples given there should be added a lost *Boythorp* NFK, first recorded in 1182 (EPNS NFK, 2, p. 138); the growing evidence for the group tends to support interpretation as a common noun rather than a pers.n.
47 VEPN, 3, p. 127, noting also a later example from YOW.
48 SSNY, p. 67. For another uncertain instance of the same term see below, p. 55, n. 54.
49 SSNEM, p. 102; Cameron, *Lincolnshire place-names*, p. 9, takes it as an ON pers.n. *Barni*.
50 EPNS YOW, 4, p. 225.
51 EPNS NTT, p. 291.

early examples of the names may have been taken up and transferred to later settlements.[52]

It might be suggested that there is little to be gleaned from the compounds noted so far about the origins and functions of *thorps*. Some of the points arising – particularly the possible implications of, on the one hand, fairly frequent royal ownership and, on the other, occupation by young men – will be discussed further in due course (pp. 151–2). But, unless we make something of some boggy instances, or push the rather heterogeneous associations with woodland (perhaps we could imagine a more functional sense than has previously been suggested for the recurrent Woodthorpe?), there is little here that is indicative of the kind of livelihood that was pursued in a *thorp*.

References to livestock, for example, are rare and uncertain. A good possibility is Gristhorpe YON, which may involve pigs (ON *gríss*), although a recorded personal name (derived from the animal) is also possible.[53] A similar compound may be *Sunthorpe* YOE, perhaps 'swine-thorpe' as a number of early spellings suggest (e.g. *Suin-, Swynthorp* 1238, 1297).[54] Fellows-Jensen proposes OE **wither* 'wether, castrated ram' for the lost Norfolk *Witherestorp*.[55] In Langthorpe YOE and Sausthorpe LIN lambs (OE/ON *lamb*) and sheep (ON *sauthr*) could be involved, though again in both cases there are equivalent recorded ON personal names (nicknames in origin, derived from the animals).[56] Similar is Bullerthorpe YOW, *Bullokesthorp* in 1251, where *bullock* may also be used as a personal name, this time of English origin, rather than the animal.[57] There are some suggestive possibilities

---

52 On the *gaukr* names see Fellows-Jensen, 'Place-names in *-þorp*', p. 46. For *pūca* see *eadem*, 'Scandinavian settlement names in East Anglia', pp. 45–60 at 53: she alternatively suggests a cognate Danish *púki*; see also *eadem*, 'Torp-navne i Norfolk', p. 56. Note that our statistics in Table 3.6 assume the English form.

53 Pigs are preferred by CDEPN, p. 264, and allowed by SSNY, p. 59. Older works assume the pers.n.: DEPN, p. 206, EPNS YON, p. 104.

54 It should be noted, however, that forms in *Sun-* are earlier, from 1187×1207, and more persistent. EPNS YOE, pp. 16–17. Swinthorpe LIN (*Sonetorp* 1086), cited there as a parallel, is widely regarded elsewhere as containing an ON pers.n. *Súni* (SSNEM, pp. 117–18; Cameron, *Lincolnshire place-names*, p. 122). Swinethorpe LIN (*Suenestorp* 1181) contains the ON pers.n. *Sveinn* or the equivalent noun meaning 'young man, servant' (SSNEM, p. 132; Cameron, *Lincolnshire place-names*, p. 122). In both of these names, as perhaps in *Sunthorpe* YOE, there seems to have been reinterpretation as *swin* 'swine'.

55 We have not found this name: Fellows-Jensen cites *Witherestorp* as a single undated form in 'Torp-navne i Norfolk', p. 56.

56 For Langthorpe EPNS YOE, p. 48, favours the pers.n.; SSNY, p. 62, allows both alternatives. For Sausthorpe the apparent genitive singular *sauths* has led most to favour the pers.n. (DEPN, p. 405; CDEPN, p. 529; Cameron, *Lincolnshire place-names*, p. 106); only Fellows-Jensen (SSNEM, p. 131) mentions 'sheep', although she thought the pers.n. more likely.

57 So EPNS YOW, 4, p. 94. A comparable case is Bowthorpe YOE, which could involve a pers.n. or OE *bula* or ON *boli* 'bull' (SSNY, p. 55).

here, but we do not find clearly recurrent compounds with qualifiers readily interpretable as animal names in the plural: contrast the numerous instances of OE *scēap* 'sheep' combined with *lēah*, *tūn* and *wīc*.[58]

If animals are hard to pin down, clear references to crops are no easier to find. It has been suggested that Mawthorpe LIN contains OE/ON *malt* 'malt', but once again there is a personal name alternative.[59] In the case of Cawthorpe, found three times in Lincolnshire, together with the apparently identical Calthorpe NFK, there is a recurrent group, and the compound could conceivably involve OE *cāl* or ON *kál* 'cabbage, kale'.[60] If the farms were arable, it is intriguing that the word OE *sulh* 'plough' seems to appear in Souldrop BED, but this has generally been given a topographical interpretation.[61] In fact, the best clue to one aspect of the agricultural activity that went on in *thorps* is probably the frequent combination with OE *myln* 'mill': 11 instances of Milnthorpe, Millthorpe and the like are noted, 6 of them recorded before 1300 (although none, intriguingly, before 1200; see, however, the discussion of mills in Domesday below, pp. 132–5).[62]

One more compound, of some interest in view of what we will later suggest, might be recorded here. Minsthorpe YOW (*Manestorp* 1086, *Menethorp* 1166) has been considered to contain OE *(ge)mǣne* 'common' or *(ge)mǣnnes* 'community'.[63] Similar suggestions, alongside other alternatives, have been made for Menthorpe

58 EPNE, 2, p. 101.

59 SSNEM, p. 129, makes the suggestion, partly in view of recurring Maltby (ibid., p. 59). Cameron, *Lincolnshire place-names*, pp. 85, 87, follows DEPN (pp. 312, 318), in accepting the ON pers.n. *Malti* for both Mawthorpe and Maltby. SPNN, pp. 296–8, argues that the instances of Maltby contain the pers.n. but that Mawthorpe does indeed involve *malt*.

60 There is a general preference, however, for a recorded personal name on the basis of philological detail. One might have expected *cāl* or *kál* to give some spellings in *Col-* rather than *Cal-*; cf. VEPN, 2, pp. 123–5. The lack of such spellings is not conclusive (cf. Calmoor HMP, Calden BRK), but it may have helped inform the widespread acceptance of the pers.n.: DEPN, pp. 83, 92; Cameron, *Lincolnshire place-names*, p. 30; SPNN, p. 244; CDEPN, p. 111. Fellows-Jensen (SSNEM, p. 106) observes – without much enthusiasm – that the qualifier has also been 'tentatively' explained as ON *kál*, and indeed H. Lindkvist, *Middle-English place-names of Scandinavian origin* (Uppsala, 1912), p. 183, to which she refers, is very circumspect about the idea. However, the appearance of a possible fifth member of the group in *Cawthorpe felde* LEI, first found in 1529, may perhaps begin to tip the balance against a pers.n (EPNS LEI, 4, p. 277).

61 EPNS BED & HNT, pp. 42–3; DEPN, p. 431; CDEPN, p. 560. It seems that *sulh* could also mean 'furrow', and that from here there was an extension to 'gully, furrow-like valley', which is considered appropriate to the lie of the land in the case of Souldrop.

62 Fellows-Jensen, 'Place-names in *-þorp*', p. 46, notes that this may reflect a compound **myln-þorp*; and, very interestingly, that there are at least nine equivalent names in Denmark which – given that mill is ultimately a Latin loan-word – may perhaps have entered Denmark via the English of the Danelaw.

63 EPNS YOW, 2, p. 37; SSNY, p. 63.

YOE and for two instances of Manthorpe LIN.[64] Any suggestion of communality, however, is worthy of note in the present context.

Dating the names and the settlements

Dating named *thorp* settlements is not, of course, straightforward. This section examines place-name and documentary evidence: archaeological investigation will be summarised elsewhere (Chapter 5).

Some seventeen Danelaw *thorps* are recorded in documents that purport to date from before the Norman Conquest of 1066: most of these instances survive only in post-Conquest copies, some of doubtful authenticity. Six *thorps* have a claim to a first date of record during the second half of the tenth century:[65]

Scroppenthorp NTT (to *Scroppen Þorpe* 958 (14th c.) S 679)

Thorpe Lidget YOE (*Ðorp* 959 (12th c.) S 681)

Thorpe Morieux SFK (*æt Þorpæ* 962×91 (11th c.) S 1494)[66]

Wifelesthorp LEI (*æt Wifeles Ðorpe* 972 (13th c.) S 749)

Longthorpe NTH (*æt Þeorp* c.971×84 (12th c.) S 1448a)[67]

Finnesthorp NTH (*æt Finnesthorpe* c.971×84 (12th c.) S 1448a)[68]

Although none of these survives in a contemporary copy, all of the documents are broadly historically trustworthy, and it would be too sceptical to deny that the group confirms that some Danelaw *thorps*, at least, were in existence by the second

---

64   Menthorpe is taken to include a pers.n. by EPNS YOE, p. 261, accepted by SPNLY, p. 195; the 'common' interpretation is advanced by DEPN, p. 322. There is also a Menethorpe in the county, but its early forms (including *Menigthorp* and *Meningthorp* in the thirteenth century) suggest a different origin (EPNS YOE, p. 145; DEPN, p. 321). For Manthorpe an ON pers.n. is preferred by Cameron, *Lincolnshire place-names*, p. 86, and DEPN, p. 313; OE/ON *manna* 'of the men, of the community' is allowed as an alternative by SSNEM, pp. 114, 129, and CDEPN, p. 396. A seventeenth-century Manthorpe RUT is considered by EPNS RUT, p. 151, to be more probably the pers.n. than *manna*. For *mann* in a comparable context (recurring *Man(nes)howe*) see D.N. Parsons, 'Field-name statistics, Norfolk and the Danelaw', in P. Gammeltoft and B. Jørgensen (eds), *Names through the looking-glass: festschrift in honour of Gillian Fellows-Jensen* (Copenhagen, 2006), pp. 165–88 at 169.

65   This is discounting Dogsthorpe NTH and a simplex *Thorp* (possibly the same place) which appear in a text copied into MS E of the *Anglo-Saxon Chronicle* under AD 963. This is part of a complex of documents forged in the twelfth century: see above, p. 39, n. 3.

66   Certainly in East Anglia: the identification with Thorpe Morieux is conventional but not certain.

67   See above, p. 35, n. 37. The same composite document, other parts of which may be a little later than 984, contains two references to an *Eadric on Þorp/Torp*, which may well refer to the same Peterborough estate, later known as Longthorpe, but need not.

68   From the same composite text as the previous name: *Finnesthorp* is unidentified (cf. EPNS NTH, p. 165; SPNN, pp. 122–3, on the pers.n., ON *Finnr*).

half of the tenth century. Beyond this, however, there are many questions of date that are difficult to answer: what proportion of the *thorps* are this early? How much earlier might they be? How long did *thorp*-names go on being coined?

A few landholders named in Domesday Book appear to have given their names to places. The lost 1086 *Toketorp* NFK probably reflects the *Tóki* who had held land there in the time of King Edward.[69] Kettlethorpe, in North Cave YOE, is the 1086 *Torp* where one Chetel had held in 1066, although the personal name qualifier is not noted in the written record of the place-name before the thirteenth century (*Ketolthorp* 1285).[70] And whereas the Germund who gave his name to Grainthorpe LIN (*Germundstorp* 1086) does not appear in Domesday Book, a late medieval note in a cartulary claims that it was Count Alan of Brittany – a known major 1086 landholder – who enfeoffed Germundus with the land here.[71] Other identified examples involve rather later individuals. For Domesday *Esetorp* LIN, the corresponding entry in the Lindsey Survey of *c.*1115 runs in *Esatorp ij. carucatas quas Buselinus tenet*; thereafter the place-name incorporates the name of the early-twelfth-century tenant: it is modern Buslingthorpe.[72] The Úlfketill who held Oakerthorpe DRB (*Ulkilthorpe* 1154×89, 1175) can probably be assigned to the twelfth century on the basis of the local *Hugo filius Hulfchetel* 1179×98.[73] Herringthorpe in Rotherham YOW is remarkable, since the forms *Henrithorp* 1194×9 and *Heringthorp* 1307×27 apparently reflect both the given and family names of an early post-Conquest holder, Henry de Hareng – the Heryng family remained at the site through several generations.[74] *Bochardistorp* 1235 is now Thorpe in the Glebe NTT: it is first recorded as a simplex in Domesday Book, but for a while took the name of the family who held it, perhaps beginning with John Bochard, who was there in the early thirteenth century.[75] Thorpe Morieux SFK is also a Domesday simplex, but was known alternatively as *Guvetorp* in 1201; this form contains the name of Gua, mother of Roger de Murious, mentioned in the 1201 document.[76]

There are further probable identifications from the twelfth and thirteenth

---

69   O. von Feilitzen, *The pre-Conquest personal names of Domesday Book* (Uppsala, 1937), p. 33.
70   SSNY, p. 69 (no. 29); EPNS YOE, p. 225.
71   Cameron, *Lincolnshire place-names*, p. 52. A further instance may be Ganthorpe in Terrington YON: this is *Gameltorp* 1086, which presumably reflects the name of Gamel, a 1066 tenant here. However, in this case it has been argued – from the later run of spellings – that the original name of the place was *Galmethorp*, with the ON pers.n. Galmr, implying that the Domesday form of the name was in a sense accidental (SSNY, p. 58).
72   SSNEM, pp. 105–6.
73   EPNS DRB, 2, pp. 335–6.
74   EPNS YOW, 1, pp. 185–6.
75   EPNS NTT, p. 257.
76   DEPN, p. 469.

centuries, but none that has been noted earlier than Domesday Book.[77] This is unsurprising, of course, given the very limited source material surviving from the pre-Conquest Danelaw. On the basis of negative evidence it is likely enough that plenty of the *thorps* with personal name qualifiers found in Domesday Book recall earlier landholders, since the Domesday tenants that are known had different names (e.g., the only recorded TRE holder of *Ianulfestorp* YOE is one Healfdene).[78] A more tangible indication that many of the personal name qualifiers must have taken root earlier than the late eleventh century arises from the proportion of Old Norse among the personal name qualifiers: by 1086 we have seen that these are found across the Danelaw in a ratio of 80:20, Old Norse to English; in Yorkshire the equivalent ratio is 89:11. These figures are comparable with, if a little lower than, those for *bȳ*-names, and an argument made in connection with that type might be repeated here.[79] Since the place-names contain a significantly higher ratio of ON personal names than the general landowning population recorded by Domesday Book – calculated at 70:30 Old Norse to Old English in Yorkshire, lower elsewhere – it appears likely that in general they are the product not of a general eleventh-century 'Anglo-Scandinavian' population but of more characteristically Scandinavian communities.

Having drawn this comparison with the *bȳ*-names, however, there are various indications which could suggest that the *thorps* as a group should be considered as rather later – or at least rather longer-lived – than the *bȳs*. First, there is the incidence of combination with post-Conquest-type elements, particularly personal names introduced by the Normans. Among *bȳ*-names, at any date, these are very rare in the Danelaw 'proper' (as opposed to the north-west, west of the Pennines, where there is a cluster of this type of formation).[80] Among *thorp*-names they are markedly more common, accounting by our reckoning for 9 per cent of the personal-name qualifiers that can be safely assigned to languages of origin in the pre-1300 record.[81] Examples include Waterthorpe DRB (*Walterthorpe* 1276), Donisthorpe LEI (*Durandestorp* 1086) and Rogerthorpe YOW (*Rogartorp* 1086). A

---

77 For example, Clawthorpe, EPNS WML, 1, p. 58; Thorpe Arnold, EPNS LEI, 2, pp. 277–8.

78 A superficial search suggests that TRE tenants are frequently not noted for *thorp* place-names, making this assumption surprisingly difficult to substantiate. The low status of the places perhaps accounts for this phenomenon. It should also be noted, of course, that Domesday vills are frequently divided between several tenants, not all of whom are necessarily named.

79 Abrams and Parsons, 'Place-names', p. 398.

80 Ibid., pp. 399–400.

81 Fellows-Jensen, 'Place-names in -*þorp*', p. 41, gives a total of 13% in her pre-1500 corpus. The contrast with *bȳ* emerges very clearly in Fellows-Jensen's study of the East Midlands: she finds only 2 post-Conquest names among 146 *bȳ*-names with personal-name qualifiers recorded by 1500; in the equivalent group of *thorp*-names she finds no fewer than 26 out of 110 (SSNEM, pp. 18,

second criterion, rather slight in itself, but generally accepted, tends to point in the same direction: this is that certain short ON personal names based on the element Thor-, such as Tóki, Tóli and Tósti, become very common in the eleventh-century record but appear to be rare before that time.[82] Such forms are very infrequently combined with bȳ, but rather more commonly so with thorp.[83] Thirdly, a much smaller proportion of linguistically ON nominal and adjectival qualifiers are found with thorps as compared with bȳs.[84] On the basis of the pattern of attestation in thorp-names it could certainly be argued that the use of nouns and adjectives as qualifiers is generally a later phenomenon belonging more to an 'Anglo-Scandinavian', or Middle English, period than to the Old Norse culture prevailing when many of the personal-name compounds were coined.

Comparison and contrast with the bȳ-names could be further developed in various directions, but it is time to make the point – to draw attention to the elephant sharing the room occupied by the last three paragraphs – that the name-groups differ in one striking respect. Bȳ is never found as a simplex place-name, and in compounds hardly ever exhibits a change of qualifier; thorp-names are characterised, as we have noted, by a high number of simplexes and frequent instability in compounds. Thus, while it is a fair assumption that the qualifiers in bȳ-names date from the original coining of the compound, this would clearly be a false assumption in the case of the thorps. Indeed, several of the names detailed above – Kettlethorpe, Buslingthorpe, Thorpe Morieux – were demonstrably either

---

81 cont.
  29, 93–4, 99). It should be observed, however, that rather a high proportion of her 26 names can be otherwise explained, and do not appear in our conservative figures cited in Table 3.5. Cameron, 'Scandinavian settlement, part II', p. 141, finds no post-Conquest pers.ns in his corpus of bȳs from 1086, but three or four among his thorps; cf. ibid., p. 143.

82 SSNEM, pp. 277–8; Abrams and Parsons, 'Place-names', p. 400. Note that SPNN, p. 374, regards the etymology of Tóki, specifically, as uncertain.

83 For example, Toketorp NFK, Tolethorpe RUT and Towthorpe YOE (Toletorp 1086).

84 Once more, calculations by different scholars at different times produce varying results, but in every case the distinction between bȳs and thorps is marked. Thus, figures for Yorkshire derived from SSNY, pp. 13, 15, 50, 51, produce 91% ON among the bȳs, against only 47% among the thorps. In the East Midlands, Cameron finds 77% ON among bȳs (K. Cameron, 'Scandinavian settlement in the territory of the Five Boroughs: the place-name evidence' in K. Cameron (ed.), *Place-name evidence for the Anglo-Saxon invasion and Scandinavian settlements: eight studies* (Nottingham, 1975), pp. 118–19), but only 3/11 (= 27%) among thorps ('Scandinavian settlement, part II', p. 142); Fellows-Jensen's equivalent figures (from SSNEM, pp. 18, 24, 94, 96) are 45% ON in the bȳs against 34% in the thorps. Though we do not have comparable figures for bȳ-names, our total for nouns and adjectives as qualifiers in Danelaw thorp-names is 57% ON by 1086, falling to 39% by 1300 (above, p. 52, and Table 3.6). Lund, 'Thorp-names', pp. 224–5, draws attention to the relatively low Norse ratio in qualifiers that are not pers.ns, suggesting that they show that we are not dealing with 'a Danish place-name element productive in a Danish milieu'.

simplexes or compounds with different qualifiers before they came to incorporate the names of datable people. In these circumstances, it is clearly not safe to date the origin of the *thorp* at *Toketorp* by the eleventh-century fashion for the name *Tóki*, or that at Williamthorpe DRB by the linguistic and cultural effects of the Norman Conquest.

What can be said for the Danelaw *thorps* based on analysis of their qualifiers, therefore, must be hedged around with caution. Most striking is a clearly significant association with ON personal names, an association which becomes more marked the earlier and further north we go. Given the extensive evidence for the use of *thorp* in Scandinavia, especially Denmark, in the early Middle Ages, it would seem perverse to deny the likelihood that the use of *thorp* in Danelaw England owes a good deal to its use among Norse-speaking immigrant communities who would have arrived in the later ninth or tenth centuries.

Yet that instability, combined with the formal difficulties in distinguishing Old Norse and Old English cognates, allows a logical challenge which was pursued to the extreme by Niels Lund in 1976. Lund suggested that practically all the Danelaw *thorps* may have been early English *thorps* (or *throps*) in origin, arguing that all the Scandinavian qualifiers would have been later additions.[85] This seems to us an extreme and unlikely position. Nevertheless his argument cannot be ignored and the evidence upon which it is based will be re-examined in the next chapter.

---

85 Lund, 'Thorp-names'. He argues that, parallel to so-called Grimston-hybrids, the *thorp*-names represent 'a take-over of existing villages already called something + *thorp*' (p. 225).

4

English throps

In comparison with their Danelaw counterparts, the *throps* of 'English' England have been little studied. There is much less material to consider under the various headings below, partly because of this neglect, and partly because there are many fewer names in the group: there is also less variation to discuss in, for instance, the language of the qualifiers. Nonetheless, to facilitate comparison we shall present the material in the same general sequence as with the Danelaw names, above.

Size and status

Although the same observation can be made, that *throps* tend not to grow into large places, little solid evidence for their probable early dependent status has been collected, and Smith simply noted a couple of examples that were hamlets within other parishes.[1] Nor has it been Fellows-Jensen's purpose to present the measurable evidence for this group of names in the same way that she analyses the Danelaw group. Study of the early levels of fiscal assessment remains to be done, therefore, as do more sophisticated calculations of settlement loss and parish numbers. From our material – which is not at all sophisticated in this respect – it appears that the incidence of loss is relatively lower than in the Danelaw: 26 names out of 100 are marked as absent from the twentieth-century map, as opposed to the figure of 46 per cent lost or shrunken places identified by Fellows-Jensen in the Danelaw. On the other hand, our rough figure for parishes points to a similar pattern as presented by the *thorps* further north: 16 of 100 *throp*-names became parishes, while Fellows-Jensen cites 18 per cent for the Danelaw.[2] These

---

1 EPNE, 2, 215.
2 In these two calculations we have used our collection of *throp*-names first recorded by 1500 to compare with Fellows-Jensen's Danelaw corpus of the same date.

Figure 4.1 Roadsign to Throop DOR. A simplex name located in the large ancient estate of Puddle.

aggregated figures inevitably mask localised variations; in Wiltshire, for instance, none of the ten medieval *throps* ever held parish status.[3]

More striking, however, are the similar patterns of place-name usage. As in the Danelaw, simplex names are frequent: of 77 names recorded by 1300, 21 (27 per cent) appear first in simplex form – the equivalent calculation for the *thorps* further north was 23 per cent (Figure 4.1).[4] As in the Danelaw, simplex names are sometimes unstable: examples include Thorpehall Farm in Southchurch ESX (*Thorp* 1086, *Southorp* 1275) and Stoneythorpe in Long Itchington WAR (*Torp* 1199, *Samsonesthowrp* 1220). And, as in the Danelaw, directional qualifiers are characteristic. Indeed, whereas they accounted for 7 per cent of the pre-1300 *thorp*-names, they reach an extraordinary 27 per cent (21/77) of the equivalent *throp*-corpus. Smith duly interprets this as evidence of dependence on 'some larger or older settlement'.[5] In addition, there are a number of *throps* which take the local

3   S. Draper, *Landscape, settlement and society in Roman and early medieval Wiltshire*, BAR British Series 419 (Oxford, 2006), p. 44, table 3.
4   Fellows-Jensen gives a calculation for simplex *throps*, recorded by 1500, as 12/54 (22%), to be compared with her Danelaw proportion, identical to ours, of 23% ('Place-names in *-þorp*', p. 41).
5   EPNE, 2, p. 215. Smith himself might be thought to offer a challenge to this interpretation when he explains Southrop GLO as 'the most southerly of the *þrops* in the district' (EPNS GLO, 1,

parish-name as qualifier: as in the Danelaw, this phenomenon is more commonly attested in later records (e.g. *le Hatfeld Throp* HRT in the fifteenth century and *Bedon Thropp* BRK in the sixteenth),[6] but it is found relatively early in *Ebblesburnthorpe* WLT, recorded in 1289 and relating to Ebbesborne Wake parish.[7]

Finally, there is the date of first record. It will be recalled that a good proportion of Danelaw *thorps* first appear later than 1086: from her corpus to 1500 Fellows-Jensen calculated 39 per cent, from ours to 1300 we calculated 41 per cent. Yet the proportion among the English *throps* is strikingly higher: 74 per cent (40/54) according to Fellows-Jensen,[8] 73 per cent (56/77) according to us. This is an intriguing observation because, as we shall see, it appears to sit uneasily with Smith's influential argument that the *throps* are older as a class than the *thorps*. In the current context it strongly reinforces the impression given by the simplexes and the directional names, suggesting that – at whatever date they were coined – the *throps* do not in general denote places that were substantial and central settlements: in this respect they appear closely comparable with the Danelaw *thorps*.

Qualifiers

One very clear distinction between the *throps* and the Danelaw *thorps* emerges from a study of their qualifiers. As we have seen, in the Danelaw personal names make up the largest group of qualifiers, accounting for between 46 and 61 per cent of the compounds by a conservative count. Outside the Danelaw the figure is just 18 or 19 per cent: 10/56 by our calculation, 8/42 according to Fellows-Jensen.[9] Unfortunately it is hardly possible to break down the small numbers involved here to give any useful indications of distribution: our examples come 1 each from Northamptonshire and Berkshire, 2 from Buckinghamshire and 3 each from Hampshire and Gloucestershire. Only 2 of these names are recorded in 1086, out

---

5 *cont.*
  pp. 45–6). It is of course possible that some such names worked in a rather wider geographical context, but the many examples in which *throp* can be explained as a minor settlement within a smaller unit or parish tend to suggest that the latter is the usual usage – e.g. Sedrup in Hartwell BUC, Southrope in Herriard HMP, Astrope and *Westthorpe* in Puttenham HRT. Southrop GLO, therefore, although it became a parish, was perhaps in origin a dependent settlement of the *Leach* estate (surviving in Eastleach Martin and Eastleach Turville) to its north. For another suggestion that a directional *throp* may refer to another *throp* rather than the estate centre see EPNS WLT, p. 26.
6 EPNS HRT, p. 260; U. Wagner, *Studies on English place-names in Thorp* (Basel, 1976), p. 10.
7 EPNS WLT, p. 393.
8 Fellows-Jensen, 'Place-names in -*þorp*', p. 45.
9 Fellows-Jensen, 'Place-names in -*þorp*', p. 41.

of some 15 compounds in all by this date, but again the numbers seem too small to give good indications of chronological trends. What can be said is that 19 per cent of personal name qualifiers across the south and south-west sits fairly coherently with the 28 per cent found in the Danelaw half of Northamptonshire, and therefore – given that we can see the figures increase the further north we look in the Danelaw – that there is something of a continuum across the country in this respect: there is no sharp jump across the line of the A5, as the raw figures might suggest.

The personal name qualifiers outside the Danelaw are almost all English. Of the ten accepted in our pre-1300 material, eight have been considered to be certainly Old English, one is possibly so, and the tenth is a Middle English surname (Colethrop GLO, apparently containing the family name of one Hugh Cole, a thirteenth-century tenant; the surname is itself possibly derived from an OE Cola).[10] Among a further handful of uncertain examples there is one that could be an Old Norse personal name: a twelfth-century Katestrop in Amersham BUC could contain ON Káti.[11] The only other possible trace of Old Norse influence on a throp-qualifier outside the Danelaw is found in an identical-looking later-recorded name, Catesthorp in Winchcomb GLO.[12] Whatever the true explanation of these names – ON personal name Káti or kati 'boy', or ME Cate – it is clear that Old Norse is at best marginal to the personal nomenclature found combined with throp outside the Danelaw. The same can be said for Continental or Norman influence. At first record none of the throps contains a personal name of post-Conquest type (save, in a sense, the ME surname Cole). A couple turn up later: Williamstrip GLO is originally Hetrop 1086, but becomes Williamsthorp by 1287, apparently with the

---

10 EPNS GLO, 2, p. 183.

11 Wagner, Studies, p. 25.

12 EPNS GLO, 2, p. 32. Catesthorp is first recorded in the fifteenth century, which is why it does not make our primary material. Smith tentatively derives this from an ME personal name Cate, ultimately from Old Norse Káti. This ON personal name is thought to occur in England, but it is not particularly common. For three possible independent instances of the pers.n. in England (as Catus, Cadi, Cade) see SPNLY, p. 163. It is therefore a little surprising to find it twice in a context where Old Norse is otherwise absent. Slightly more satisfactory in accounting for the recurrence, perhaps, is the possibility that instead we could have here ON kati 'boy', and that these examples might belong to the group of 'young men' names. This possibility has also been considered by Fellows-Jensen (SSNEM, p. 107) for Caythorpe LIN and Caythorpe NTT. Note that in the GLO and BUC instances the word, or name, has a genitive (or plural) in -es-, which would be indicative of borrowing into English, although – for what it is worth – the limited documentary record does not record *cate 'boy' as a loanword in Middle English. In the two instances of Caythorpe the spellings are instead consistent with a Scandinavian inflection, singular or plural. The alternative is to interpret these names also as containing the personal name Káti, which begins to strain faith in coincidence.

name of the 1086 tenant, Willelm;[13] Stoneythorpe WAR is a simplex *Torp* from 1199 onwards, but an alternative name-tradition is first recorded as *Samsonesthowrp* 1220, probably after the Thomas Sanson who held the manor in 1202.[14]

Just as Old English dominates the personal name qualifiers, so it can account for all of the identifiable nouns and adjectives combined with *throp*. There is potential ambiguity with Old Norse, of course, in words like *north*, *south* and *west*, but since there are no clear Old Norse qualifiers in this corpus, there is little reason to suspect it in ambiguous cases. Likewise there is no sign of French: Fellows-Jensen includes Castle Thorpe BUC, with OFr *castel*, under this heading, but by our reckoning this falls on the Danelaw side of the Ouse.[15]

The range of qualifiers attested outside the Danelaw is more restricted than that found within it. No doubt this is partly a function of the much smaller corpus; partly also, as has been noted, it will result from the fact that directional terms are so proportionately common. Before 1300 there are 21 instances of 'east', 'south', 'west', 'middle', 'high', 'up' and – a less certain instance – 'nether'. After 1300 there are a further 17. (Incidentally, there are intriguing distributions here: in both the earlier and later groups 'east' and 'west' are better represented than 'south', while 'north' is wholly absent from both. In the Danelaw 'east', with ON *austr*, and 'west' are also more common than 'north' and 'south', but all four do occur.)

Of the remaining qualifiers, a few identify *throps* by local topography, as Eathorpe WAR (Figure 4.2) and Eythrope BUC (with OE *ēa* 'river') and Brookthorpe GLO (OE *brōc* 'stream'). In contrast to the Danelaw, however, there are no names involving trees or woodland terms in the pre-1300 corpus, although a single instance of Old English *æsc* 'ash-tree' is found a little later in Eastrip WAR, recorded as *Asshetrop* in 1327, *Asshethrop* in 1406.[16] Nor are there any early names suggesting grass or reeds, as there were further north. Again, there is a possible fourteenth-century exception in *atte Besthrop*, recorded as a local surname in Duntisbourne Rouse GLO in 1327. This may be a further instance of Old English **bēos* 'bent-grass' to add to the Danelaw group (above, p. 53), although it is worrying both that the single surname-form is not supported by any further local documentation and that more secure instances of **bēos* appear limited to the east of England.[17]

Crops and animals are no better represented. Calthorpe in Banbury OXF might possibly contain OE *cāl* 'cabbage, kale' and belong with a group that has been

---

13   EPNS *GLO*, 1, p. 30.

14   EPNS *WAR*, pp. 134–5.

15   Fellows-Jensen, 'Place-names in -*þorp*', p. 41.

16   EPNS *WAR*, p. 94.

17   For the local name, see EPNS *GLO*, 1, p. 74, where no suggestion is made for the etymology, probably wisely. For the regional restriction of **bēos*, see *VEPN*, 1, pp. 84–5.

discussed in the Danelaw (above, p. 56), but OE *col* '(char)coal' and OE *colt* 'colt' are possible alternatives.[18] Two *throps* could contain OE *cocc* 'cock, fowl': Cockrup in Coln St Aldwyn GLO and Cokethorpe in Hardwick OXF;[19] and beside them from the Danelaw can be set Cockthorpe NRF, an original simplex (*Torp* 1086) which is first attested with the affix, as *Coketorp*, in 1254.[20] A group of three may be suggestive of a specialised function, but is perhaps insufficient to rule out other possibilities, particularly the same word used as a personal name or byname.[21]

Figure 4.2 Eathorpe WAR (the 'river' *thorp*) on the confluence of the rivers Itchen and Leam, where access to water is still important to the villagers.

Kings, princes and bishops are all absent from the non-Danelaw corpus. However, one of the more striking parallels with the Danelaw is found in the category of groups of people who are presumably tenants or workers. The best relatively early example is Swanthorpe in Crondall HMP, first recorded as *Swanethorp* in 1233. Of this, Richard Coates has written: 'OE *Swānaþrop* "herdsmen's secondary settlement", with the implication that the site is a permanent village replacing an earlier seasonal herdsmen's settlement.'[22] Leaving aside, for the time being, any further implications, this does seem likely to be a

---

18   EPNS OXF, 2, pp. 412–13; DEPN, p. 83.
19   EPNS GLO, 1, p. 30; EPNS OXF, 2, p. 324.
20   DEPN, p. 115. Clearly in favour of the bird here, however, is Chaucer's suggestion in *The Parlement of the Foules* of a proverbial association between cock and *thorp*: 'The cok, that orlogge ys of thropes lyte', 'the cock that is the timepiece of little *thorps*' (J.A. Burrow and T. Turville-Petre (eds), *A book of Middle English* (Oxford, 3rd edn, 2005), p. 297). Does this suggest that *thorps* do not have parish churches with bells?
21   VEPN, 3, pp. 143–7, especially at 146.
22   R. Coates, *The place-names of Hampshire* (London, 1989), p. 159.

name involving the genitive plural of Old English *swān* 'herdsman'. It would, of course, be a close parallel for possible instances we have seen involving the cognate ON *sveinn*, and the rather more secure instances of Boythorpe, Knapthorpe and so on. Nor is it an isolated 'English' example. The same compound may recur in *Swanthorp*, a lost place in Chelmsford Hundred ESX.[23] And then there is the late-recorded instance of *Inchthrop* in Cirencester GLO, first recorded in 1540. For this ME *enche* 'manorial tenant' has been suggested. Legally these were specialist workers such as ploughmen or shepherds who held *enchelonds* and worked full-time for the lord. In the context of naming, however, a general gloss 'workman' has been offered, or a more specific 'goatherd' or simply 'youth, boy'.[24] Whatever the precise application(s), these names look likely to be related to the Boythorpe types of the Danelaw.

Other names may suggest resident workers, although interpretation is uncertain. A fourteenth-century name, *Boutherop* in Eastleach Martin GLO (*Burithrop* in 1310), is confidently interpreted by the EPNS editor as containing the genitive plural of OE *(ge)būr* 'peasant'.[25] However, similar spellings for Burdrop in Sibford Gower OXF and Burderop in Chisledon WLT – the latter the only one of the group first recorded before 1300, in 1249 – are assigned to OE *burg* 'stronghold', and in the Chisledon instance it is said that 'there is a rectangular camp here'.[26] The extraordinarily named Cock-a-troop Cottages in Mildenhall WLT were more simply *Crokerestrope* in 1257: this name appears to contain OE **croccere* 'potter', although it has been implied that this is less a prosaic descriptive name than a rather fanciful one, recalling prolific finds of Roman pottery in the neighbourhood.[27]

In sum, while several types of compound noted with *thorp* in the Danelaw are unrepresented or poorly represented outside it – those involving wood and vegetation terms, high-status owners, ecclesiastical connections, mills and communal ownership – others recur across the divide: in particular, directional qualifiers and terms suggestive of groups of workmen or youths. There is also, it might be noted, a single OE *pūca* 'goblin' in Puckrup GLO, recorded from the thirteenth century,[28] and evidently to be related to the group in the Danelaw (discussed above, pp. 54–5).

---

23   EPNS ESS, p. 569. Unfortunately the form is not assigned a date.
24   EPNS GLO, 1, pp. 64, xi.
25   EPNS GLO, 1, p. 31.
26   EPNS OXF, 2, p. 405; EPNS WLT, pp. 281–2.
27   EPNS WLT, p. 301. On 'Crocker'-names and their distribution and significance see C. Dyer, 'Place-names and pottery', in O.J. Padel and D.N. Parsons (eds), *A commodity of good names: essays in honour of Margaret Gelling* (Donington, 2008), pp. 44–54.
28   EPNS GLO, 2, p. 71.

Dating the names and the settlements

Five throp-names are attested in documents that do, or may, pre-date Domesday Book. They are:

> Thorpe SUR (*in loco qui dicitur Thorpe* 672×674 (13th c.) S 1165)[29]
> Uppthrop WOR (*Uppþrop* 990 (e.11th c.) S 1363)[30]
> Thrupp NTH (*æt Þrope* 956×1002 S 1497)[31]
> Gestingthorpe ESX (*æt Gyrstlingaþorpe* 975×1016 S 1487)
> Adelstrop GLO (*Tatlestrope* ?11th (12th c.) S 1548)[32]

Three of these tend to confirm the use of *thorp/throp* by at least the later tenth century – unlike the Danelaw group of comparable date they survive in more or less contemporary form. More striking is the case of Thorpe, a parish in Surrey, which promises to take the written record of the place-name element back to the later seventh century. The relevant document is not straightforward, however. It is a charter recording an extensive early royal grant of land to the monastery of Chertsey, but the earliest surviving copy is of the thirteenth century, and like many such endowment charters it is open to suspicion of being a forgery, the wishful thinking of later members of the community. In general, however, modern scholars are inclined to accept that the core of the charter records a genuine grant of the seventh century, although Stenton's judgement that it is 'distended with spurious matter' has been echoed, in one form or another, by most commentators.[33] If some details of the document may have been altered to fall into line with a later historical reality, then perhaps the addition of Thorpe could be one of them.[34] The transaction, as it survives, concerns a grant of 200 hides of land at Chertsey, together with just 5 at Thorpe. As the map published by John Blair

29 Plus many spurious later charters: see above, p. 33, n. 32.
30 Identified by EPNS *WOR*, p. 186, with Upthorpe Farm in Alderminster, but this seems impossible. See A.J. Robertson (ed.), *Anglo-Saxon charters* (Cambridge, 1956), pp. 132–3, 377–8. *Uppthrop* is presented as *oðre naman*, 'the other name', of an estate of two hides at *Mortun*: EPNS *WOR*, p. 102, correctly identifies this with Moreton's Farm, in Bredon, which is far too far from Alderminster for the identification. To account for the phrasing of the document, incidentally, it is possible that the two hides granted *on Mortune* represent a constituent element, *Uppthrop*, of a larger Moreton estate. See further below, p. 145.
31 See above, p. 35, n. 38.
32 Also in S 1250, a spurious charter purportedly of the eighth century.
33 See the various views summarised in Sawyer, *Anglo-Saxon charters*.
34 It should be noted that Scharer (cited by Sawyer, *Anglo-Saxon charters*) proposes the exact opposite: that an original small grant of land at *Thorpe* might have been inflated to add the remaining Chertsey holdings. However, S.E. Kelly, in her forthcoming *The Charters of Chertsey Abbey*, does indeed regard the reference to Thorpe as a probable addition: she notes that the phrasing is clumsy and that the assessment of hides in *mansae* looks anachronistic.

illustrates,[35] the small parish of Thorpe is readily understood as a minor dependency of its large and important neighbour Chertsey. The question is whether Thorpe is necessarily an early dependent unit, as implied by the putative date of the grant, or whether it may be a later development, anachronistically added to the charter at a much later stage to ensure that the ancient origins of this holding were as established as those of the main estate. Since the document is not extant before the thirteenth century, it is a question that cannot be answered with certainty, but it is one of some significance to the discussion which follows.

In 1956 A.H. Smith published an important account in which he argued that *throp*, in English England, belonged to an early stratum of Anglo-Saxon name-giving.[36] He based this conclusion not on the documentary record – there is no mention of Thorpe SUR and the Chertsey endowment – but on the distribution map. He argued that the element was absent from Kent and Sussex in the south-east because the earliest Anglo-Saxon settlers of these parts had come from a region in which the term was not used, and that it was absent from Devon and Cornwall in the far south-west because the term had ceased to be productive by the time of the Anglo-Saxon conquest of this region. In the case of Devon (where the element is indeed very rare, although not completely absent, as Smith asserted) such argumentation would probably have suggested to him a latest *terminus* for *throp*-naming in the counties further east somewhere around the early eighth century AD.[37]

This proposal is cogent and authoritatively stated.[38] Yet voices of doubt have been raised. Stressing that 'the uniformity of the evidence [i.e. either side of the Danelaw line] is most striking', Urs Wagner was reluctant to accept that the corpus could be divided into two large groups with distinct origins. He argued that the lateness of much of the evidence, especially outside the Danelaw, was more in keeping with recent coinage, into the twelfth century and later, than with a group of ancient names that would have had to have escaped record for centuries. Accepting the indications that 'in the Danelaw, there can be little doubt that ... the place-name element owes its origin to Danish *thorp*', Wagner concluded that, in general, the *throps* of the south and south-west represented the 'spread of

35 J. Blair, 'Frithuwold's kingdom and the origins of Surrey', in S. Bassett (ed.), *The origins of Anglo-Saxon kingdoms* (Leicester, 1989), pp. 97–107, at 102.

36 *EPNE*, 2, pp. 215–16.

37 *EPNS DEV*, 1, pp. xv–xviii.

38 In a review of *EPNE*, R.M. Wilson (*Review of English Studies*, 9 (1958), pp. 414–24 at 415) argues that Smith's account of *throp* 'provides evidence for the position of the Anglo-Saxons on the Continent', which is splendidly circular.

Scandinavian *thorps* from their homeland, the Danelaw'.[39] More recently, Fellows-Jensen, writing on the geography of the groups of place-names inside and outside the Danelaw, has noted:

> that the distribution pattern of the *þrops* forms a kind of attenuated tail to that of the *þorps*, and that both the *þorps* and the *þrops* tend to cluster along and near to the two ridges ... that run in a broad sweep from Yorkshire to the south-west. It would seem that it was on these uplands that secondary settlements were likely to be called *þorp* by Danes and *þrop* by the English.[40]

Such an account implies that the distribution of the *throps* may be governed by factors other than the circumstances of the earliest Anglo-Saxon settlements, and it is clear that Fellows-Jensen also had serious doubts about Smith's chronology. She went on to stress that the *throps* are often rather late-recorded, later even than the Danelaw *thorps*, suggesting that the English names 'may be younger as a class',[41] and, like Wagner, has floated the idea that some of the *throp*-names may have arisen under the influence of Danish *thorp* as a loan-word.[42]

In common with these scholars, we feel that both the distribution map and the general pattern of attestation, as analysed above, tends to support a relatively late date for most of the *throp*-names. Before rehearsing that case, however, we ought to weigh up some possible indications to the contrary. The early record of Thorpe SUR, if genuine, is one, of course. Beside it might be put a few of the compound names. Most striking is Gestingthorpe ESX, where the qualifier, *Gyrstlinga-*, the genitive plural of a group-name, **Gyrstlingas*, is apparently a well-known type in eastern English place-names. In general the type clearly belongs earlier rather than later in the Anglo-Saxon period (even if not to the initial colonisation phase, as scholars used to believe).[43] Yet this example is not straightforward. While it is perhaps to be interpreted as the '*thorp* of the **Gyrstlingas*, the followers of one **Gyrstel*', two alternatives have been proposed. One is that these are not the followers of an eponymous leader, but rather a group from a 'gorse-place', a

---

39 Wagner, *Studies*, pp. cxiii–cxv.

40 Fellows-Jensen, 'Place-names in -*þorp*', p. 40.

41 *Ibid.*, p. 45.

42 Fellows-Jensen, 'Torp-navne i Norfolk', pp. 47–59 at 49.

43 The evidence for the antiquity of the -*ingas* type is clearly set out in EPNE, I, pp. 300–1. Work of the 1960s and 1970s, summarised by M. Gelling, *Signposts to the past: place-names and the history of England* (1978; Chichester, 3rd edn, 1997), pp. 106–9, threw grave doubt on whether the places so named should be associated with the immigration-phase of Anglo-Saxon settlement, but did not greatly shake this evidence for the ancient appearance of the names. The paradox is explored in some detail in D.N. Parsons, *Pre-Viking place-names of Northamptonshire* (forthcoming).

Gyrstling – and group-names formed from topographical features have not been considered as old as those formed from personal names.[44] The other possibility, favoured by A.H. Smith, is that Gestingthorpe is, although the forms do not show it, a two-stage place-name: a *thorp* dependent on a now-lost primary place-name *Gyrstlingas*.[45]

The reason for Smith's interpretation, presumably, is that – unlike -*ingahām* or -*ingafeld* names – this -*ingathorp* is not supported by a secure pattern of repeated names of the same type. It is true that there are possible parallels, but they are not strong. We have already noted Morningthorpe NFK, where the Domesday forms vary between simplex and qualified versions: this certainly gives some support to the complex two-stage interpretation that this is more likely to be the *thorp* of a lost place *Morningas* than an original '*thorp* of the *Morningas*'.[46] There is also Epping(e)thorp in Essex, a form noted three times in the fourteenth and fifteenth centuries. EPNS ESX is not sure whether this denotes a hamlet in Epping, or is an alternative name for the main estate: 'it is possible', writes Reaney, 'that *Yppinges* interchanged with *Yppingaþorp*, "the village of the upland dwellers".'[47] Given the indications that a *thorp* is usually a small dependency, the latter seems an unlikely interpretation. Further, it should be noted that here we very probably have a group-name based on a topographical feature rather than a personal name. Thus, although it is possible that in this complex – Gestingthorpe, Eppingthorp and Morningthorpe – there *could* be an indication of the early use of *thorp/throp* among surviving English place-names, it is far from certain.

Other possible indications of early date also prove difficult to pin down. Thus Adlestrop GLO and Bigstrup BUC are generally considered to contain the personal names *Tǣtel (or Tātel) and *Biccel, respectively. Such personal names, short names with -*el* suffixes, are well known in Old English, but tend largely to belong to the earlier Anglo-Saxon period:[48] to find two of them in a small corpus would be suggestive of an early date for the whole class of names. Yet this evidence is not really conclusive. On the one hand, although the name-type is generally early in Old English, it is not sharply restricted: a man with the very name *Tātel* worked as a

---

44 Watts suggests the derivation from gorse: CDEPN, p. 249. In this he is partly following E. Ekwall, *English Place-Names in -ing*, (1923; Lund, 2nd edn, 1962), p. 35, although Ekwall thinks gorse may be used as a person's nickname meaning something like 'rough, bristly'. On the chronology suggesting that 'the personal type was of great antiquity ... [whereas the] geographical type continued in use throughout the OE period', see EPNE, 1, p. 300.

45 EPNE, 2, pp. 209, 215.

46 Above, p. 45, n. 26.

47 EPNS ESX, p. 22.

48 P. Kitson, 'How Anglo-Saxon personal names work', *Nomina*, 25 (2002), pp. 91–131 at 125.

moneyer in Mercia in the middle of the ninth century, for instance, while another moneyer, a certain *Wædel*, is found as late as the eleventh century at Bath.[49] And on the other hand, the place-name interpretations here are not necessarily entirely secure. In the case of Bigstrup, for instance, although the first element could certainly be OE **Biccel*, alternative possibilities suggest themselves, for while **Biccel* is unattested as a personal name, Bickley, from an OE **Biccanlēag*, is a frequently attested English place-name, found at least six times in various counties.[50] It is conceivable that this is a *thorp* attached to a now-lost instance of Bickley. Alternatively, if *Wædel* might be from Continental Germanic (see above), then presumably Bigstrup could similarly contain the Old High German personal name *Bichilo*, on the basis of which OE **Biccel* is hypothesised.[51]

In names such as Thorpe SUR and Gestingthorpe ESX, then, there are hints that some *thorp* place-names in southern England could have been coined relatively early in the Anglo-Saxon period. Given that the term is inherited from the Germanic of the Continent, where it is also used as a place-name element, and that it is attested in Old English glosses dating from the later seventh century, we might not unreasonably suspect that it appears in some place-names coined, say, between the fifth and seventh centuries. Yet on the other hand are the points raised by Wagner and Fellows-Jensen, which we think are generally supported by our own analysis of the material. These points tend to suggest a relatively late date for most of the *thorps* and *throps*: they certainly seem to cast considerable doubt on Smith's argument that those outside the Danelaw are to be dated centuries earlier than most of those inside it.

Key to the argument is the coherence of the distribution, geographically and contextually, across the country. The *thorps* of the Danelaw, and the *throps* outside it, have significant features in common – notably the prevalence of simplex forms and of directional qualifiers – that suggest that they may be of similar type and status across the corpus. These similarities could perhaps arise from the application of a common, inherited Germanic term at two distinct historical

---

49   For *Tatel*, who worked for kings Berhtwulf (840–52) and Burgred (852–74), see J.J. North, *English hammered coinage I* (London, 1994), pp. 97, 100. It is not inconceivable that the moneyer held the estate at Adlestrop, although it is hardly certain. For *Wædel* see V. Smart, *Sylloge of coins of the British Isles 28: cumulative index of volumes 1–20* (London, 1981), p. 75. Apparently the same name, as *Wadel* – perhaps the same man – is found among Domesday landowners in Somerset, Devon and Cornwall: von Feilitzen, *Pre-conquest names*, pp. 407–8, suggests that the etymon could alternatively be OGer *Wadilo*. F. Colman, *Money talks: reconstructing Old English* (Berlin and New York, 1992), p. 121, similarly allows Continental Germanic, but prefers OE (cf. her comment on p. 34).

50   DEPN, p. 41; VEPN, I, p. 96.

51   EPNS BUC, p. 161.

periods, as implied by Smith's account, but there are indications which suggest otherwise. For one thing, there is no sign of any kind of sharp line between the two types. The distribution through Gloucestershire, Wiltshire, Oxfordshire, Northamptonshire and Leicestershire is effectively continuous and coherent, spatially and typologically. Although we have noted a major distinction in the proportions of Danelaw and non-Danelaw names incorporating personal-name qualifiers, it is apparent, on closer inspection, that there is a continuum in this usage running from north to south, and that personal-name qualifiers thin out gradually through the Midlands and southern Danelaw before reaching 'English' territory: this regional shading does not look much like a simple distinction between Viking Scandinavian and ancient English practice.[52]

Secondly, so many of the names are first recorded relatively late that it is hard to believe that any large group of them could derive from an ancient stratum of name-giving. Certainly, it is accepted that individual place-names, especially of minor or dependent places, can escape the written record for a long time, but Wagner notes that comparable OE elements like *wīc* and *stoc* are generally much better recorded in pre-Conquest sources,[53] and Fellows-Jensen stresses that the corpus of non-Danelaw *throps* is concentrated in an area where local nomenclature in Anglo-Saxon charters is particularly well-recorded.[54] If the names had all been established by the eighth century, as Smith implies, it is extraordinary that none of them is mentioned in a boundary-clause to an Anglo-Saxon charter of the tenth or eleventh centuries. Moreover, there are indications on both sides of the Danelaw line that the element remained comprehensible and relevant after the Conquest. The frequent change or addition of qualifiers at this date must suggest this: it does not prove that names could be coined so late, but would be a remarkable characteristic of a group of names laid down hundreds of years earlier and obsolete thereafter.[55]

We tend to believe, therefore, that the *thorps* and *throps* across the country

---

52 It is, perhaps, significant that the best case for an ancient English example, Thorpe SUR, lies outside the main distribution, and is almost isolated. However, the fifteenth-century field-name *le Thrope*, in Molesey, not far from Thorpe, complicates the matter.

53 Wagner, *Studies*, p. cxiv.

54 Fellows-Jensen, 'Place-names in *-þorp*', p. 45.

55 Wagner (*Studies*, pp. cvi–cvii) draws similar conclusions from the fact that thorp-names are frequently preceded by the definite article in later medieval records: *le Thorpe*, *la Trope*, *le Westhorp* and so on. He argues that this suggests that 'at the time when the article was used ... thorp was (still) a meaningful name'. Note also that in discussing the name Drope, recorded only from 1540, Pierce accepted a Middle English transfer of the element from the English south-west Midlands into the Vale of Glamorgan as being more likely than a loan from Old Norse; very early English coinage is not to be reckoned with in south Wales, of course: G.O. Pierce, *The place-names of Dinas Powys hundred* (Cardiff, 1968), pp. 253–4.

predominantly reflect one phase of medieval settlement (albeit perhaps a long-lived one, with regional distinctions), rather than two widely separated phases. The marked association with Scandinavian elements, especially personal names, in the Danelaw must suggest that *thorps* were significant to the settlement-pattern in this area between perhaps the later ninth and eleventh centuries. Their continuing vitality in many areas into at least the twelfth century is implied by the changing qualifiers at this date. We accept the possibility that some names are much more ancient than this, but in general the characteristics and distribution of the whole corpus suggest that examples of these are probably rather few.

Closely bound up with these matters is the question of how far the Danelaw *thorps* may be built on a foundation of pre-Viking Anglo-Saxon *throp* or *thorp* settlements. This is a question practically impossible to resolve on place-name evidence. On the one hand, it is conceded that qualifying elements – so often seen to be unstable – are not a simple, reliable guide to the origins of these names, as they may be for other types;[56] on the other, the association with Scandinavian personal names, in particular, is so very strong, especially in the northern Danelaw, that it would seem perverse not to accept the probability of a Scandinavian origin for many, if not most, of the settlements so named. But nagging uncertainty will inevitably remain in individual cases.

Fellows-Jensen has made a bold attempt to try to identify ancient *thorps* within the Danelaw on the basis of their later status and prosperity: she points to certain *thorps* that became medieval parishes and are assessed at relatively high taxable rates in Domesday Book. As a primary example she cites Fridaythorpe on the Yorkshire Wolds, which is part of the landscape surrounding the deserted medieval settlement of Wharram Percy, where archaeologists have laboured for years. As noted earlier, the area contains a number of *thorps*, including Mowthorpe, Raisthorpe and Towthorpe, which are known to be outlying dependencies of otherwise-named parishes.[57] Then there is Fridaythorpe, which is both a parish and has an exceptionally high taxable value at Domesday (Figure 4.3). Unlike the other *thorps* in the immediate vicinity it may also have an Old English personal name as first element. In consequence, it is easy to agree with Fellows-Jensen that there are 'reasons for believing that Fridaythorpe may have been an old established settlement before the arrival of the Danes'.[58]

However, the modality in this conclusion ('may have been') is important. For Fellows-Jensen's own analysis throws some doubt on the criteria exploited here. Thus, taking first parish status and the language of the qualifier: by her analysis,

---

56 The point made forcibly by Lund: above, p. 61.
57 Above, p. 39.
58 Fellows-Jensen, 'Place-names in -*þorp*', p. 39.

Figure 4.3 The church at Fridaythorpe YOE. The village lies close to Wharram Percy on the Wolds, the name deriving from a personal name of unknown origin, either Old German *Frigdag*, OE *Frigedæg*, or ON *Frijádagr*. Typical of *thorps* more generally, the church is both small and architecturally simple.

11 of 52 Danelaw *thorp*-names that have English personal names as qualifiers are parishes. That equates to 21 per cent, and it is certainly of interest that this is higher than the 17 per cent that she calculates for Danelaw *thorp*-names with Scandinavian personal names as qualifiers (30 parishes out of 177 names). Here are some grounds, again, for agreeing with the contention – for the group with English personal names – that 'since the parochial status of these villages points to their having been well-established in the eleventh century, their foundation may have antedated the arrival of the Danes'. But 30 parishes which combine *thorp* with Scandinavian personal names is not a negligible number, and again we can agree that 'the question is whether the parochial status of these settlements reflects their age or the fact that the Danes developed their resources particularly quickly'. Clearly, if growth between *c.*900 and *c.*1050 could account for the wealthier, more significant-looking *thorps*, then it begins to cast doubt on parochial status as a dating criterion. And we might think so particularly when we turn to the third group, the Danelaw *thorps* with post-Conquest-type personal names. Here, Fellows-Jensen finds that 8 of 34 became parishes, which at 24 per cent is the

highest yet. Of these she comments: 'although the *þorps* with parish status could be old settlements that were partially renamed in the eleventh century, it seems more likely that they are in fact young settlements'. And she goes on to suggest, for some specific examples in east Lincolnshire, that rapid eleventh-century development had transformed the status of the landholdings. If this could be the case for over 20 per cent of the *thorps* with late personal names as qualifiers, it is difficult to be sure of the significance of the similar number of *thorps* with Old English personal names as qualifiers.

Not surprisingly, Domesday assessments suggest a similar – rather confused – story to the one indicated by parish status. Fellows-Jensen calculates that nine Danelaw *thorps* with Scandinavian personal-name qualifiers are assessed at eight carucates or more, and observes that all nine of them lie on the Yorkshire Wolds, suggesting to her 'that, at the time of the compilation of Domesday Book, the Wolds were exceptionally prosperous',[59] a prosperity which she is happy to ascribe to conditions within the previous 150 years. Yet if this could be so, it surely shakes the argument that Fridaythorpe should be considered an ancient, pre-Danish settlement because it was valuable by the end of the eleventh century.

In fact, various indications – most of them individually recognised by Fellows-Jensen – tend to suggest that *thorps* occupy a dynamic, developing, early medieval landscape. Thus, in one context, it is suggested that the coastal *thorps* of south-east Lindsey, Lincolnshire, were developed in connection with the salt industry in the post-Conquest period, but that the settlements (already with *thorp*-names?) were probably in seasonal use much earlier – and in two cases at least, at Aisthorpe and Theddlethorpe, grave covers of the mid- to late tenth or early eleventh century built into the walls of the later churches may suggest a more permanent presence by that date.[60] We are left to wonder whether the names in *thorp* were originally bestowed at a time when the settlements were in only seasonal use, or whether they belong to one of the later phases. Elsewhere in Lincolnshire the relationship between pre-Conquest stone sculpture and *thorp*-names has also seemed suggestive of settlement evolution. North of Lincoln, forming part of the regular 'ladder' system of parishes lying along Ermine Street and the Lincoln Edge, are three adjacent parishes, Cammeringham, Brattleby and Aisthorpe, which each yield similar Anglo-Scandinavian stone sculpture, again of the second half of the

---

59   Fellows-Jensen, 'Place-names in -*þorp*', p. 44.
60   *Ibid.*, pp. 43–4; 'Torp-navne', pp. 54–5. Fellows-Jensen's discussion reports the work of Arthur Owen in, e.g., A.E.B. Owen, 'Salt, sea banks and medieval settlement on the Lindsey coast', in N. Field and A. White (eds), *A prospect of Lincolnshire* (Lincoln, 1984), pp. 46–9. For the grave-monument at Theddlethorpe St Helen, see P. Everson and D. Stocker, *British Academy corpus of Anglo-Saxon stone sculpture, 5. Lincolnshire* (Oxford, 1999), p. 264, and P. Sawyer, *Anglo-Saxon Lincolnshire* (Lincoln, 1998), p. 15. For Aisthorpe, Everson and Stocker, *Lincolnshire*, pp. 95–6.

tenth century. If, in general, the statistics relating to -*ingahām*, -*bȳ* and -*thorp* names point to a hierarchy of status, then – it is argued – in this case that hierarchy no longer appears to have been clearly relevant after *c*.950.[61] If this evidence can be accepted – and certainly we would support the points made from the analysis of place-name types – then it implies that, under certain circumstances, *bȳ*- and *thorp*-names that would not have been coined much before *c*.900 could attain parish status within half a century. Indeed, a possible implication of the work on the sculpture in northern Lincolnshire is that it was the second half of the tenth century which saw the establishment of parishes in this region, a process involving a fundamental reorganisation of ecclesiastical units and boundaries.[62] This, if correctly identified, would evidently be a mechanism by which some relatively new dependent settlements of the previous generations could have been quickly promoted in status.

Another transformation in settlement structure has been proposed for the Yorkshire Wolds in the period after AD 900. Both Gillian Fellows-Jensen and Margaret Gelling have recognised that an archaeologically identified reorganisation of settlement and agricultural holdings here in perhaps the tenth century may have had a significant effect on the place-name pattern.[63] And – as a later section of this book will explore in more detail – this phenomenon in eastern Yorkshire is symptomatic of a series of changes that appears to have affected great swathes of England in the later Anglo-Saxon period. In particular, in the ninth and tenth centuries, across a wide belt of the country, small dispersed settlements seem to have been swept away and replaced by compact, centralised, 'nucleated' villages. Associated, to some extent, with these changes were revolutionary developments in farming practice whereby individual arable holdings were replaced by large communal 'open' fields divided into strips assigned to separate farmers. Reorganisation of settlement and agriculture in this way – now recognised as a commonplace by archaeologists and landscape historians – must have had profound effects on many aspects of Anglo-Saxon society, of which place-naming was surely one. And with regard to the specific question of *thorp*-names, two broad possibilities arise: first, older names that existed before agricultural and/or ecclesiastical reorganisation may subsequently have become applied to new units or to units with new characteristics; second, the upheavals provide an excellent context for the coining of new names.

---

61 Fellows-Jensen, 'Torp-navne', p. 54; D. Stocker and P. Everson, 'Five towns funerals: decoding diversity in Danelaw stone sculpture', in J. Graham-Campbell *et al.* (eds), *Vikings and the Danelaw: select papers from the proceedings of the thirteenth Viking congress* (Oxford, 2001), pp. 223–43, at 227.

62 Stocker and Everson, 'Five towns funerals'.

63 Fellows-Jensen, 'Torp-navne', pp. 51–4; M. Gelling, 'Anglo-Norse place-names on the Yorkshire wolds', in Gammeltoft and Jørgensen (eds), *Names through the looking-glass*: pp. 85–93 at 92.

We shall return to some of these points in our conclusions. For the moment, the aim has been to suggest that there are circumstances in which small and dependent places of, say, c.900 could have achieved significant status during the tenth and eleventh centuries, and that it is therefore not necessary to assume that Danelaw *thorps* with parochial status and/or high taxable values in Domesday Book are ancient settlements that must have been founded in the early Anglo-Saxon period. Of course, it is not possible to assert the inverse: we could not argue that *thorps* which are substantial in the eleventh century are *not* old, pre-Viking-period establishments – and in any individual case this is certainly worth investigating – but that is not to concede that they *must* be so old. In our view their later size and value is not sufficient evidence to demonstrate that any Danelaw *thorps* necessarily descend from pre-Viking English-named *thorps* or *throps*.[64]

In this discussion of status and date we have strayed a little from the statistical basis of the study, which shows very clearly that *thorps* are generally small and of low status. Having drawn particular attention to the minority which grew into something more substantial, it is worth re-emphasising that the weight of evidence tends to suggest that all *thorps* originally shared these characteristics of dependency, and that the exceptions, which become larger and more significant places, are likely to have grown from humble origins.[65] The rate at which this growth was achieved appears impossible to calculate, but – to conclude – there are enough possible contexts in the later Anglo-Saxon period for us to be wary of assuming that it could only happen to long-established settlements.

None of this, we concede, amounts to a proof that Niels Lund was wrong to suggest that a stratum of early English *thorp/throp* names underlies the *thorps* of the Danelaw. It is perfectly possible that there were some such names, but we think it is very hard indeed to isolate them. And from the point of view of the construction of the names themselves, there are no real clues. As we have seen, outside the Danelaw there is very little to suggest archaic name-formation in the *thorps*; Gestingthorpe ESX is the best example of an unconvincing bunch. Within the Danelaw, there is even less which suggests antiquity. When names in *thorp* are placed beside those in *hām*, an undeniably early OE element, the difference

---

64 On the basis of a palaeo-botanical study suggesting that cultivation at Thorpe Bulmer DRH was uninterrupted between the Roman period and the later Anglo-Saxon, Fellows-Jensen suggests that the settlement is of great age ('Torp-navne', p. 49). This may indeed suggest that the *thorp* here is not a late colonisation of wasteland, as was once the paradigm, but this work does not appear to establish continuity of the particular *settlement-site*, and – of course – it cannot show that any earlier settlement was also named *Thorpe* (see below, p. 117)

65 In connection with the stone sculpture at Aisthorpe LIN, it is worth noting that only 4 of 70 *thorps* in Lincolnshire and neighbouring 'Stamfordshire' have such sculpture, which tends – again – to support the minor status of such settlements (Stocker and Everson, 'Five towns funerals', p. 229).

between them is very striking: as well as being frequently combined with -*ingas* group-names, *hām* is characteristically combined with monosyllables that are difficult to explain, and for which unrecorded personal names provide the philologists' usual escape-route. The qualifiers of *thorp*-names, in contrast, on both sides of the Danelaw line, are overwhelmingly intelligible, which suggests that the compounds, at least, do not generally reach back into the obscurity of the earliest Anglo-Saxon centuries.

One small group remains for those who want to point to tangible evidence of an early English stratum of *thorps* in northern England. Two *throp*-names – Throphill (*Trophil* 1166), near Morpeth, and Thropton (*Tropton* 1177), near Rothbury – have been identified in Northumberland, a territory which seems in general to have remained beyond the Danelaw to the north and to have escaped Scandinavian linguistic influence on its place-names. These examples are likely, therefore, to present a native English form. It is striking, however, that in neither case is *thorp* the generic, as in the vast majority of settlement-names. This must throw some doubt on the relevance of the Northumberland instances to an understanding of usage further south. They do not simply support a suggestion that *thorp* place-names would have extended from Dorset to Northumberland before the interruptions of the Viking period, because they are not of the same type as the predominant model further south. They do certainly tend to support other evidence, notably the pre-Viking glosses, which confirm that the word was native to English before the Scandinavian settlements of the ninth century, but it is very difficult to deduce from them any other significant clues about usage further south. One even wonders here whether the word is correctly identified, or whether the word had developed a distinctive sense here that is not usual elsewhere: there is, for instance, no sign of a *throp*- or *thorp-tūn* anywhere else.[66]

It might be added that Smith also includes the Yorkshire (West Riding) instances of Thrope in Kirkby Malzeard (*Trope* 1198) and Throapham (*Trapun* 1086, *Thropon* 1352) in his conspectus of native English *throp*-names.[67] These instances, which he took to support the Northumbrian ones, are established entirely on the evidence of the metathesis, a linguistic criterion which, as we have discussed above (pp. 33–4), is slippery at best. Since these names are simplex generics, and are not in close geographical association with Throphill and Thropton (which lie at least 100 miles further north), it is not self-evident that they belong with and

---

66 Ekwall (DEPN, s.n. Throphill) suggests that 'A better etymology for Thropton is given by the meaning "cross-roads" evidenced for *þrop*', but unfortunately it is argued in Appendix 1, below, that 'cross-roads' is probably a ghost-sense suggested by imprecise glossing.

67 EPNE, 2 pp. 215–16 and map.

support the Northumbrian names against the many conventional generic *thorps* of Yorkshire.[68]

Along with previous commentators, therefore, we conclude that it is simply very difficult to deduce how far Old English practice may underlie the *thorps* of the Danelaw, just as it is difficult to determine whether any of the names outside the Danelaw are ancient. Rather, we are drawn back to the various observations that can be made about the names that survive for us to examine. With the single exception of Thorpe SUR, which is not entirely straightforward, we have not seen any evidence of *thorps* recorded before the tenth century and – on both sides of the Danelaw line – it might be suggested that much earlier dates are improbable. To the north and east the high frequency of Scandinavian qualifiers indicates that, as they stand, the majority of names are no older than the late ninth century. To the south and west the absence of *thorp*-names from the rich record of Anglo-Saxon charters suggests that they were not thick on the ground at an early date. Across the country there is little in the nature of the qualifiers in compounds to point to antiquity, and there are various indications – including the general intelligibility of the qualifiers and the frequent late date of first record – which suggest that they are relatively recent coinages in the late Anglo-Saxon period, and that they remained commonplace, not archaic, after the Norman Conquest. All this, taken with the impression of a continuous distribution across the south-west Midlands and across the Danelaw line, as discussed above, tends to support the contention that, in general, the known *thorp* and *throp* settlements are likely to belong not to two widely separated phases, as Smith would have it, but broadly to one phase, which begins, loosely, in the second half of the Anglo-Saxon period.

Thus far, then, we have examined *thorps* and *throps* either side of the Danelaw line and concluded that the surviving distribution may generally represent a continuum of usage in the late pre-Conquest period. It is not clear how far early Old English names may underlie those in the Danelaw: the theoretical possibility remains, but we have found little specific evidence to support it in individual cases. It remains to ask whether an alternative theory is possible: rather than the *thorps* of the Danelaw depending upon Old English antecedents, is it possible that usage in 'English' England derived from practice introduced into the Danelaw by Scandinavians?

---

68 It might also be noted that the identification of the word is not quite certain in these instances. Although apparently confident in EPNE, Smith is less whole-hearted in the subsequent publication of the details in EPNS YOW: in particular he notes that the forms of Throapham are actually consistent with the dative plural of an unknown OE *þrāp (EPNS YOW, 1, p. 145); in the case of Thrope he is bothered by the regular early forms in *Trop*, rather than *Throp* (EPNS YOW, 5, pp. 203–4).

It has been noted above (pp. 70–1) that some previous commentators have proposed this as a possibility. Fellows-Jensen drew attention to what might be a parallel spread of the ON element *toft* into the south-west Midlands.[69] No one doubts that *toft* is ultimately a Viking-age introduction into eastern England, and it appears clear that this term, like so many others that were borrowed into English from Norse, must have spread gradually into local usage beyond the Danelaw boundary.[70] In this case, the spread is tangible, in so far as *toft* is twice recorded in twelfth- and thirteenth-century field-names in Gloucestershire,[71] and this may therefore be a significant parallel to a putative spread of *thorp* from the Scandinavian east to the English west. However, in various respects, *thorp* and *toft* are quite different. For one thing, the distribution of *thorp*, or *throp*, goes much further south and west than that of *toft*: unlike *toft* – which has only been noted in Gloucestershire west of the Danelaw[72] – it quite clearly reaches Wiltshire, Berkshire, Hampshire and Dorset and beyond into Somerset and Devon. For another, *thorp/throp* is a known English element, attested in pre-Viking sources. Taken together, these observations give no strong support to the idea that *thorp* in 'English' England is solely or principally to be derived from Scandinavian usage. The almost complete absence of Scandinavian qualifiers in the *thorp*-names south of the Danelaw (above, pp. 65–6) tends to point in the same direction. While it is, of course, possible that *thorp* as a loanword carried a new concept into new territory, and thereby spread a surprisingly long way, this does not appear a necessary, nor particularly likely, explanation.

In fact, one further piece of evidence tends to underscore this conclusion because it suggests that the Old English cognate was in use in Midland place-

---

69 Fellows-Jensen, 'Torp-navne', p. 49.

70 For *toft* in England see EPNE, 2, pp. 181–3, and P. Gammeltoft, '"I sauh a tour on a toft, tryelyche i-maket", part two: on place-names in -*toft* in England', *Nomina*, 26 (2003), pp. 43–63. For a detailed discussion of the spread of Scandinavian terms into the medieval literary texts of the south-west Midlands, see R. Dance, *Words derived from Old Norse in early Middle English: studies in the vocabulary of the south-west Midland texts* (Tempe, 2003); however, Dance discusses neither *thorp* nor *toft*: neither, it seems, would belong to the register of his texts.

71 *Wivetoft* c.1220 EPNS GLO, 2, p. 177 and *Hundestoft* 12th EPNS GLO, 1, p. 205; *Ibid.*, 4, p. 178, for the date of the latter. The qualifier in the former is obscure: Gammeltoft, '"I sauh a tour"', p. 63, suggests OE *wīfa* 'woman', a supposed masculine side-form of OE *wīf*, the evidence for which is minimal; in the latter the qualifier is *hund*(*r*) 'dog', either OE or ON, pers.n. or common noun (Gammeltoft, '"I sauh a tour"', p. 58).

72 It has also been noted in Essex, but EPNS ESX, p. 591, gives frustratingly limited information. *Toft* has also supposedly been noted in a Kent place-name: J.K. Wallenberg, *The place-names of Kent* (Uppsala, 1934) takes it to be the generic element in *Goretop* (*Garestoft* 1289, *Goretuffe* 1395, *Gooretoft* 1471, *Gortoffe* 1545) in Worth parish. P. Cullen was unconvinced and favoured Middle English *tuffe*, *tufte*, 'a tuft, a cluster of trees or bushes' ('The place-names of the lathes of St Augustine and Shipway, Kent', PhD thesis (University of Sussex, 1997), pp. 513–14).

names before the period of Scandinavian settlement. It is appropriate, therefore, to describe it in the final section of the chapter.

The charter

The Anglo-Saxon charter numbered 214 in Sawyer's list records the sale of a five-hide estate by Burgred, the last pre-Viking king of Mercia, to one Wulflaf. The transaction is dated AD 869, a year after Burgred had had to deal with a Viking occupation of Nottingham – it is true – but five years before his kingdom was conquered and eight before it was settled in some planned way, according to the *Anglo-Saxon Chronicle*.[73] The document survives as a single sheet, which may be a ninth-century original or perhaps a copy made in the following century: there seems no reason to doubt its testimony.[74] From our point of view that testimony is important, in the first place, because the estate that changes hands is called *on Upþrope*. This is an example of a *thorp* (as metathesised *throp*) in use in the Midlands in a pre-Viking context. Certainly, even if the Vikings were already in evidence and causing problems, the document is surely too early to reflect Norse linguistic influence, and indeed there is no hint of it in the other names it records.

It is unfortunate, however, that this critical place-name is unlocated. There are no clues in the main text of the charter as to where it might be, save that it is in Mercia:[75] there are half a dozen places named Upthorp(e) in our database, including examples in Northamptonshire, Huntingdonshire and Worcester-shire;[76] moreover, we have seen plenty of evidence that directional qualifiers might be unstable. It might be hoped, however, that a passage appended to the charter by the main scribe would give more than enough detail for an identification. It begins:

> Est autem terruncula prememorata his falerata agellulis constipataque on Sceomman hrycge Willering wic & on Midhelte Cynemunding wic & on Sigeres felda Ud[d]ing wic

> Moreover, the aforementioned little estate is embossed and bounded around by these little properties: Willhere's *wīc* on *Sceomman* ridge, Cynemund's *wīc* in *Midhelte* and Ud[d]a's *wīc* in Sighere's open land

---

73 D. Whitelock, *The Anglo-Saxon Chronicle: a revised translation* (London, 1961), pp. 46–8.

74 N.P. Brooks and S.E. Kelly, *Charters of Christ Church, Canterbury* (forthcoming), no. 92.

75 Brooks and Kelly, *Charters of Christ Church*, note that the assessment of the estate in *manentes* is characteristic of Mercia rather than Kent, where sulungs were preferred. In fact the Kentish associations of this charter are wholly unclear: it is unknown what interest, if any, Christ Church Canterbury ever had in the estate.

76 For the two in Worcestershire, one of them also with a pre-Conquest record, see above, p. 69, n. 30.

Yet none of these six place-names has been identified either, and certainly they are not readily to be found near the known locatable instances of Upthorp(e). There is still a further clue, because the passage goes on to mention 'inland' related to the granted estate *æt Peodan beorge*. This name also is elusive: Padbury BUC is perhaps the most similar-looking surviving name, but the run of spellings for that tends to suggest a name in -*byrig*, dative of *burg* 'stronghold', rather than *beorg* 'hill'. Although substitution or confusion in transmission would be perfectly possible with these elements, it does not help secure the identification, and – again – the minor place-names detailed above have not been traced near Padbury.

Thus this is a *thorp* that remains unidentified: to such an extent, in fact, that it is the only one in our database that cannot be placed even tentatively one side or other of the Danelaw boundary, and it has therefore not appeared in most of the statistics quoted above.[77] Yet its importance is not greatly diminished: it crucially shows the term being used in an English context before the historical date of Scandinavian settlement, and it does so in a name, with a directional qualifier, which is typical of the great swathe of *thorps* that runs through the Midlands. If we are right to argue that the name-type represents a single settlement-phase shared across the Danelaw boundary, then this is evidence to suggest that it is a phase that was taking shape in Anglo-Saxon England before the arrival of Scandinavian newcomers.

Still this does not exhaust the significance of the *Upthrop* charter, because its phrasing goes on to give hints about the structure of the estate into which the settlement fitted, and about the organisation of agriculture practised there. These hints will be of significance to our further thinking. Before coming to them, however, we want to step to one side and examine our corpus from a rather different point of view.

---

77 As one of a group of seven unidentified or lost OE place-names it might be suggested that it is more probable that this Upthrope was located in the Danelaw, where strong Scandinavian linguistic influence could account for the loss or erasing of earlier forms, rather than outside where such names would have been more likely to survive.

5

Thorps: the archaeological evidence

Cameron's study of the East Midlands, more precisely the Five Boroughs, sought to explain the position of *thorps* in the wider landscape.[1] His conclusions continue to influence how these places are viewed within the developing settlement hierarchy of the period c.850–1250. In the following two chapters Cameron's hypothesis acts as the starting point for our re-evaluation of these places, but unlike him, we do not restrict ourselves to the *thorps* of the Danelaw. Rather, and taking our cue from the linguistic evidence presented in the previous two chapters, we will treat *thorps* and *throps* across the country together as a single group. As we have seen, analysis of the place-names themselves has begun to point us in various directions, stressing in particular that these were in origin small and dependent places. It does not, however, give us a picture of the physical appearance of these places, nor of their precise location in the landscape. Neither are the names particularly informative when it comes to understanding how these places might have functioned (although the hints of groups of workmen are duly noted). All these facets of rural settlement are perhaps more usefully examined from archaeological and topographical perspectives, and this is our aim in the next two chapters. Does the material evidence for *thorps* support the linguistic evidence? Or is it contradictory? And what additional clues might it offer in our attempt to address the simple question we have posed ourselves: what is a *thorp*? In this chapter we draw on archaeological material that was unavailable to Cameron thirty years ago to suggest both when *thorp*-places were being established and what form they took in their earliest phases. But, as we shall see, this is still not always an easy task.

Dating thorps

The analysis of the preceding chapters has suggested that *thorps* in the Danelaw owe a great deal to the Scandinavian settlements of the later ninth and tenth

---

1   Cameron, *Scandinavian settlement*; Cameron, 'Scandinavian settlement, part II', pp. 139–56.

centuries, although there is a suggestion in S 214 that the place-name type was already to be found in English nomenclature by the mid-ninth century. The appearance in the Danelaw of the earliest *thorps* in documents from the second half of the tenth century is consonant with this picture, suggesting that some, perhaps many, of the names were coined in the period c.880 × c.950. Since very few Danelaw documents earlier than AD 950 survive, we cannot expect much greater resolution. Outside the Danelaw – with the single, disputed, example of Thorpe SUR – the earliest recorded names also belong to the second half of the tenth centuy. In parts of this region, documents of the tenth century and before are much more widespread, and one might have expected, if the place-name type had been common at an earlier date, to find evidence for it. Instead we find a suggestion, in the frequent late date of record, that the names may often have been coined later, not earlier, than the tenth century.

Thus we can hypothesise that there may have been a revolution in place-naming in or around the first half of the tenth century. (To some extent this could 'simply' represent Scandinavian settlement, but in this case there is the intriguing relationship to pre-existing English usage and to developments outside the Danelaw thereafter.) The impression from the historical record, rightly or wrongly, is that *thorps* were something of an overnight phenomenon, arriving so suddenly that within a generation or two (at least in those parts of the country such as Yorkshire, Lincolnshire and north Norfolk where they lie thickest on the ground) the face of the English countryside was dramatically redrawn. Parallels might be drawn with church construction a century or so later: it has been estimated that between c.1075 and c.1125 anything from 1000 to 2000 parish churches were built across England – a phenomenon likened by one commentator to the appearance of 'mushrooms in the night'. This is an allusion that might equally apply to *thorps*.[2]

In other senses, too, drawing an analogy between churches and *thorps* is helpful. Just as church building presents a physical manifestation of broader changes affecting medieval rural society in the two decades either side of 1100, so we might ask whether the origin of *thorps* should be sought in an earlier period of large-scale and rather rapid landscape realignment and reapportionment. But before jumping to such conclusions, churches also offer a salutary note of caution. We know that many of the 'new' churches of the late eleventh and early twelfth centuries were not the first to be built at a particular location, but were rather simply stone replacements for earlier timber structures. When *thorp*-names are encountered for the first time in the written record, we must ask ourselves what

2   R. Morris, *Churches in the landscape* (London, 1989, rev. edn 1997), pp. 140–67.

was there before: did names given in the first half of the tenth century refer to newly established settlements, or could they represent a renaming of the existing landscape?

Renaming is certainly always a theoretical possibility, although it is hard to pin down in the record: Cameron notes that documented evidence remains 'extremely slight',[3] and even the slight evidence is usually controversial or problematic. Thus, one of the most straightforward cases is the renaming of English *Northworthy* as Viking *Derby*,[4] yet it has recently been suggested that this is not a simple case of a new name applied to the identical location: instead it may be the outcome of competing designations of an uncertainly located Anglo-Saxon settlement and a Scandinavian adaptation of the name *Derventio*, which would have denoted the Roman fort at Little Chester, upriver from the present town.[5] Complications and uncertainties similarly attach to the partial renamings that might be evidenced in the early record of some *thorps*. Banthorpe LIN appears in Domesday Book both as *Barnetorp* and *Barnetone*, but it is impossible to know whether the single instance of *Barnetone* preserves an earlier version of the name, represents a scribal error, or – conceivably – denotes a related but separate settlement to the *thorp*.[6] Likewise, although Martinsthorpe RUT is first attested as *Martinestoch*, in 1176 – which seems not to be an error, since *Martinstok* is found also in 1286 – it is impossible to be sure that OE *stoc* has simply been replaced by *thorp*, because the two names may perhaps have designated separate settlements.[7] Rather, it has to be concluded that the nature of our early documentary record tends not to permit the secure identification of straightforward name-change.

That does not mean, however, that it did not happen. Indeed, in at least one category of Danelaw names widespread renaming of earlier settlements is generally considered probable. These are the Grimston-hybrids, which combine OE *tūn* with Scandinavian personal names, and have been judged – on the basis of this linguistic structure and their usually favourable sites – to represent

---

3   Cameron, 'Scandinavian settlement, part II', p. 139.
4   EPNS DRB, 2, p. 446, citing Æthelweard's late-tenth-century statement (relating to events of 871): 'in loco qui Northuuorthiege nuncupatur, iuxta autem Danaam linguam Deoraby'.
5   J. Carroll and D.N. Parsons, *Anglo-Saxon mint-names. Vol. I: Axbridge–Hythe* (Nottingham, 2007), pp. 112–13, 117–19.
6   SSNEM, p. 102, favours scribal error.
7   EPNS RUT, p. 200.
8   Gelling, *Signposts*, pp. 231–4. Note that there is some controversy here, too, about the nature, if not the fact, of the replacement. The conventional view has been that the original English place-name would have involved *tūn*, and that a new qualifier, the name of the new owner, was simply substituted. It may be more likely, however, that *tūn* was adopted by the Scandinavians, and that the new place-names replaced a wider variety of older ones (D.N. Parsons, 'How long did the Scandinavian language survive in England? Again', in J. Graham-Campbell *et al.*, (eds), *Vikings and the Danelaw* (Oxford, 2001), pp. 299–312, at 308–9).

Scandinavian takeovers of existing Anglo-Saxon settlements.[8] If this type of renaming could take place in this class of names, then it must be possible that the *thorps* may also be new designations for older places. The establishment of a solid chronology for their foundation, both individually and as a group, is therefore an essential prerequisite if they are to be fully understood; and it is archaeology that offers this much needed clarification.

It might be noted that with the exceptions of Theddlethorpe LIN, Aisthorpe LIN and Thorp Arch YOW, no *thorp* churches contain pre-eleventh-century stone sculpture, despite lying in areas where such material is not uncommon.[9] This may point to the relatively late date of church construction in *thorps*, but it does not help to date the origins of the village themselves, which might have turned to church building long after they had come into existence. To do this we need to turn to the excavated evidence. No *thorp*, however, has been the subject of concerted or systematic archaeological investigation. In the absence of major excavation campaigns, however, we do have data recovered, often in advance of recent building or the digging of pipe trenches, from small-scale interventions within the historic cores of a considerable number of *thorps*. This information clearly holds the potential to elucidate the earliest phases of these places, but using it for this purpose presents immediate problems. Where excavation has taken place, locations have been dictated by modern development, rather than chosen to address the research questions that lie at the heart of this book. As a result potentially datable material often comes from parts of these settlements beyond the earliest occupation zone, while settlement cores might remain unexplored. Complicating matters still further, the limited number of explorations within particular *thorps* (often restricted to one or two reported interventions in any settlement) makes it particularly difficult to assess whether the material we have is representative of the *thorp* as a whole or simply reflects very localised, and perhaps abnormal, activity. As more comprehensive surveys of medieval villages have shown, the nature of the material evidence they produce can vary considerably from one part of the settlement to another.[10] Thus there are important caveats to consider when dealing with the available evidence and many interpretative pitfalls that lie in the path of the unwary. The temptation is to collate the information and

9   Everson and Stocker, *Lincolnshire*, pp. 95–6, 265; J. Lang, *British Academy corpus of Anglo-Saxon stone sculpture, 3. York and Eastern Yorkshire* (Oxford, 1991); J. Lang, *British Academy corpus of Anglo-Saxon stone sculpture, 6. Northern Yorkshire* (Oxford, 2001); E. Coatsworth, *British Academy corpus of Anglo-Saxon stone sculpture, 8. Western Yorkshire* (Oxford, 2008), pp. 265–6.

10   M. Aston and C. Gerrard, '"Unique, traditional and charming": the Shapwick Project, Somerset', *Antiquaries Journal*, 79 (1999), pp. 1–58; N. Cooper and V. Priest, 'Sampling a medieval village in a day: the "Big Dig" investigation of Great Easton, Leicestershire', *MSRG Annual Report*, 18 (2003), pp. 53–6; Jones and Page, *Medieval villages*, pp. 79–104 and 155–200.

to present a composite picture of *thorp* history. But, again, the evidence from other surveys would advise against this approach: it is clear that, despite sharing much in common, all villages or hamlets followed unique developmental paths.[11]

The results from excavations at Weaverthorpe YOE highlight some of the problems of interpretation that need to be overcome.[12] Modern Weaverthorpe is a linear village lying on both sides of the road from Rudston to Wharram-le-Street (Figure 5.1). The principal house, sitting within landscaped gardens, is located a short distance to the east of the main village. The church of St Andrews stands isolated a few hundred metres to the north, on the edge of a now-empty banked and ditched rectangular enclosure. Planned extension of the churchyard into this enclosure prompted the excavations, which revealed the stone footings of two medieval halls and associated buildings. The northern hall, the smaller of the two, was dated by pottery evidence to the twelfth century, although the documented manorial descent may associate it perhaps with a change of ownership in c.1069. The other hall and its annexes appear to have been constructed sometime after 1220. Evidence of earlier activity on the site was restricted to the recovery of a number of residual Romano-British pottery sherds and a possible sleeper trench designed to take a horizontal weight-bearing timber. This was backfilled with soil and rubble and contained fragments of bowls made from Stamford Ware, a type of pottery in production from AD 900 to 1200.[13] A compelling case can therefore be made for the creation of a church–manor complex north of the village in the post-Conquest period (the grant of Weaverthorpe church to Nostell Priory was confirmed in 1114–21).[14] Only the Stamford Ware found in association with structural remains points towards the possible pre-Conquest origin of the village. While the date range of this pottery type spans nearly three centuries, the fact that it was not found here with either ceramics dating to the twelfth century or the later buildings perhaps indicates that it had been deposited in the tenth or eleventh centuries. The total absence of other early medieval material might also be cited as evidence for a post-900 foundation date, in which case these partial remains might indeed represent part of the earliest plan of the medieval village. But it remains the case that nothing more than this single building is known of the layout of the settlement at Weaverthorpe in the pre-Conquest period. Frustratingly, these excavations cast no light on when the tofts and crofts along the village street were originally laid out.

11   Jones and Page, *Medieval villages*, pp. 223–43.
12   T. Brewster, 'An excavation at Weaverthorpe Manor, East Riding, 1960', *Yorkshire Archaeological Journal*, 44 (1972), pp. 114–33.
13   M. McCarthy and C.M. Brooks, *Medieval pottery in Britain AD 900–1600* (Leicester, 1988), pp. 153–6.
14   J. Bilson, 'Weaverthorpe church and its builder', *Archaeologia*, 72 (1921–2), pp. 51–70.

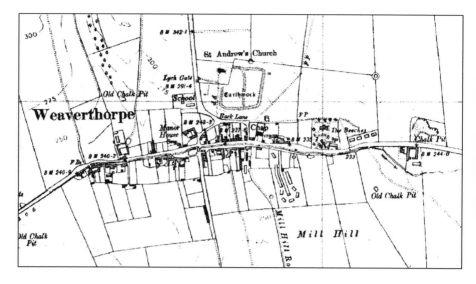

Figure 5.1 Weaverthorpe YOE in the mid-twentieth century. A linear village on the edge of the Yorkshire Wolds.

The principal elements of the modern Weaverthorpe layout – regular village with manor complex beyond – are echoed at the deserted site of Low Caythorpe YOE. Here a hollow-way running through a series of well-preserved tofts and crofts marks the location of the single-street village.[15] To the east is the site of a double-banked manorial complex, the target of excavations in the 1960s.[16] These revealed a chronological sequence remarkably similar to that demonstrated at Weaverthorpe: in summary, investigations here revealed a single late Saxon timber building that was replaced in stone during the twelfth century. This was in turn rebuilt in the fourteenth century and, after alteration, finally abandoned in the mid-sixteenth century (Figure 5.2). The village itself may have been deserted by the second half of the fifteenth century.

Permission to level the earthworks at Kettleby Thorpe LIN in 1964 prompted the survey of the then-surviving earthworks (unfortunately already mutilated by the quarrying of gravel in the mid-nineteenth century) and the excavation of a series of trenches across the village site (Figure 5.3).[17] As the aerial photograph shows, the village earthworks here are extensive and irregular, although there are

15   *MSRG Annual Report*, 4 (1989), p. 31.
16   G. Coppack, 'Low Caythorpe, East Yorkshire: the manor site', *Yorkshire Archaeological Journal*, 46 (1974), pp. 34–41.
17   E. Russell, 'Excavations on the site of the deserted medieval village of Kettleby Thorpe, Lincolnshire', *Journal of the Scunthorpe Museums Society*, 3/2 (1974), pp. 1–40.

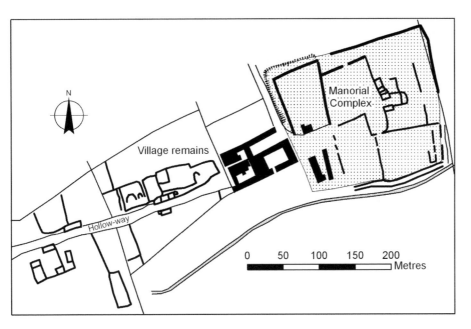

Figure 5.2 Village and manorial earthworks at Low Caythorpe YOE. The village earthworks immediately to the west of the manorial curia have been obscured by the modern farm buildings but sufficient remains to reconstruct its linear pattern.

components within the plan – such as those areas to the east and south-west – which exhibit signs of planning. Settlement growth can be traced from the distribution of pottery across the village. The earliest fabric was a single sherd of locally made Torksey Ware (900–1200)[18] found in proximity to building 1. This area also produced Stamford Ware, as did the three plots immediately to its north. A further sherd of Stamford Ware, which may have been disturbed, came from within the quarry. Minimal though the evidence is, we might tentatively postulate that the ceramics point to an original village core in the eastern part of the village established after 900. Kettleby Thorpe's Domesday Book entry implies a population of more than 20 in 1086, meaning that it was a not insignificant place if they all lived within the village itself.[19] The village subsequently grew, initially expanding to the north-west, where pottery dating to the late twelfth century was recovered, and later in the thirteenth century to the south. None of the metalwork, however, can be associated with the earliest phases of the village.

18   McCarthy and Brooks, *Medieval pottery*, pp. 151–3.
19   DB Lincs, 25.13: 'In [Kettleby] Thorp Klakkr and Leofwine had 10 bovates of land taxable. Land for 2 ploughs. Gilbert, Hugh's man, has 1 ploughs. 2 sokemen on 2 bovates of land; 3 villeins with 2 ploughs. Meadow, 60 acres. Value before 1066, 60s; now 100s. Exactions 20s.'

These three excavations are the most extensive to have been undertaken in *thorps*. Yet, as we have seen, they offer little more than a few tantalising glimpses into the early phases of these places. It might be suggested, however, that they do begin to offer up some useful lines of enquiry, among which, perhaps, the most notable is the absence of evidence for their existence before the start of the tenth century. Does this point towards their establishment in a late Saxon or, more appropriately given their location, an Anglo-Scandinavian context? Secondly, as we might expect, there is discrepancy between the material evidence for settlement and the date of first reference in historical sources. Weaverthorpe, Caythorpe and Kettleby Thorpe are first evidenced only in the Domesday survey,[20] so archaeology has

Figure 5.3 Oblique aerial photograph of the earthwork remains of Kettleby Thorpe LIN, showing evidence for quarrying at the centre of the village and the Lincoln–Grimsby railway line, which has cut through outlying parts of the medieval settlement.

provided important antedatings in these instances, although happily still remaining within the parameters of what we might term the *thorp* moment (tenth and eleventh century) suggested by the pre-Conquest documentation.[21]

The recovery of late Saxon wares – including St Neots Ware Type 1 (850–1050),

---

20 For Kettleby Thorpe see n. 17 above. DB Yorks, 2B 18: 'In Weaverthorpe, 18 carucates, with these outliers, [Low] Mowthorpe, 5 carucates and Sherburn, 3 carucates, there are 26 carucates taxable; 15 ploughs are possible there. Archbishop Aldred held this as one manor. Now Archbishop Thomas has it. Waste. Value before 1066, £14. To this manor belongs Helperthorpe, where there are 12 carucates taxable, 6 in soke, and 6 in sake and soke. Waste.' DB Yorks, 2B, 15: 'In [Low] Caythorpe three are 4 carucates taxable; 2 ploughs can plough. This land was and is St. Peter's. Value before 1066, 40s.'

21 It should be noted that the absence of pre-900 pottery is normal in villages of all name-types, not just *thorps*, although more recent exploration of inhabited settlement cores is beginning to redress this balance.

22 McCarthy and Brooks, *Medieval pottery*, pp. 157–61.

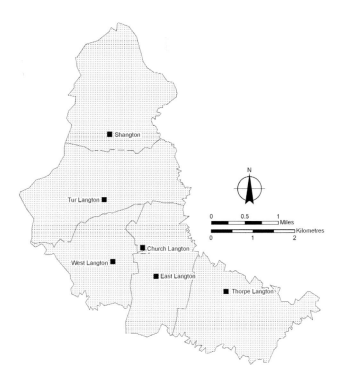

Figure 5.4 The extent of the Langton estate LEI. Thorpe Langton occupies the most south-easterly part of this early medieval land division. Many other *thorps* occupy this type of peripheral position away from the estate centre.

Stamford Ware and Thetford Ware (later ninth century to early twelfth century)[22] – as the earliest pottery from *thorps* is a recurrent theme in the available literature. Excavations close to the church of Bruntingthorpe LEI produced two sherds of Stamford Ware together with local coarse wares and the tibia of an ox.[23] At Edmondthorpe LEI, an eleventh-/twelfth-century Stamford Ware pitcher was found, again near the church.[24] A further indication that later ecclesiastical buildings continue to signal the focus of earlier occupation comes from Thorpe Langton LEI, where a cluster of pits, postholes and boundary ditches associated with late Saxon and medieval pottery were exposed close to the parish church (Figure 5.4).[25] Such features suggest a settlement of some substance and

23 TLAHS, 47 (1971–2), p. 66.
24 TLAHS, 79 (2005), p. 149: these sherds were recovered from a deposit thought to relate to the addition of two buttresses to the thirteenth-century church tower. It is likely, therefore, that the Stamford Ware pitcher had been disturbed during these works and subsequently redeposited.
25 MSRG Annual Report, 17 (2002), p. 49: the excavators themselves described the area under investigation as lying within the 'historic core' of the village.

Figure 5.5 The thatched church of All Saints, Ixworth Thorpe SFK. The brick porch hides a Norman doorway. (Photograph reproduced by kind permission of Suffolk County Council Archaeological Services.)

permanence given the physical definition of the properties in its earliest phases. This is paralleled at Kirkby la Thorpe LIN, where a series of ditches and pits was found in the western half of the site, all containing late Saxon and early medieval fabrics.[26] By contrast, settlement mobility is suggested by finds made at Ixworth Thorpe SFK, where the thatched church (Figure 5.5) now stands isolated on a hill: around it were found quantities of pottery of late Saxon date, while the present village has produced nothing earlier than the twelfth century.[27]

Fieldwalking on the ploughed-out remains of the deserted village of *Fregsthorpe* RUT produced mainly Stamford Ware, shelly and sandy coarse wares and Lyveden–Stanion Wares, offering a date range from the tenth to thirteenth centuries.[28] As the surveyors noted, the archaeological evidence for *Fregsthorpe*'s origins appear to corroborate Cox's suggestion that the name, not recorded before 1300, may have been coined as late as 1050–1250.[29] The earliest phases of occupation at Keythorpe

---

26 *MSRG Annual Report*, 15 (2000), p. 27: the report also concludes with the tantalising statement that '[A] subsequent watching brief during development revealed further late Saxon/early medieval features.'

27 *MSRG Annual Report*, 8 (1993), pp. 50–1. The south door of the church is built in the Norman style (N. Pevsner, *Suffolk* (Harmondsworth, 1961), p. 284).

28 *MSRG Annual Report*, 1 (1986), p. 27; *MSRG Annual Report*, 10 (1995), p. 31.

29 EPNS RUT, pp. xl and 150.

Hall Farm LEI appear to be indicated by ceramics of tenth- or eleventh-century date.[30] Fieldwalking has also produced material associated with occupation and dating to the eleventh century but no earlier both north and south of the church at Morningthorpe NFK.[31] At Garthorpe LEI the investigation of the churchyard produced pottery dating from the eleventh century from a disturbed subsoil,[32] while a survey of the remains of Hothorpe NTH recovered Stamford Ware and further quantities of shelly coarse wares from across the deserted village earthworks, demonstrating settlement here probably by the early eleventh century but certainly by the twelfth.[33]

In many other instances, the earliest proof of occupation on the present village site post-dates the Norman Conquest. At Gunthorpe LEI and Leethorpe LEI nothing has been found before the twelfth century.[34] Thorpe-by-Water RUT has produced only two sherds of Potters Marston pottery (1100–1300).[35] The laying of a major pipeline through the deserted village of Casthorpe LIN revealed nothing earlier than the thirteenth century despite the discovery of 'several stone walls and surfaces that probably constitute remains of the abandoned settlement'.[36] Another pipeline dissecting the village of Lubberthorpe LEI produced Potters Marston pottery, together with Lyveden (1225+), Nuneaton (1250–1400) and Midland Purple Wares (1375–1550), but nothing earlier.[37] Pits containing eleventh- and twelfth-century pottery at Millthorpe LIN,[38] and a medieval pit and posthole together with several other undated features at Eathorpe WAR comprise the earliest physical evidence for settlement in these places.[39] Medieval subsoils were

30 TLAHS, 56 (1980–1), p. 119: pottery was said to have been found over a distance of several hundred metres both north of the medieval fishponds and south of the stream to the east of the modern farm.

31 S. Addington, 'Landscape and settlements in South Norfolk', Norfolk Archaeology, 38/2 (1982), pp. 97–139, at 105.

32 TLAHS, 75 (2001), p. 143.

33 MSRG Annual Report, 11 (1996), pp. 43–4: it was the surveyor's belief that the parts of the village explored represented a planned extension of the original village core over existing ridge and furrow. The earliest part of the village, it was suggested, lies under the early-nineteenth-century mansion. Given the date of the pottery from the surviving tofts and crofts, an eleventh- or perhaps even tenth-century establishment date for Hothorpe might be entertained. Hothorpe appears small in the Domesday survey, but this may in part be explained if it was returned with Threddingworth, of which it was a chapelry.

34 Leicestershire HER no. MLE 5346; Leicestershire HER no. MLE 4071.

35 Pers. comm. Paul Blinkhorn.

36 MSRG Annual Report, 11 (1996), p. 38.

37 TLAHS, 57 (1981–2), p. 90.

38 MSRG Annual Report, 15 (2000), p. 27. Cameron, Dict. LIN, p. 88: Millthorpe was first recorded in the late twelfth century.

39 MSRG Annual Report, 18 (2003), p. 70.

encountered during a watching brief within the shrunken core of Thorpe St Peter LIN,[40] a fourteenth-century graveyard soil was identified at Trusthorpe LIN,[41] and a medieval midden was excavated at Thrupp OXF.[42] Conversely, it is extremely rare to find evidence for occupation beneath *thorps* which pre-dates *c.*900. At Calthorpe NFK, however, the recovery of a quantity of Thetford-type wares together with a single sherd of Ipswich-type ware (*c.*725–850) might point to origins in the middle Saxon period.[43]

Such findings merit comment, despite the intrinsic dangers already identified in dealing with *thorps* together as a group. In recent years archaeological efforts focused on issues relating to rural settlement origins have shifted from the investigation of deserted to surviving villages. Methodologies have changed too; open-area excavations and fieldwalking campaigns appropriate for the study of the deserted sites have given way to sampling techniques more suited to the limited spaces (roadside verges, private gardens) available in living villages. Research-led investigations now regularly use test-pitting as a means of obtaining information from all parts of modern settlements.[44] As developer-led interventions are often undertaken on a small scale, and since their location is dictated by areas of development rather than research questions and thus represent a random or haphazard sampling of the archaeology, the evidence they produce is easily comparable to that obtained from test-pitting, meaning the two can often be put together to create a broader picture of settlement history.

These new approaches have revolutionised our understanding of the earliest stages of village formation. The chronological gap which was once thought to exist between the final ceramic phases present on middle Saxon farmstead sites (pre-850) – a pattern of dispersed settlement abandoned across the central belt of England in favour of nucleated villages – and evidence for the existence of these new nucleated centres, which was largely absent before *c.*1100, has now been filled.[45] Many villages show signs of considerable continuity of location and occupation.[46] It is possible to identify, lying below many, a small core nucleus, often established before 850, from which the later medieval village grew. If this is

---

40 *Ibid.*, p. 64.

41 *Ibid.*, pp. 64–5. This soil layer pre-dates any surviving fabric in the church itself; N. Pevsner and J. Harris, *The buildings of England: Lincolnshire* (London, 1995), pp. 769–70.

42 *SMA* (1999), pp. 30–1.

43 *MSRG Annual Report*, 7 (1992), p. 28; A. Davison, 'The field archaeology of the Mannington and Wolverton estates', *Norfolk Archaeology*, 42/2 (1995), pp. 160–84.

44 C. Gerrard with M. Aston, *The Shapwick Project, Somerset: a rural landscape explored*, Society for Medieval Archaeology Monographs 25 (London, 2007).

45 C. Lewis, P. Mitchell-Fox, and C. Dyer, *Village, hamlet and field: changing medieval settlements in central England* (Macclesfield, 2nd edn, 2001), pp. 21–4.

46 Jones and Page, *Medieval villages*, pp. 87–92.

not yet a commonplace, it is a settlement history that can no longer be considered rare or anomalous.

Given this, it is the absence of any such evidence from the *thorps*, perhaps with the exception of Calthorpe NFK, which is noteworthy. This is the more so since many of our *thorps* lie within areas with long and continuous ceramic traditions. There may be an exception in Leicestershire, where there may have been a brief aceramic phase before 900, potentially depriving us of earlier evidence, but this is certainly not the case in Norfolk or Northamptonshire. On the balance of the available evidence, it is possible to propose that as a group *thorps* look as though they were indeed taking shape at a relatively late date. Using pottery as a guide, a large proportion seem to have their origins in the tenth century. Others may have been created later, although the majority had clearly been established before 1100. If not 'mushrooms in the night', when set against the longer chronology of English village formation as it is now understood, spanning the 400 years between 850 and 1250, the appearance of *thorps* in the landscape nevertheless occurred rapidly.

Moreover, while *thorps* might often develop in places that had been previously farmed, they do not seem to owe their existence, or to have grown directly from, any earlier settlement associated with this activity. *Thorps* were founded in locations that had not previously been occupied. The archaeological evidence would suggest these were indeed new settlements, built in addition to others that already dotted the English countryside. Furthermore, since both the date of first record and the archaeological material are largely consistent with one another, we might conclude that these places were *thorps* from the outset, rather than older settlements that took the appellation -*thorp* as a substitute for an older nomenclature. Such as they are, our conclusions remain in line with the Cameron hypothesis, reinforcing his notion that *thorps* were both late arrivals in the English landscape and new settlements in the sense that they were sited in places where there is little evidence for earlier occupation. With this in mind, we now turn to the question of what *thorps* looked like.

Settlement morphology

Discussion of early *thorp* plans is clearly hampered by the lack of large-scale excavation that has been undertaken on this group of settlements. What archaeological data have been extracted from within the historic cores of surviving *thorps* tend to comprise, as we have seen, little more than the recovery of small assemblages of material culture and occasional evidence for the existence of timber buildings. While this may be used to suggest when a particular *thorp* was taking shape, it reveals little which might usefully aid the reconstruction of the actual form and layout such settlements might have adopted. Invaluable in this respect, then, are those deserted *thorp* settlements which have now been ploughed out and where it has been possible to undertake fieldwalking – and thus recover datable evidence for their earliest phases of occupation – over their whole area. Where such results can be used in combination with the plotting of either surviving earthworks or those that can be traced through soilmarks or cropmarks, it is possible to begin to establish the relationship that exists between the earliest phases of occupation and those which were found on the eve of shrinkage or desertion – processes and events which might post-date the foundation of the settlement by many centuries. This information can then be taken to the interpretation of earthwork surveys of *thorps* for which no other archaeological data exist and, with extreme caution, some level of back projection can be attempted in the absence of other pointers to their settlement origins. Moreover, establishing the form that *thorps* took in the late Middle Ages helps to bridge the nearly 1000 years that separate their origins from the first systematic depiction of their layouts on the first edition OS maps of the late nineteenth century.

Fregsthorpe RUT is one example of a deserted *thorp* now being ploughed out by modern farming. Fieldwalking revealed a compact spread of medieval pottery associated with a series of degraded earthworks (Figure 5.6).[47] These marked a regular block of closes lying on either side of a single street. A modern field boundary running parallel to and fifty metres south of the street is mirrored by a stone scatter to the north. These appear to mark the extent of the tofts. The pottery spreads beyond these, particularly on the north side, indicating that the toft was backed by a croft of approximately the same dimensions as the toft. A later earthwork survey identified a shallow scarp coincident with the edge of the pottery scatter, clearly representing the remains of the croft boundary. Five tofts and crofts to the north of the hollow-way are defined by the eroded remains of property banks, varying in width between thirty and fifty metres; while to the south the row contains an additional toft on the western side, breaking the symmetry of the settlement layout. This last toft and croft was the only one which failed to produce pottery earlier than the second quarter of the thirteenth century and might, consequently, be a later addition to the original village plan. Across all the other ten plots, Stamford Ware was found spanning the tenth to thirteenth centuries, although in a second fieldwalking programme the pottery was dated no earlier than the eleventh century, perhaps accounting for *Fregsthorpe*'s absence from Domesday Book.[48] This pottery was found both on the tofts and within the crofts and would suggest that, as originally laid out, *Fregsthorpe* was planned as a regular,

47 MSRG *Annual Report*, 1 (1986), p. 27.
48 MSRG *Annual Report*, 10 (1995), p. 31.

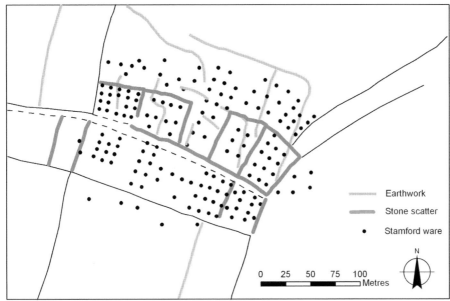

Figure 5.6 Composite plan of the results of earthwork survey and fieldwalking on the deserted site of *Fregsthorpe* RUT. The coincidence of early ceramic material with surviving earthwork remains is particularly striking, suggesting little alteration of plan before final abandonment.

rectangular settlement. The slightly radial pattern of the northern toft and croft boundaries, it has been suggested, indicates that the village was laid out over existing open fields.[49]

In the early eighteenth century the village of Hothorpe NTH was said to contain around 20 houses. In 1801 the present Hall was built, disrupting the village plan and displacing part of its population. When the park was laid out thirty years later, those that remained were relocated to the parish of Theddingworth across the county border into Leicestershire.[50] The earthworks here consist of a series of long and thin tofts and crofts (Figure 5.7). Those to the south-east of the hall appear to have been laid out over the ridge and furrow of the open fields, while the block to the east abuts the cultivated area but does not seem to overlay it. The impression that this was the original core of the village is substantiated by fieldwalking results which found pottery of the eleventh and twelfth centuries associated with these earthworks.[51] Outlying sherds to the south-east of the hall do, however, tend to point to the fact that this regular row of tenements may have originally spread

49 Ibid., p. 31.
50 RCHME, *An inventory of the historical monuments in the county of Northamptonshire. Vol. 3: archaeological sites in north-west Northamptonshire* (London, 1981), pp. 141–2.
51 *MSRG Annual Report*, 11 (1996), pp. 43–4.

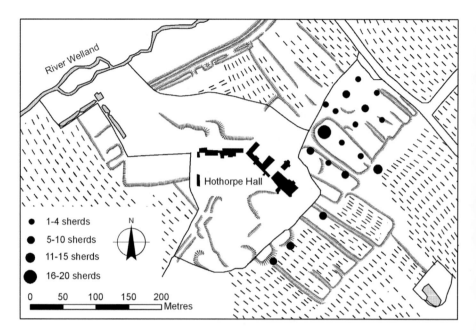

Figure 5.7 Fieldwalking results overlaid on upstanding earthworks at Hothorpe NTH. The pottery evidence suggests that the tofts and crofts visible as earthworks were all occupied during the eleventh and twelfth centuries.

under the hall. If so, the row may have been just short of 300 metres in length, and accommodated up to 10 properties.

The trace of the single street at Kingsthorpe NTH survives, together with a number of house platforms associated with the former village (Figure 5.8). To the south stands a square moated site.[52] The main evidence for the extent and form of medieval settlement, however, is an extensive scatter of pottery defining an area approximately 400 by 250 metres that straddles the hollow-way. Although the pottery dates mainly from the twelfth to fourteenth centuries, the manor is listed in 1086 with Armston NTH. Impossible though it is to disaggregate these two manors and therefore make a valued judgement about the size of population at Kingsthorpe at the time of Domesday, it is wholly possible that the site of the later village was already occupied by this date, the evidence for which might lie below this pottery scatter.

On the first edition OS map the village of Calthorpe NFK comprised a loose collection of properties with two principal foci: the manor–church complex standing at the western end of the village street, and a second group of houses and

---

52 RCHME, *An inventory of the historical monuments in the county of Northamptonshire. Vol. 1: archaeological sites in north-east Northamptonshire* (London, 1975), pp. 74–7.

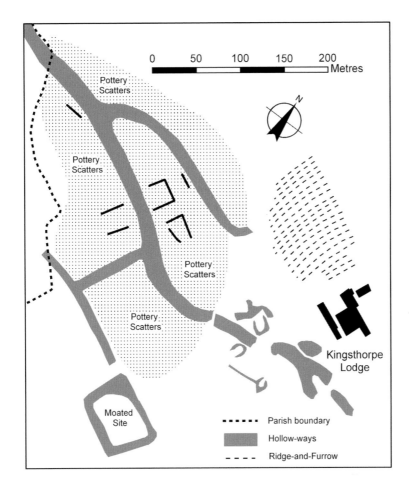

Figure 5.8 Kingsthorpe in Polebrook parish NTH. In the absence of earthworks other than the hollow-ways, the extent of the settlement can be established by plotting medieval pottery disturbed during modern ploughing.

other buildings 350 metres along this street to the east (Figure 5.9). Between the two was much open ground and a couple of isolated properties to the north of the street. Fieldwalking in these spaces produced little by way of occupation evidence from south of the street, suggesting that this lay under the village fields in the medieval period. But to the north the gaps in the nineteenth-century village plan were filled by the recovery of both Thetford-type pottery and medieval wares. Accordingly, it would appear that the village began as a more regular linear settlement, presumably comprising a single row of tofts and crofts to the north of its main street.[53]

53 *MSRG Annual Report*, 7 (1992), p. 28.

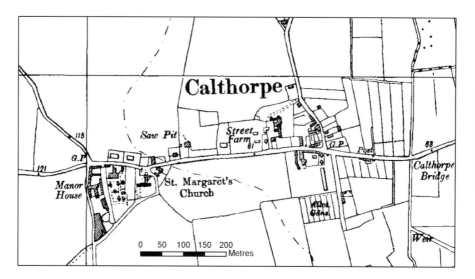

Figure 5.9 Calthorpe NFK in the mid-twentieth century. In its current form, the village looks polyfocal in plan, but it is clear from pottery recovered in the area west of Street Farm, to the north of the village street, that it began as a linear settlement.

Attempting to draw out the characteristics of *thorp* plans from just four examples is unwise. Nevertheless, it might be cautiously postulated that, under certain circumstances, *thorps* in their earliest phases might adopt regular, linear and compact layouts, containing plots of near-equal size, the settlement as a whole articulated by a single village street. These basic characteristics are found again at the deserted village site of Thorpe-in-the-Glebe NTT (Figure 5.10).[54] Surrounded by the ridge and furrow of its open fields, the village extends over a distance of 430 metres along a single village street, now a hollow-way. Building platforms and crew-yards are clearly visible running along the entire northern side of this street, although the presence of a headland immediately to their rear suggests that these were tofts without crofts. The church stood centrally within the southern row, with the manor house to its east and other platforms beyond, and to the west a group of larger tenements. There are problems, however, in establishing the relationship of this regular plan with the earliest phases of occupation. In the Domesday survey of 1086 the manor was waste and the recorded population nil.[55] If deserted at this time then there is the clear possibility

---

54 Cameron and O'Brien, 'Thorpe-in-the-Glebe'.
55 DB Notts, 1.60: 'In Thorpe [in-the-Glebe] 10 bovates of land taxable. Land for 10 oxen. Outlier. Waste. Meadow, 12 acres. Value 2s; before 1066, 40s.' DB Notts, 9.91: 'In the King's Thorpe [in-the-Glebe] 7 bovates of land taxable, which belong to Wysall. Soke. Waste. Meadow, 30 acres. Value before 1066, 40s; now 12s.'

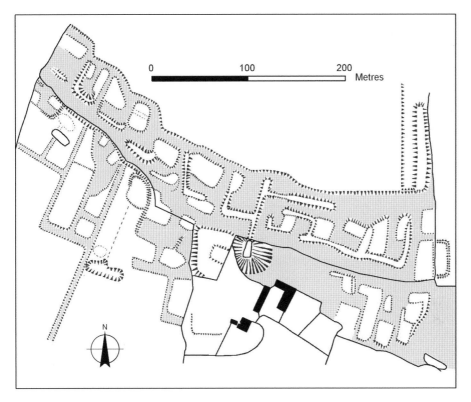

Figure 5.10 Earthworks at the deserted settlement of Thorpe-in-the-Glebe NTT. House platforms and other upstanding features have been picked out by shading the more low-lying surfaces which lie around them.

that, when repopulated, the opportunity may have been taken to lay out the village anew, removing any trace of its former plan. Indeed, it remains possible that the new village may have even been re-established on a different site altogether from the old one.

Thorpe in Earls Barton NTH, now deserted, lies on the north bank of the river Nene. Its earthworks trace the plan of two rows of closes on either side of a central street (Figure 5.11). Four tofts can be defined to the west and a further five to the east, all separated by low banks and backed by a scarp marking the extent of each plot. In 1086 it had a recorded population of four, which would have been easily accommodated within this rectangular block.[56] Stone scatters to the north of the earthworks indicate an extension to the village. Pottery contained within it does

56 DB Northants, 56.59: 'Robert holds from the Countess [Judith] 3 virgates of land in *Widetorp*. Land for 1 plough; it is there, in lordship, with 4 villeins. Meadow, 4 acres. The value was 4s; now 10s.'

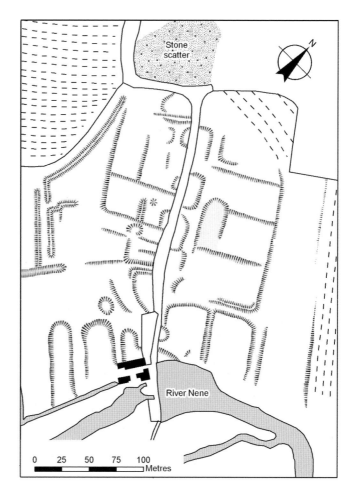

Figure 5.11 Thorpe in Earls Barton parish NTH. A double row of closes on either side of a central village street are clearly visible above the bridging point over the river Nene.

not pre-date 1100, suggesting that this part of the village was added in the twelfth century.[57]

Single-street layouts are also features of 'English' *throps*. Althorp NTH village was probably cleared by the Catesby family at the beginning of the sixteenth century. There is little coherence to the surviving earthworks that bound the hollow-way at its north-western end; however, ridge and furrow suggests that the area covered by these formed the core of the settlement, although other parts of

---

57   RCHME, *An inventory of the historical monuments in the county of Northamptonshire. Vol. 2: archaeological sites in central Northamptonshire* (London, 1979), pp. 42–3.

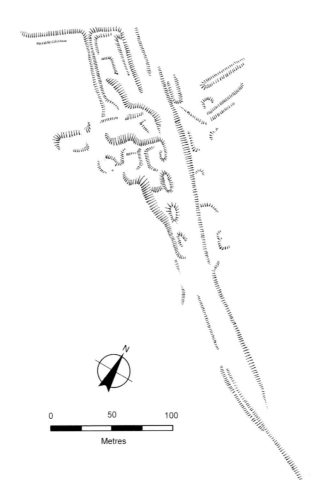

N

0   50   100
Metres

Figure 5.12 The deserted settlement of Althorp NTH, which had probably been cleared by the first decade of the sixteenth century. The earthworks thus reflect the shape of the settlement as it had developed by the end of the Middle Ages.

the village, perhaps along the southern side of the street, may have been lost (Figure 5.12).[58] Certainly the recorded population of ten in 1086 indicates that a larger area than is now visible should have been required.

Even into the nineteenth century many *thorps* retained their simple linear plan. This is the case for Althorp LIN, Bonthorpe LIN, Deenethorpe NTH, Menethorpe YOE, Millthorpe LIN, Scotterthorpe LIN, Thorpe-le-Fallows LIN (where only a post-enclosure road disrupts the plan), Wigsthorpe NTH and Yaddlethorpe LIN. Linear

58 RCHME, *North-west Northamptonshire*, pp. 1–2.

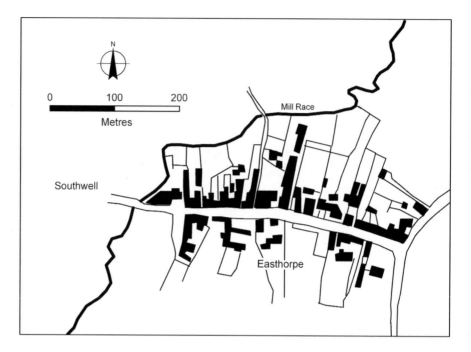

Figure 5.13 The linear plan of Easthorpe, next to Southwell NTT. On the other side of the town, Westhorpe is also a linear settlement.

plans are also a feature of Easthorpe and Westhorpe, attached to Southwell NTT (Figure 5.13). Of the 'English' *throps*, Heythrop and Dunthrop OXF are good examples. The compact layouts of other nineteenth-century *thorps*, where the shape of the surrounding fields appears to define their rectilinear plan, might also be categorised within this group of single-street settlements. They include villages and hamlets such as Boothorpe LEI, Ewerby Thorpe LEI, Haisthorpe YOE, Knapthorpe NTT, Thorpe-on-the-Hill LIN, Thorpe Langton LEI, Woolsthorpe NTT and Yawthorpe LIN. This also seems to have been a feature of the medieval village of Ixworth Thorpe SFK before its later migration. Here the position of the church at the head of the village street is reminiscent of Calthorpe NFK, both layouts finding parallels in the plans of Ashwellthorpe NFK, Bassingthorpe LIN, Caythorpe LIN, Edmondthorpe LEI, Friesthorpe LIN, Gunthorpe NTT, Northorpe LIN, Thorpe-by-Newark NTT (Figure 5.14) and Woolsthorpe LEI. Elsewhere, churches might be located outside the main core of the village. Weaverthorpe YOE acts as the model, but the layout is repeated in the plans of Bilsthorpe NTT, Biscathorpe LIN, Bruntingthorpe LEI, Burythorpe YOE, Helperthorpe YOE, Owthorpe NTT (Figure 5.15), Thorpe Achurch NTH, Thorpe Bassett YOE and possibly Aisthorpe LIN.

Far rarer among the *thorps* are those based around a street grid, of the kind seen

Figure 5.14 The thirteenth-century tower of the church of St Lawrence, Thorpe-by-Newark NTT. The short nave indicates that the village was never very big in the Middle Ages.

Figure 5.15 View south and east over Owthorpe NTT into the Vale of Belvoir beyond. The parish contains good agricultural soils.

at Abthorpe NTH (Figure 5.16), Astrop NTH, Castlethorpe NTH, Osgathorpe LEI and Ullesthorpe LEI. To generalise from the total corpus, we can see that by the nineteenth century both *thorps* and *throps* might take a variety of settlement forms; but overwhelmingly they tended towards linear single-street plans with regular rows of tofts and crofts. We are convinced that this was not simply the product of their small size: many settlements in -bȳ, for instance, were no larger than the *thorps*, and yet their street plans were invariably more complex, as at Granby LEI, Laceby LIN and Swaby LIN. Nor was it a product of post-medieval changes, for such regularity and simplicity is certainly present in the late medieval forms of the deserted *thorp* villages – and scatters of pottery suggest that it was characteristic of their earlier phases too.

Conclusions

The archaeological evidence establishes, as well as any flawed and incomplete dataset can, that *thorps* were in all probability late arrivals in the English landscape, with many laying down roots in the tenth and eleventh centuries. They grew up in

Figure 5.16 Main Street, Abthorpe NTH, looking towards the church of St John the Baptist, which is set on a large rectangular green at the centre of the village.

places where there is a marked absence of evidence for permanent occupation before AD 900. In their early phases, *thorps* tended to be small, compact places, exhibiting clear signs of planning. Their layout characteristically took the form of a single village street and regularly sized tofts and crofts. These attributes, we suggest, can be found across both *thorps* and *throps*. In this context a further observation made by Cameron might usefully be revisited. He noted that, in Domesday Book, a number of places in -*bȳ* were represented by more than one settlement: examples include North and South Conesby LIN, Great and Little Gonerby LIN, and East and West Graby LIN.[59] He suggested that this indicated that some *bȳs* had grown substantially by 1086 and had spawned subsidiary settlements. By contrast, Domesday Book contains no example of a double *thorp*. In the light of our discussion concerning *thorp* plans there may be an alternative explanation for this phenomenon. The irregularity of plan exhibited by the *bȳs* may, in part, be a late product of these places developing their nucleated form from more than one original settlement focus. Where these expanded to form a single conglomeration, the resultant plans are generally more complex than those settlements which have grown from a single nucleus.[60] If the distance between the early cores was sufficiently large, these could remain separate despite any expansion, hence the double settlements. Double settlements of the late Middle Ages may therefore be survivors of, or successors to, local settlement which began as a dispersed set of individual centres. They need not necessarily be

---

59 Cameron, 'Scandinavian settlement, part II', pp. 142–3.
60 C. Taylor, 'Polyfocal settlement and the English village', *Medieval Archaeology*, 21 (1977), 189–93.

products of later expansion. By contrast, all the evidence points towards *thorps* beginning as single centres. As they expanded, new areas of occupation were added to the earlier core rather than away from it. The reasons why *thorps* should tend towards nucleation and why it might not surprise us that *bȳs* should begin as polyfocal settlements is a subject to which we will return. In the next chapter, however, we turn to where these places were established and how, potentially, they may have functioned.

6

Thorps in the landscape

If, as we have suggested, *thorps* were new settlements, established in places that generally seem to exhibit no signs of permanent occupation before the tenth century, are we right to see them as pioneer settlements? This was certainly how Cameron saw his East Midlands group, based on an assessment of their position in the landscape. His conclusions have already been outlined in our introduction (see pp. 15–16), but they are worthy of brief reiteration here. Particular place-name groups, he argued, were not evenly distributed across the landscape. Old English place-names, particularly those in -tūn and -hām, together with the Grimston-hybrids, appear to cluster in the main river valleys, surrounded by easily worked and fertile soils. In contrast, place-names in -bȳ seem frequently to adopt positions along the minor streams which fed the main watercourses, occupying less rewarding soils; while, as a group, *thorps* are found away from watercourses, on the higher and more intractable clays of the watersheds.

The preponderance of Scandinavian personal names used as qualifiers for the bȳs, and the more common occurrence of post-Conquest names attached to *thorps*, supported the idea that these two families of names belonged to different periods of settlement history, bȳs forming earlier than *thorps*. Coupling this evidence with their position in the landscape, Cameron concluded that each name type represented successive phases of land colonisation. Within an empty landscape, the earliest settlers would be attracted to the best land and would quickly take up positions where this could best be exploited; hence the location of -tūns and -hāms in the valley bottoms. Those arriving in an already settled landscape would invariably be forced into less desirable locations, first along the secondary tributary streams (the bȳs) and finally up on to the interfluves (the *thorps*).

Distilled from this study, and boldly stated, Cameron was arguing not only that *thorps* were late arrivals in the landscape but that they were founded in areas that had little or no history of settlement or cultivation; that they were places from which their inhabitants sought to bring problematic, and previously unbroken, ground into cultivation for the first time. Thirty years on, and again with new evidence to hand, these ideas are also ready for re-evaluation.

Thorps as pioneer settlements?

The study of early medieval landscapes and settlements has moved forward rapidly over the last quarter of a century through the use of extensive survey. In some thorp heartlands, such as the counties of Leicestershire, Norfolk and Northamptonshire, the advent of landscape archaeology in the late 1970s and early 1980s resulted in extensive exploration of the countryside using a combination of prospection techniques, foremost among which has been systematic fieldwalking. In other areas, such as Lincolnshire, Nottinghamshire and Yorkshire, large-scale surveys of this type remain rare. Nevertheless, when viewed nationally, thousands of hectares have now been covered, allowing the presence or absence of pottery and other objects found on modern ploughsoils to be noted.

From these distributions crude reconstructions of changes in land use over time have been attempted. One critical formula has been to recognise low-density scatters of pottery as deriving from manuring.[1] Since this material can be dated, albeit often only to broad date ranges, it has proved possible to define which land was under cultivation and when, and to chart the growth and contraction of ploughed land. Other land uses are suggested by the absence of this material. Palaeoenvironmental data can be used to test and refine the arable/non-arable division of the landscape gained through the exploration of distributions of pottery and other artefacts. The study of pollens carries the potential to reveal the range of plants, grasses and trees growing in particular locales.[2] Accordingly, over large parts of the country it is now possible to be relatively certain of the varying ratios of woodland to pasture to arable, and to thus define the regional characteristics of the early medieval landscape.

The backdrop to land exploitation in the early medieval period and the framework which structured subsequent activities was the organisation and the use made of land in the Romano-British period. One outstanding result of recent large-scale survey work has been to show the sheer intensity of settlement in the

---

1   G. Foard, 'Systematic fieldwalking and the investigation of Saxon settlement in Northamptonshire', World Archaeology, 9 (1978), pp. 357–74; R. Jones, 'Signatures in the soil: the use of pottery in manure scatters in the identification of medieval arable farming regimes', Archaeological Journal, 161 (2004), pp. 159–88.
2   P. Dark, The environment of Britain in the first millennium AD (London, 2000); for a very recent demonstration of how useful palaeoenvironmental evidence can be in filling other evidential gaps see S. Rippon, Beyond the village: the diversification of landscape character in southern Britain (Oxford, 2008).

countryside of lowland England before AD 400 and to demonstrate just how much land appears to have been brought under the plough.[3] The pattern of settlement was generally dispersed; big villa complexes intermixed with isolated farmsteads and the occasional larger hamlet or village. Farmsteads are often distributed at a density of one per 1–2 km².[4] Villas might favour river terraces and spring line locations, but farmsteads spread across the landscape regardless of the quality of soils. They are encountered in equal numbers on heavy clays and shallow chalks, on loams and sands, or on gravels and alluvial deposits. Halos of pottery found around these farms indicate extensive arable cultivation, perhaps equivalent to, or even on occasion surpassing, the area taken into open or common fields on the eve of Black Death.[5] Where Hoskins, writing in the 1950s, postulated that Anglo-Saxon colonists had faced the task of clearing the English Midlands of its primordial forest, by the 1990s a picture had emerged of a more open, domesticated and ordered landscape into which they settled.[6] Ideas of continuity rather than disjuncture between the landscapes of Roman and early medieval lowland England are now favoured by landscape archaeologists.[7]

It is extremely unlikely, therefore, given the ubiquity of evidence for Roman settlement and farming, that thorps represent the first settlements in particular areas or the first attempt to bring their surrounding land under cultivation. And evidence to this effect is not difficult to find. In north-east Northamptonshire alone we find the following examples. In Apethorpe parish a courtyard villa was excavated in 1859.[8] Barnwell parish, containing the hamlet of Crowthorpe, was traversed by a Roman road and has produced evidence for at least four separate Roman settlements.[9] Likewise, Polebrook with Kingsthorpe was crossed by a

3   J. Taylor, *An atlas of Roman rural settlement in England*, CBA Research Report 151 (York, 2007).

4   e.g. T. Beaumont James and C. Gerrard, *Clarendon: landscape of kings* (Macclesfield, 2007), pp. 30–36; Jones and Page, *Medieval villages*, pp. 49–56; S. Parry, *Raunds Area survey: an archaeological study of the landscape of Raunds, Northamptonshire* (Oxford, 2006), p. 56.

5   e.g. C. Hayfield, *An archaeological survey of the parish of Wharram Percy, East Yorkshire. 1. The evolution of the Roman landscape*, BAR British Series 172 (Oxford, 1987); V. Gaffney and M. Tingle, *The Maddle Farm Project: an integrated survey of prehistoric and Roman landscapes on the Berkshire Downs*, BAR British Series 200 (Oxford, 1989). It would be a mistake, however, to interpret manure scatters as evidence for permanent cultivation. Ley-farming was a practice well known to the Romans. For perhaps as much as half the time, then, areas which produce evidence for ploughing may have been rested and laid to grass. See G. Kron, 'Roman ley-farming', *Journal of Roman Archaeology*, 13 (2000), pp. 277–87.

6   W.G. Hoskins, *Leicestershire: an illustrated essay on the history of the landscape* (London, 1957), p. 2.

7   S. Rippon, 'Landscapes in transition: the late Roman and early medieval periods', in D. Hooke (ed.), *Landscape: the richest historical record*, Society for Landscape Studies Supplementary Series 1 (Amesbury, 2000), pp. 47–61.

8   RCHME, *North-east Northamptonshire*, pp. 8–10.

9   Ibid., pp. 12–15.

Roman road and populated by three associated settlements.[10] A single focus of occupation and burials lies within Lilford-cum-Wigsthorpe.[11] The early medieval landscape of Warmington, within which Eaglethorpe can be found, was preceded by an even longer history of cultivation including late prehistoric field systems, Roman settlement and extensive Roman manure scatters.[12] A similar pattern emerges from investigation of the land around Thorpe Achurch and Thorpe Waterville.[13] In the north-west part of the county there are indications of intensive occupation in the Iron Age around Flore and the hamlet of Glassthorpe,[14] and Roman settlement of the land in the vicinity of the villages of Hothorpe and Thorpe Ludenham.[15] Seven separate Roman settlement sites have been found in Ravensthorpe parish,[16] and in Norton parish, including the hamlet of Thrupp, are the settlement remains of the small Roman town of *Bannaventa* (straddling Watling Street), an outlying Roman villa and three other settlement nuclei.[17]

Northamptonshire is not peculiar in this respect. Roman pottery finds in the vicinity of Thorpe Langton LEI reveal a dense pattern of settlement and intensive manuring of the surrounding countryside (Figure 6.1). Close scrutiny of thorp landscapes across the country reveals much the same earlier history; to list fully the results of archaeological investigation would simply be to labour the point. But it might be noted that *Bannaventa* is not the only small Roman town to be found with the orbit of a thorp. *Delgovicia* is thought to lie within Shiptonthorpe parish YOE, and the town of *Ad Pontem* grew from a vexillation fort on the Fosse Way in the area later occupied by Thorpe-by-Newark NTT.[18] Other Roman military installations have been located at Osmanthorpe NTT[19] and Longthorpe NTH, near Peterborough,[20] while there is evidence for an extensive pre-AD 400 field system around Edenthorpe YOE and Roman settlement and manuring in Calthorpe NFK.[21] Sibthorpe NTT contains a Roman villa, while other places in the same county, such

10   Ibid., p. 74.

11   Ibid., p. 61.

12   Ibid., pp. 106–8; M. Shaw, 'A changing settlement pattern at Warmington, Northants', *MSRG Annual Report*, 8 (1993), pp. 41–8.

13   RCHME, *North-east Northamptonshire*, pp. 94–5.

14   RCHME, *North-west Northamptonshire*, pp. 91–2.

15   Ibid., p. 138.

16   Ibid., p. 168.

17   Ibid., pp. 150–53.

18   M. Millett, *The Romanization of Britain: an essay in archaeological interpretation* (Cambridge, 1998).

19   M. Bishop and P. Freeman, 'Recent work at Osmanthorpe, Nottinghamshire', *Britannia*, 24 (1993), pp. 159–89.

20   S.S. Frere and J.S. St Joseph, 'The Roman fortress at Longthorpe', *Britannia*, 5 (1974), pp. 1–129.

21   D. Riley, *Early landscape from the air: studies of cropmarks in south Yorkshire and north Nottinghamshire* (Sheffield, 1980), pp. 60–1, figures 8 and 9. Davison, 'Mannington and Wolverton'.

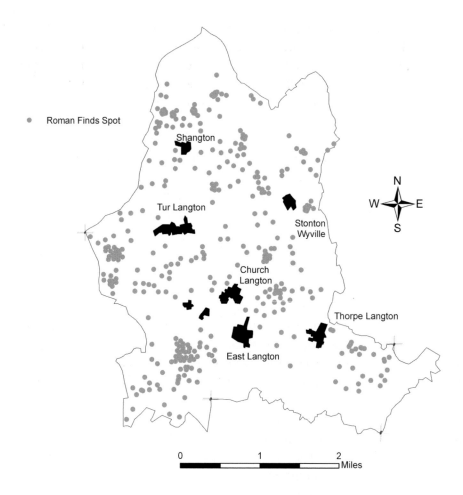

Figure 6.1 Map of the group of Langton parishes in south Leicestershire, showing finds of Romano-British date and the sites of modern villages on medieval sites, including Thorpe Langton LEI.

as Perlethorpe, Gleadthorpe and Besthorpe NFK, have produced evidence for rural settlement and field systems.[22]

   None of this need prove continuity, however. Indeed, the failure of the Roman small towns to develop into substantial settlements in the medieval period suggests much reduced levels of occupancy and land exploitation, while Unwin argues from his north Nottinghamshire examples that later township boundaries appear to show little correspondence with Roman field boundaries.[23] In fact,

22   T. Unwin, 'Townships and early fields in north Nottinghamshire', *Journal of Historical Geography*, 9/4 (1983), pp. 341–6; A. Davison, 'Besthorpe', *Norfolk Archaeology*, 45/1 (2006), p. 124.

across the country extensive field survey is beginning to create a mixed picture of what was happening in the countryside during the late Roman–early medieval transition. In some areas there are clear signs of economic downturn, supporting the traditional view that the collapse of the market and reduced rural populations led to a retreat off the claylands in favour of the lighter soils of the river valleys. The scale of this movement, however, can now be questioned. Around Raunds NTH,[24] Whittlewood BUC & NTH[25] and Medbourne LEI[26] there are signs of continued occupation of villa and farmstead sites throughout the fourth and into the early fifth centuries. A proportion, sometimes as many as a quarter, of these sites have produced local early medieval handmade pottery sherds indicative of continued occupancy of certain sites, even if others appear to have been abandoned.

When the landscapes of *thorps* are explored for evidence of settlement and farming activity which might broadly be dated to the period AD 400–850 – that is, the period immediately preceding what we have termed the *thorp* moment – there is plenty to suggest that these were vibrant spaces. In the township of Eaglethorpe NTH, for example, mapped pottery clusters reveal a pattern of dispersed farmsteads from which the land was worked.[27] At Ixworth Thorpe SFK three areas of early Anglo-Saxon settlement have been identified in the south of the parish, and a further one to the north.[28] Spreads of Saxon pottery found in Martinsthorpe RUT might indicate the manuring of infields.[29] And again at Thorpe Langton LEI at least three small scatters of pottery lying below the later open fields of the medieval village have been interpreted as pre-AD 850 farmstead sites (Figure 6.2).[30] Large pagan Saxon cemeteries have been found outside Thorpe Malsor NTH and Morningthorpe NFK,[31] and in Tattershall Thorpe LIN what is thought to be a late-seventh-century smith's grave has been excavated.[32]

Two common themes appear from these surveys. First is that areas within

23 Unwin, 'Townships'.

24 Parry, *Raunds*, pp. 92–5.

25 Jones and Page, *Medieval villages*, pp. 49–56.

26 R. Knox, 'The Anglo-Saxons in Leicestershire and Rutland', in P. Bowman and P. Liddle (eds), *Leicestershire landscapes*, Leicestershire Museums Archaeological Fieldwork Group Monograph 1 (Leicester, 2004), pp. 95–104.

27 *MSRG Annual Report*, 7 (1992), p. 40.

28 *MSRG Annual Report*, 8 (1993), pp. 50–1.

29 S. Sleath and R. Ovens, 'Martinsthorpe', *Rutland Record*, 14 (1994), pp. 167–74.

30 *TLAHS*, 64 (1990), p. 108; *TLAHS*, 65 (1991), p. 108.

31 B. Green, A. Rogerson and S. White, *The Anglo-Saxon cemetery at Morning Thorpe, Norfolk* 1, East Anglian Archaeology 36 (Gressenhall, 1987); *SMA*, 7 (1977), p. 4; *SMA*, 8 (1978), p. 12; *SMA*, 10 (1980), pp. 44, 46; *SMA*, 18 (1988), pp. 69–70.

32 D. Hinton, *A smith in Lindsey: the Anglo-Saxon grave at Tattershall Thorpe, Lincolnshire*, Society for Medieval Archaeology Monograph Series 16 (London, 2000).

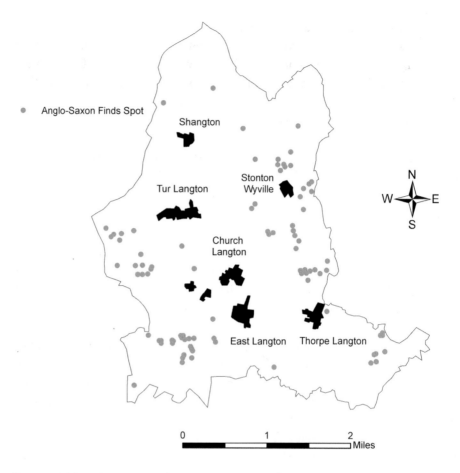

Figure 6.2 Map of the group of Langton parishes in south Leicestershire, showing Anglo-Saxon ceramic found by fieldwalking and the sites of modern villages on medieval sites, including Thorpe Langton LEI.

which *thorps* would later form might have a lively post-Roman history. Example after example indicates that these landscapes were fully occupied and utilised. The second point is that, alongside apparent continuities, there was some sort of fundamental break preceding *thorp* foundation. The settlement pattern clearly changed, for evidence of early medieval settlement is not found below *thorps* (see above pp. 85–97) but has been found within their presumed territory. Sometimes the distance of the settlement shift was not great. Early Saxon settlement in Bowthorpe NFK was found only 200 metres beyond the later medieval village.[33] At Thorpe End, Raunds NTH, the pre-850 settlement focus was likewise found immediately outside the later hamlet.[34] *Thorps*, therefore, represent a relocation of

33   G. Trimble, 'An Anglo-Saxon settlement at Bishee Barnabee Way, Bowthorpe: excavations, 2001', *Norfolk Archaeology*, 44/3 (2004), pp. 525–35.

settlement focus. But they do not represent, as Cameron suggested, first-wave colonising settlements. The landscapes within which they took shape had already been brought under cultivation and many show signs of having been farmed continuously, and almost all at least episodically, since the Roman period. In fact, others have remarked on this too. Sawyer, for instance, noting earlier finds from bȳ parishes, also cites the example of Thorpe Bulmer DRH, where pollen evidence suggested an unbroken tradition of cereal growing in the vicinity from the Roman period onwards.[35] One reason why this might have been is that the quality of the land surrounding thorps has been underestimated, and it is to this issue that we now turn.

Thorps and soils

In explaining settlement location, Cameron's hypothesis contains a strong element of physical determinism. Given freedom of choice, the process of land colonisation would be dictated by relief and soils; the best land would be occupied first, the worst last. Since the publication of this study, historians and archaeologists of the early medieval landscape have moved away from this narrow reasoning to argue that social, economic and political agencies might have played an equal or greater part in how the landscape was settled and brought under cultivation. It has only been in recent years that environmental factors have again been placed at centre stage. Williamson's study of settlement in the eastern counties of England, for example, begins by acknowledging that early and high medieval rural communities were made up of farmers, and that it was the practicalities of farming life, such as the qualities of soils or the availability or otherwise of meadow land, which were the prime considerations when deciding how the land was to be used and from where it was to be exploited.[36] Williamson's reasoning is persuasive because of its simplicity and practical logic. And if we assume that it was farmers who were the principal thorp dwellers, then we too must look to the soils as the starting point for the analysis of the local, regional and national distributions of thorp places.

Across Britain the pattern of underlying geological formations, overlain by various drift geologies, has produced a complex mosaic of different soil types. The soil map of England and Wales identifies 26 dominant soil types ranging from the raw skeletal soils of the coastline fringe through rich brown earths in the lowlands

34 Parry, Raunds, pp. 234–40.
35 P. Sawyer, From Roman Britain to Norman England (London, 1978), p. 162.
36 T. Williamson, Shaping medieval landscapes: settlement, society, environment (Macclesfield, 2003); T. Williamson, 'The distribution of "woodland" and "champion" landscapes in medieval England', in M. Gardiner and S. Rippon (eds), Medieval landscapes (Macclesfield, 2007), pp. 89–104.

to the raw peat deposits of the uplands.[37] These can be further broken down into 71 soil sub-groups. Some of these soils offer conditions which guarantee high returns from agriculture and horticulture, while others offer little or no potential beyond their use as areas of rough pasture. The identification of these soils and their associations is based on complex science and contrasts with the more qualitative approach adopted by the then Minstry of Agriculture, Forestry and Fisheries (MAFF) that divides soils into five broad bands from 1 (excellent), often associated with horticulture and intensive agriculture, to 5 (very poor), soils which offer only the possibilities of rough grazing. Despite their inadequacies, the MAFF soil designations provide a national base against which we can start to examine whether soils influenced *thorp* location.

As always, there are important caveats to consider when we put together two distribution maps that are separated by so much time as are the distribution of *thorps* in the early medieval period and modern soil grades. Today's pattern of soil grades does not necessarily reflect that pertaining in, say, AD 1000. The grade 1 land of the Fens, for example, now used for intensive horticulture, has only been made rich through drainage. At the turn of the first millennium this was poor-quality land, useful for grazing but little else. Less dramatic, but nevertheless of significance in lowland England, have been improvements made to field drainage, particularly with the laying of underground pipes in the late eighteenth and early nineteenth centuries. Again, where this was done, soil quality has generally been improved.

Nonetheless, when viewed against the soil grade map, it is clear that *thorps* located in the Midland and southern counties tend to be found on grade 3 agricultural soil; that is, soils considered good to moderate in quality on which farming can be hindered because of localised fluctuations caused by varying soil depth or moisture, climate, relief or aspect, but which more generally allow a range of arable and pastoral regimes to succeed (Figure 6.3). This is a relationship which only strengthens when late recorded *thorps* are removed. Those mentioned before 1300 map neatly onto these soils (Figure 6.4). The exception is Derbyshire, where the limited amount of good to moderate soils means that some *thorps* are located on grade 4 soils, and in a few instances even on the poorest, grade 5, land. In the Yorkshire Ridings the overwhelming tendency is once again for *thorps* to be found within grade 3 country, although here there is slippage both into better-quality grade 2 and lower-quality grade 4 areas. Again, this is a pattern which becomes more convincing when matched against the earliest named *thorps* (Figure 6.5). In Suffolk and Norfolk the picture is once more mixed, although the

37   B. Avery *et al.*, *Soil map of England and Wales* (Southampton, 1975).

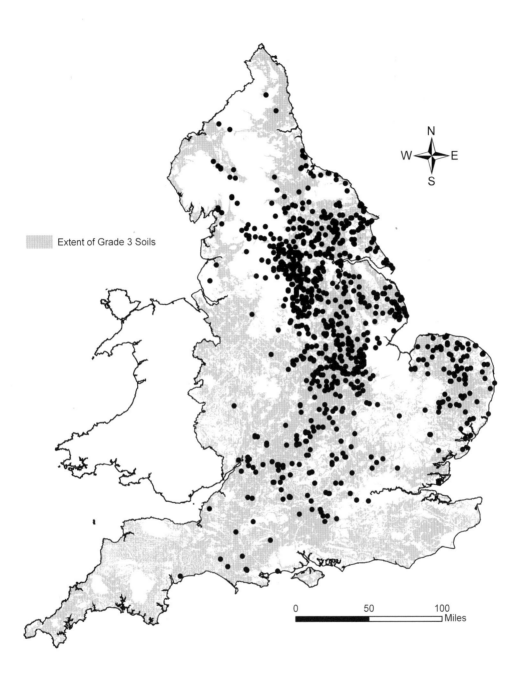

Figure 6.3 Total distribution of *thorps* mapped against MAFF grade 3 soils.

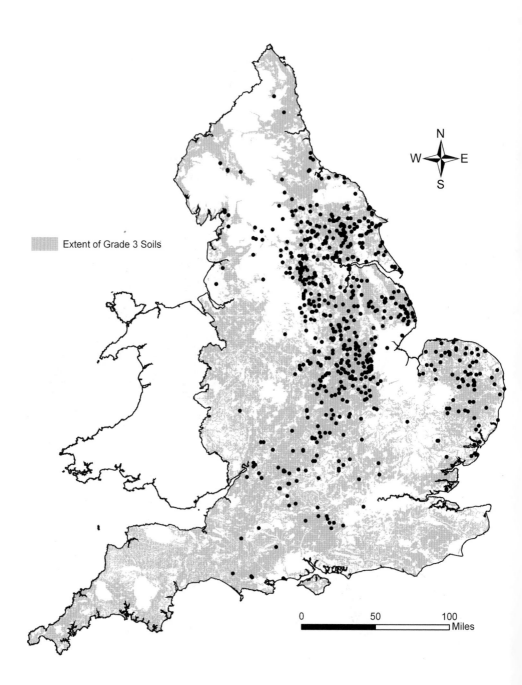

Figure 6.4 *Thorps* mentioned by 1300 mapped against MAFF grade 3 soils.

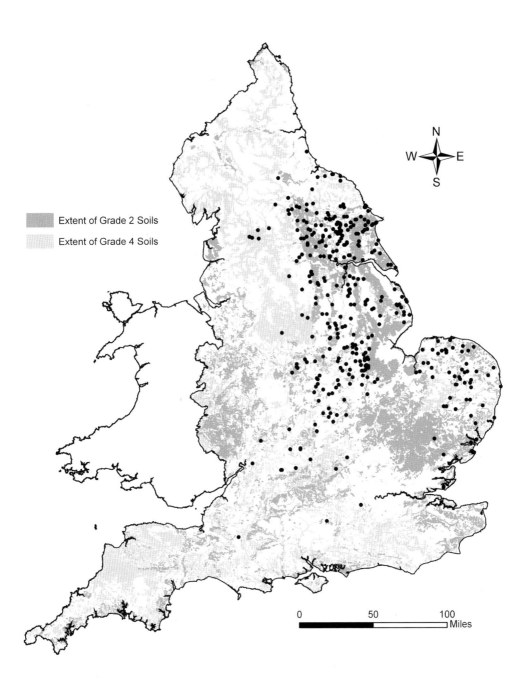

Figure 6.5 *Thorps* mentioned by 1086 mapped against MAFF grade 2 and 4 soils.

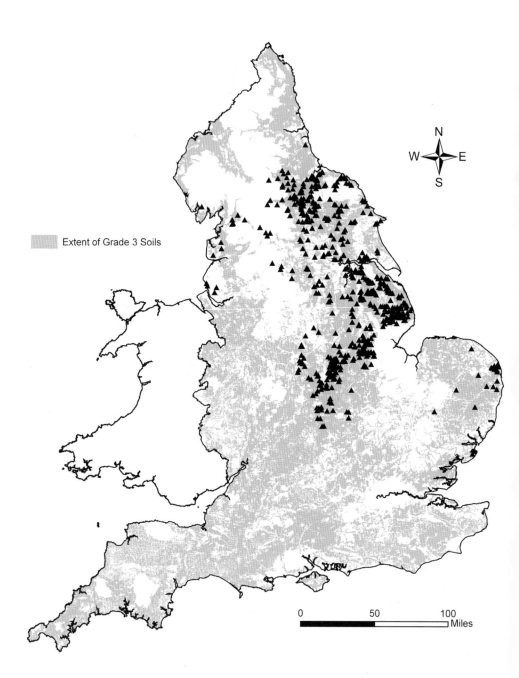

Figure 6.6 Total distribution of *bȳs* mapped against MAFF grade 3 soils.

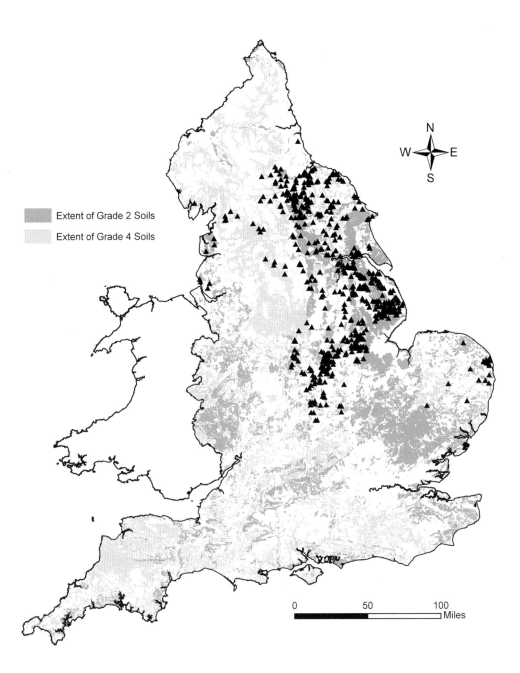

Figure 6.7 Total distribution of *bȳs* mapped against MAFF grade 2 and 4 soils.

predominant position of *thorps* is again on grade 3 with few examples found on grade 2 soils. Comparison can be drawn here with settlements in -bȳ: when these are plotted against the soil grade map they too tend to cluster on grade 3 soils, although in the North and West Ridings of Yorkshire, and in Derbyshire too, they might also take up positions on the poorer upland soils (Figure 6.6). In Lincolnshire and Norfolk the association of a number of *bȳs* with better-quality soils is misleading, for in these counties they are all found in low-lying coastal or wetland fringe areas, the very areas where drainage schemes have improved soil quality out of all recognition over the last thousand years (Figure 6.7).

When surveyed at a national scale, it is very difficult to attempt the kind of differentiation used by Cameron to explain the variant sitings of *bȳs* and *thorps*; both appear to enjoy positions on middling-quality soils. We would suggest, however, that there some grounds for arguing, albeit tentatively at this stage, that *thorps* seem to be drawn towards areas where soil conditions were generally considered by the late twentieth century at least to be relatively good, while the *bȳs* are more likely found on what were later deemed poorer soils. In other words, based on an association with soil quality our analysis of the relative positions of places in -bȳ and -*thorp* tend to contradict that proposed by Cameron. We would argue, then, that if later soil qualities at least partially reflect those that existed in the early Middle Ages, *thorps* potentially occupy positions slightly more favourable to productive farming than *bȳs*.

Conflated within each soil grade band are numerous soils of very different character. Their particular qualities might vary markedly: some may be deep and rich in organic matter, others may be shallow and thin; some may be prone to waterlogging, others to drying out; some provide the perfect seedbed for arable cultivation, others can support nothing other than grassland. The range is broad, from soils strongly favouring one type of farming to those which might be described as utility soils, able to be exploited for a variety of farming activities. Plotting the types of agricultural regimes that these soils promote provides an alternative background against which *thorps* and *bȳs* can be compared and contrasted.

Six basic farming regime soils can be isolated along the arable–pastoral spectrum: those quality soils which strongly favour arable farming; less good soils which still favour arable but which can be used for dairy farming; moderately good soils which favour dairying over arable, but on which both might successfully be undertaken; yet poorer soils used exclusively for dairying; less fertile soils used for dairying or rearing; and the poorest of all, soils useful for rearing only. The distribution of these soils across the country is not uniform. Far more arable soils are found in the eastern counties than in those in the west; likewise, such soils tend to dominate the southern counties but are rarer in the north. Since the

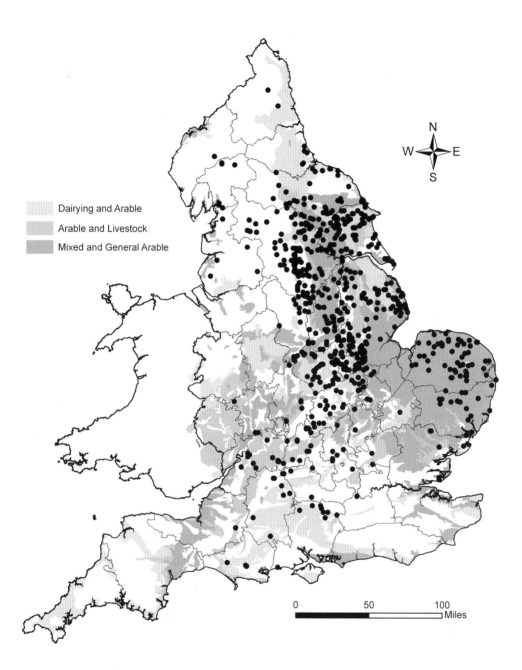

Figure 6.8 *Thorps* mentioned by 1300 mapped against all soils suitable for arable cultivation.

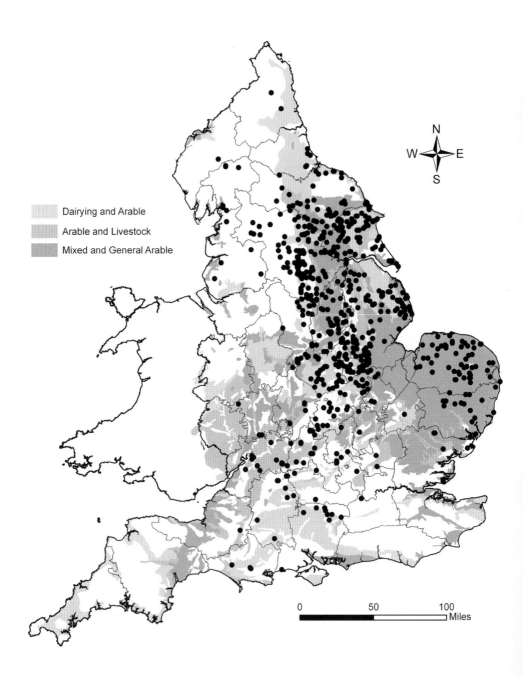

Figure 6.9 *Thorps* mentioned by 1086 mapped against soils which strongly favour arable cultivation.

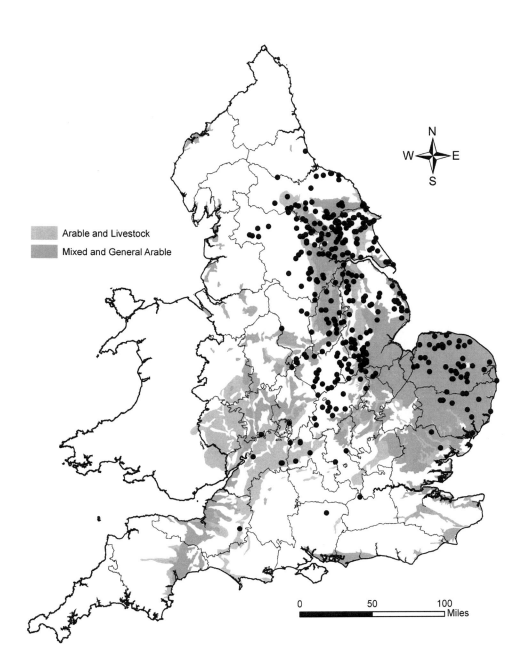

Figure 6.9 *Thorps* mentioned by 1086 mapped against soils which strongly favour arable cultivation.

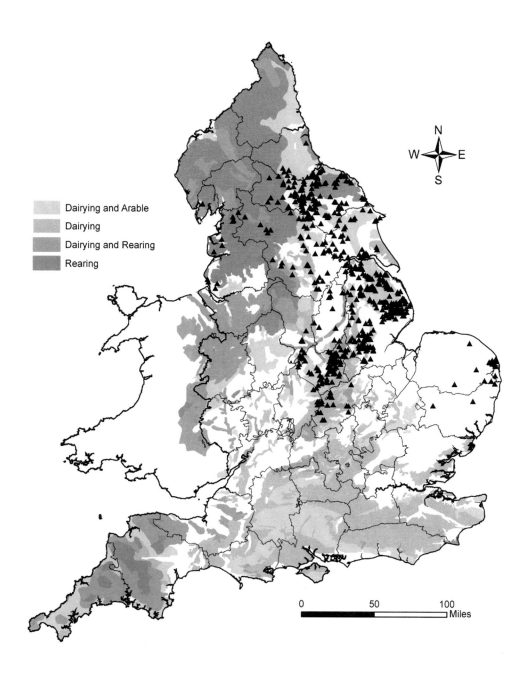

Figure 6.10 Total distribution of *bȳs* mapped against soils suitable for livestock husbandry.

majority of our *thorps* occur south or east of the Pennines, it is perhaps no surprise that the association of these places with arable soils appears so strong (Figure 6.8). Approximately half of all *thorps* are located on soils which today are used for mixed or general arable cultivation. This includes two of our south-western outliers in this group, Drupe Farm in Colaston Raleigh parish DEV and Eastrip SOM, where such soils are less common. If the utility soils – that is, those soils which offer conditions useful for both cereal production and livestock husbandry (in particular dairying) – are added, this figure rises to an impressive 90 per cent of the total number of *thorps*. It is in regions such as the North Riding of Yorkshire where the relationship with arable soils is not only most clear, but, conversely, indicates how *thorps* appear expressly to avoid the pastoral soils in the east and west. It is a picture that, once again, become more convincing when we look at the distribution of pre-1300 *thorps* (Figure 6.9). It is only the Lancashire *thorps* and a few examples occurring in Berkshire, Buckinghamshire and Northamptonshire that appear to lie beyond these soils. Here further factors can be seen at play. Despite occupying poorer soils, their grouping shows a marked gravitation towards areas of freely draining soils rather than those prone to surface inundation or to impeded water percolation. Taking these results together, we suggest the following conclusions: *thorps* strongly favour arable soils independently of their drainage properties; where they are located on the utility soils they concentrate in those areas of better-draining soils; and in areas lacking any arable soils, drainage appears to be of primary importance.

A comparison of the *thorp*–farming soil relationship with that demonstrated by settlements in -*bȳ* appears to corroborate the fact that we are looking at a real rather than coincidental phenomenon (Figure 6.10). In those Midland counties where *bȳs* congregate, especially Northamptonshire, Leicestershire and Lincolnshire (Figure 6.11), they take up positions either on soils either best used for dairy farming and rearing or on utility soils weighted towards livestock husbandry over arable. There is a similarly strong association in the North Riding of Yorkshire. In fact, *c.*75 per cent of *bȳs* are found on these soils, with a large number also occupying the shallow and thin soils of the upland areas used exclusively for rearing. West of the Pennines all the *bȳs* are found on these soils. Of the remainder, about half locate on those soils weakly favouring arable over pasture, leaving very few, such as those found in Norfolk and Suffolk, lying on exclusively arable soils. As with *thorps*, the second consideration of drainage appears to play a part in explaining some of the outliers. Those found on the east coast, for instance, cluster on ground with impeded drainage or tendencies to suffer from surface water.

Viewed nationally, then, *thorps* and *bȳs* show tendencies to congregate on particular soils with characteristics encouraging different types of farming activity.

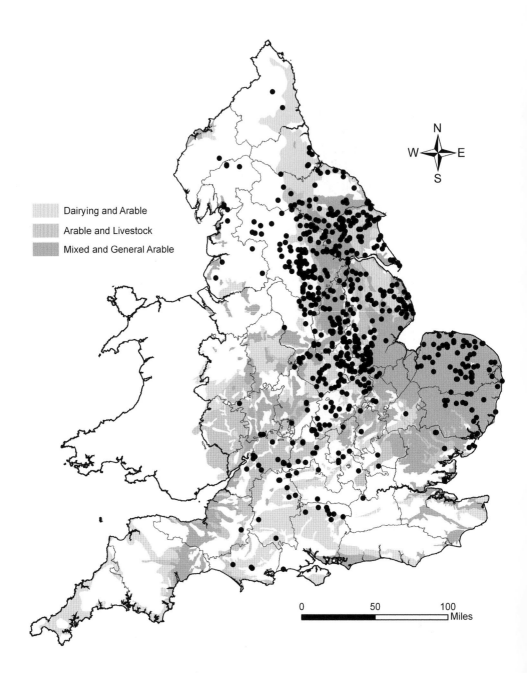

Figure 6.10 Total distribution of *bȳs* mapped against soils suitable for livestock husbandry.

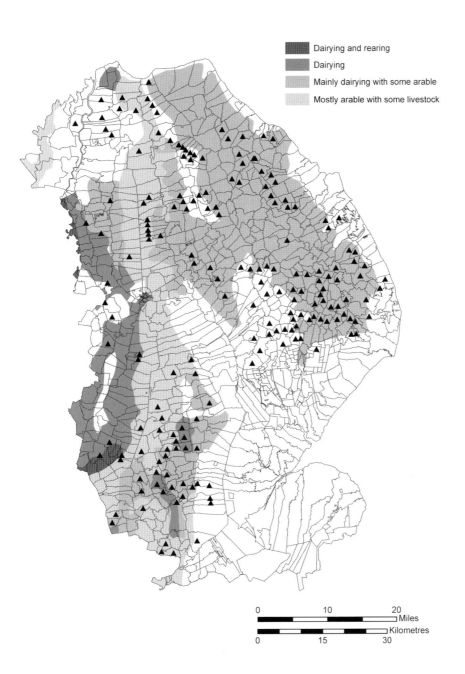

Figure 6.11 Lincolnshire *bӯs* mapped against soils suitable for livestock husbandry.

But this remains a crude indicator: decisions regarding how land was used in the early medieval period were not taken at this scale, but more locally. Is the broad picture of *thorp* and *bȳ* location supported by detailed examination of the more geographically restrictive and relevant landscapes in which they are found?

The two parishes of Norwell and Caunton NTT formerly included the townships of Willoughby (located in the north-east corner of Norwell) and Beesthorpe, Middlethorpe and Knapthorpe, all in Caunton. Both parishes are now compact and separate territorial units, but at the time of Norwell's enclosure in 1832, Middlethorpe and parts of Knapthorpe and Beesthorpe formed detached parts of Norwell Overhall manor, indicating an earlier closer relationship between the two. This is reflected in the Domesday survey.[38] In 1086 Norwell was part of the estates of the archbishop of York, and possessed soke holdings not only in Caunton but also in Willoughby and nearby Osmanthorpe.[39] Likewise, the estate of Laxton, to the north of Norwell, held soke and other rights in, among others, Willoughby, Knapthorpe and Caunton. Such interconnections indicate the earlier existence of a more extensive estate in the process of fragmentation at the time of the Conquest, to which these *thorps* and *bȳs* may one have belonged. They were not necessarily equal members, for a further layer of internal organisation is revealed by the fact that, even as late as the nineteenth century, Knapthorpe was held as part of Willoughby manor.

Found within this area are four different soil types (Figure 6.12). Four of the *thorps* – Knapthorpe, Middlethorpe, Beesthorpe and Osmanthorpe – stand on the best available soils, a mixture of moderately well-draining argillic pelosols, stagnogley soils and brown earths, today used for mixed farming or, in some areas, mainly arable or horticulture. The fifth, Besthorpe, lies to the east of the river Trent on the edge of a block of Cambric gley soils, and sandy and coarse loamy soils, which have high groundwater levels but are now used for general arable cultivation. The two *bȳs*, in contrast, lie on poorer soils. Walesby, to the north-west, lies on the interstices of the best ground and an area of brown earths and podsols, which, while producing deep, well-draining sandy soils, also contain stony and shallow soils over rock. In places these soils can support general arable, but they can also deteriorate into areas more normally used for mixed agriculture or even, where worst, forestry. Willoughby is low-lying and sited on a spur of brown alluvial soils producing loamy or clayey conditions with high groundwater levels and a tendency to winter flooding. These areas tend to be given over to either dairying or rearing. This interconnected local group of *thorps* and *bȳs*, then,

38   Middlethorpe and Beesthorpe do not appear in the survey but for Knapthorpe see DB Notts, 11.9; 12.7; 12.22; 30.3.
39   DB Notts, 5.13–16.

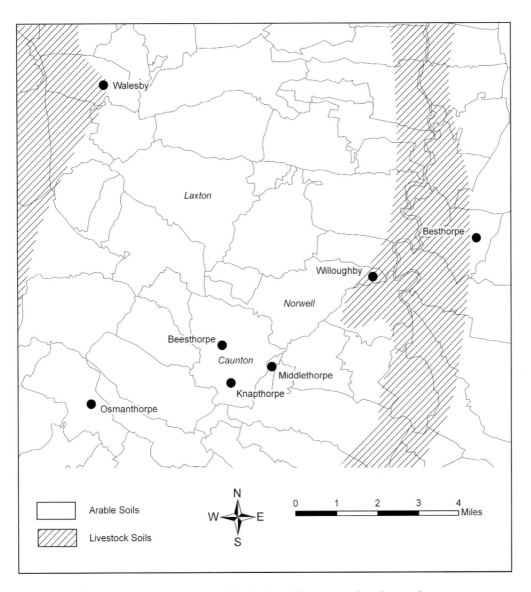

Figure 6.12 *Thorps* and *bȳs* in north-east Nottinghamshire mapped against various soils. The map appears to support the idea that *bȳs*, here exemplified by Willoughby and Walesby, favour locations where soils favour livestock husbandry, while *thorps* are found on soils appropriate for arable cultivation.

occupies precisely those environmental niches the national overview suggested. The near-perfect correlation of the extent and boundaries of Willoughby township with the interstices of the dairying and rearing soils with their neighbouring high-quality arable soils is particularly striking and argues for a careful reading of the local soil conditions and the early apportionment of land, reflecting the uses to which it could be put.

We would suggest, therefore, that this analysis begins to show that it is possible to differentiate *thorps* from *bÿs*. Moreover, we would argue that settlements which took these different names may have been performing separate economic functions within the early medieval countryside. *Thorps* housed communities involved with arable cultivation while the primary role of those living within the *bÿs* was livestock farming. So, there are perhaps some grounds to believe that it was the *type* of farming carried out in these settlements that dictated the name by which it became known. Names in *-bÿ* and *-thorp* were not interchangeable as descriptive terms, were not simply generic terms deployed on a whim by those who wanted to refer to a particular place; rather, they were mutually exclusive, carrying meanings clearly understood by contemporaries. A *thorp* could never be described as a *bÿ*, nor a *bÿ* as a *thorp*, because the two were not the same. They were easily distinguished from one another within the landscape and economy of the early medieval countryside.

Domesday mills

We will explore the wider implications of this association between *thorps* and arable soils later, but here it is perhaps worth adding one further piece of evidence to be extracted from Domesday Book which appears to support our earlier observations. As taxable resources, the survey records mills. How thoroughly this was achieved might be questioned – very few are recorded in the Yorkshire folios, for instance – but in other circuits, particularly in southern England, a more complete picture seems to emerge. The link between mills and the grinding of grain is clearly strong, but using the presence or absence of mills as an indicator or otherwise of a local arable farming economy is not without problems. These mills were water-powered: manors with no access to adequate flows would have found it difficult to build them, even if their soils encouraged the growing of grain. Secondly, mills were important seigneurial assets. The milling of grain was often a lordly monopoly, customary tenants usually being required to grind their grain at the lord's mill at a cost, a system which provided considerable income to the manor. The desire on the part of the elite to protect this asset must have encouraged the construction of mills close to early estate centres, as at Tamworth STF and Old Windsor BRK, and later near manor houses such as West Cotton

NTH.[40] On estates made up of separate manors, then, mills were more likely to be placed at their centre than on distant holdings. Both these factors have important implications when we look at the association between mills and settlements bearing *thorp*-names. Since all the evidence points to these being dependent settlements rather than manorial centres, we might expect to find a poor correlation between the two. This would be further exacerbated if, as Cameron suggested, *thorps* tended to be found away from rivers and streams, the source of the mills' power.

It is therefore surprising to find that Domesday Book guides us in a different direction (Table 6.1).[41] Instances of mills recorded across ten counties in central and southern England have been broken down by the generic place-name elements carried by those manors on which they appear. Thus, in Norfolk, 12 of 18 names in *burh* have a mill, 54 of 174 names in *tūn*, 4 of 21 names in *bȳ* and so on. These have then been rendered as percentages of the total name group, so that for the Norfolk examples 66.6 per cent of *burh* manors have mills, 31 per cent of *tūns*, 19 per cent of *bȳs* and so on. These have then been compared against the county average (all mills divided by all manors), figures provided by Darby and his co-authors of the *Domesday geography* volumes.[42] Using this statistical device, it is possible to see which manorial place-name groups appear to have a superabundance or lack of mills when viewed against the mean.

Against the county average, place-names in -*burh* score particularly highly. Only in Bedfordshire, with just two examples, do these places fail to register above the expected number. This is perhaps not unexpected: after all, the name often refers to a high-status settlement, both in secular and ecclesiastical terms, the very places where we would predict that mills might be sited. In six of the eleven counties place-names in -*hām* (including *hamm*, since these have not been differentiated) appear also to have above-average numbers of mills. The settlements with this early place-name element often sit in fertile low-lying locations, thus with access to both water for powering mills and to good soils, so this strong showing is again to be expected. Place-names in -*tūn* do surprisingly poorly, especially since they are often associated with and appear to have functioned as estate centres: only in Buckinghamshire, Derbyshire and Oxfordshire do these come in above the county

---

40 P. Rahtz and R. Meeson, *An Anglo-Saxon watermill at Tamworth. Excavations in the Bolebridge Street area of Tamworth, Staffordshire, in 1971 and 1978* (London, 1992); R. Holt, 'Milling technology in the Middle Ages: the direction of recent research', *Industrial Archaeology Review*, 13/1 (1990), pp. 50–8; Parry, *Rounds*, p. 176.

41 See above p. 56.

42 H.C. Darby, *Domesday England* (Cambridge, 1977); H.C. Darby, *The Domesday geography of eastern England* (Cambridge, 1971); H.C. Darby and I.B. Terrett (eds), *The Domesday geography of midland England* (Cambridge, 1971); H.C. Darby and I.S. Maxwell, *The Domesday geography of northern England* (Cambridge, 1962).

Table 6.1

The number of Domesday mills per county per place-name element expressed as a percentage (i.e. number of places recorded with mills per place-name generic divided by the total number of places in each county with particular place-name generic elements – figures presented in brackets). These are set against a county average based on mills recorded by manor divided by number of assessed manors in the county following Darby *et al.*

	burh	ham	tun	worth	stoc	thorp	cot	by	wic	County average
Bedfordshire	0 (0/2)	66.7 (6/9)	40.5 (17/40)	20 (2/10)	None	None	0 (0/8)	None	50 (2/4)	43.4
Buckinghamshire	50 (8/16)	46.2 (6/13)	38.7 (20/53)	100 (1/1)	75 (3/4)	0 (0/2)	25 (2/8)	None	0 (0/3)	37.7
Cambridgeshire	None	57.1 (12/21)	34.2 (14/41)	14.3 (1/7)	None	None	0 (0/1)	None	33.3 (1/3)	36.6
Derbyshire	42.9 (3/7)	0 (0/2)	33 (39/119)	0 (0/6)	None	0 (0/3)	33.3 (3/9)	33.3 (2/6)	0 (0/1)	14.5
Gloucestershire	50 (10/20)	30.7 (4/13)	28.8 (49/170)	35.3 (6/17)	0 (0/5)	50 (2/4)	10 (2/20)	None	33.3 (2/6)	34.3
Leicestershire	50 (2/4)	14.3 (1/7)	27 (24/86)	18.2 (2/11)	0 (0/1)	40 (8/20)	37.5 (3/8)	33.9 (19/56)	0 (0/1)	32.2
Lincolnshire	53.3 (8/15)	27.8 (14/54)	32.7 (50/153)	27.2 (3/11)	100 (2/2)	27.9 (19/68)	22.2 (2/9)	30.1 (64/212)	22.2 (2/9)	33.8
Norfolk	66.7 (12/18)	51.4 (72/140)	31 (54/174)	42.8 (3/7)	50 (1/2)	46.2 (18/39)	100 (1/1)	19 (4/19)	38.4 (5/13)	41.3
Northamptonshire	66.7 (6/9)	60 (3/5)	45.2 (56/129)	71.4 (5/7)	50 (3/6)	38.9 (7/18)	22.2 (2/9)	13.3 (2/15)	33.3 (2/6)	47.5
Nottinghamshire	66.7 (4/6)	40 (8/20)	25 (27/108)	14.3 (1/7)	0 (0/3)	22.2 (4/18)	25 (1/4)	23.8 (5/21)	50 (1/2)	27.3
Oxfordshire	55.5 (5/9)	81.8 (9/11)	57.1 (40/70)	50 (1/2)	25 (1/4)	40 (2/5)	12.5 (2/16)	None	0 (0/1)	46.1

average. But we might note here that results aggregate together both primary and secondary settlements – for instance, the directional tūns, Norton, Sutton, Aston and Weston – which may have skewed the figures. In fact the relationship between tūns and mills is far weaker than that for place-names in -worth, which come in at above the average in five of the eleven counties. Of the eight counties for which we have evidence for settlements in -thorp, they appear as above average in Gloucestershire, Leicestershire and Norfolk, but in Derbyshire, Lincolnshire, Northamptonshire, Nottinghamshire and Oxfordshire the number of mills falls below what we might expect. Bȳs are present in seven of the sample counties, only coming in above average in Derbyshire and Leicestershire, and in the latter only marginally. Of the elements explored, it is those places involving -cot and -wīc that perform worst of all.

On this basis, thorps perform well if not spectacularly against place-names taking other generic elements. When the figures are combined for the eleven surveyed counties, in fact, the number of thorps with mills is 33.1 per cent, against a national average for all manors of 35.9 per cent. It is only when we compare them against those other place-name elements that are considered to reflect a secondary status (cot, wīc and bȳ), the group to which thorps should belong, that we begin to see them punching above their weight. In fact, the differential between thorps, which lead this group, and bȳs, that by this reckoning perform worst of all, at 25.6 per cent, is eye-catching, for it seems potentially to echo the division we have proposed regarding the relationship between these two name groups and the soils on which they lay, supporting the notion that thorps may have been primarily arable farms that needed mills, and bȳs livestock farms that did not. We should not, of course, assume that the local situation in 1086 need reflect that which pertained 100 years earlier, when many thorps were clearly beginning to be established. Much could change on the ground over this time. But at least the pattern that emerges from this enquiry encourages us to explore further the connections that may have existed between thorps and cereal production in the early medieval landscape.[43]

A summary of the evidence

A collation of the settlement evidence for thorps has helped to redefine these

---

43 Christopher Dyer (pers. comm.) notes that, while there is a relationship between the availability of grain and mills, mills were closely connected with the consumption as well as production of grain. The most valuable mills in Domesday Book are those next to towns which produced little or no grain. So it is possible that the number of mills associated with thorps suggests that they had grain to process, but perhaps also that they had enough households to generate a demand for flour.

places. It is now practicable to question the current consensus that they were merely secondary settlements of no specialised function relating to the last wave of Scandinavian land colonisation. They certainly began to appear in the English countryside in growing numbers during the course of the tenth century and would seem to have proliferated further during the eleventh and twelfth centuries. But their place in the landscape was not, it would seem, restricted by previous patterns of settlement and land apportionment that forced them into agriculturally marginal areas. Rather, they took shape within areas boasting long histories of occupation and cultivation. Above all, they favoured those regions where soils appropriate for arable production predominated, where they might develop alongside other neighbouring settlements upon which they were often administratively and ecclesiastically dependent. They began as small single-focus nucleations, adopting regular and compact plans articulated by a single street; and they would preserve this settlement structure, where they survived, into the nineteenth century.

Most tellingly, it is in their form and in their landscape position that *thorps* can be seen to form a family of places distinct from settlements in -*bȳ*, with which they are most often associated. The latter favoured areas containing pastoral soils and were prone to develop more complex layouts than the *thorps*, perhaps an indication that they developed from a background of polyfocal, rather than single-focus, settlement. The reasons behind these morphological contrasts, we would argue, originate in functional differences. We know that arable cultivation needs a local labour force that needed to be accommodated, and the regular layout of the *thorp* plans suggests little social stratification among their populations, equal status perhaps being reflected in the equally sized tofts and crofts. Hence, *thorps* look like planned nucleations of the kind that could accommodate manorial tenants.

Certainly, by the twelfth and thirteenth centuries, many *thorps* were populated by tenants holding one to two oxgangs or half to one yardland. The Black Book of Peterborough records 12 full *villani* holding 11 acres in Longthorpe NTH, and further 6 half *villani*.[44] The hundred rolls reveal that eight tenants on the manor of Souldrop BED held land assessed at half to one virgate, and another seven held less.[45] At Heythrop OXF eight *villani* held one virgate, with only one holding a half virgate; while in the same county, at Thrupp, five *servi* held a half virgate, one a full virgate and another one quarter.[46] In both these Oxfordshire cases, however, around a half of the population were free tenants. In Astrop OXF the rolls of 1279 record two freeholders with, respectively, three yardlands and one yardland in

44 T. Stapleton (ed.) *Chronicon Petroburgense*, Camden Society 47 (London, 1849), pp. 158–9.
45 *Rotuli hundredorum*, 2 (London, 1818), p. 327.
46 *Ibid.*, pp. 740, 853–4.

addition to their messuages, eight tenants with half a yardland and four cottars with between one and three acres;[47] and of the three recorded at *Cotthrop* one held a half virgate, one a full virgate and the third three virgates.[48] Elsewhere, however, this pattern is less clear. In the hamlet of Neithrop OXF the five recorded tenants all held between one and three virgates, while at Tythrop OXF there were no half virgate holders.[49] All one can perhaps say is that these censuses of manorial holdings suggest that *thorps* housed a relatively high proportion of tenants holding relatively small amounts of arable land. This may, but of course it may not, reflect the make-up of the first *thorp* dwellers.

By contrast, if the economic basis of the *bȳs* was livestock farming, then here farmers required dedicated space for the barns, byres and other outbuildings associated with animal management; and their herds or flocks required more regular attendance than the crops in the *thorp* fields. At a macro-scale, we know that in pastoral areas settlement patterns tend towards dispersion because this gives easier access to pastures and livestock. Dairying in particular is a labour-intensive activity. And this tendency toward dispersion also affected local decision-making too. Farm complexes were often located at a short distance from one another, giving the space to accommodate the extra buildings required and provide more direct access to the fields. This offers one explanation for the origin of the polyfocal nature of the pastoral *bȳs* and the more complex nature of their later plans in comparison with those of the *thorps*. It may also account for their more jumbled plans, for access in and around larger farm complexes would inevitably lead to more irregular street patterns. There are strong grounds indeed to see within the physical layout of these places the close relationship that existed between form and function.

To suggest that agricultural specialisation lies behind place-names in -*thorp* and -*bȳs* carries broader implications. Such enterprises can only exist and flourish under a certain set of social and economic conditions. Where these are not present, local farming communities will lean towards more mixed farming regimes, where a balance is found between arable and livestock husbandry, as a means of support and survival. It is imperative, therefore, that if the conclusions of this chapter are to be substantiated we demonstrate that those conditions which might foster the development of *thorps* did indeed pertain at the moment of their origins.

---

47 E. Stone and P. Hyde (eds), *Oxfordshire hundred rolls of 1279*, Oxfordshire Record Society Series 46 (Oxford, 1968), p. 38.
48 *Rotuli hundredorum*, p. 706.
49 *Ibid.*, pp. 784–5.

7

Thorps: a hypothesis and its wider implications

Our decision to present separately in this book the linguistic, archaeological and topographical evidence for *thorps* in England was born both of convenience and of a desire for clarity. What we have disaggregated, we now want to bring back together, to see whether our individual approaches combine together to form a coherent story and to discover, of course, whether we are now in the position to address the question that has remained at the heart of this enquiry: just what was a *thorp*?

Briefly, let us restate some of the conclusions already reached in our analysis of *thorp* places. First, linguistic and archaeological indicators seem to agree in suggesting that *thorps* began as small, relatively insignificant settlements. In their earliest phases they appear to adopt simple, compact, linear plans, with a small number (rarely more than a dozen) of regularly sized building plots arranged along a single village street. It is the occasional exception which grows to any status or prosperity; generally, where they survive, they remain small, to the extent that something of their original essence can still be found in their nineteenth-century layouts when they were first systematically mapped. Secondly – and, again, both the archaeological and name evidence point in the same direction – it would appear that *thorps* were a recognisable living aspect of the settlement pattern in the later Anglo-Saxon or Anglo-Scandinavian period. Dates of first record prove that some *thorps* were established by the second half of the ninth century, and their numbers can be shown to increase throughout the tenth and into the first half of the eleventh century. Indeed, we can often trace their formation into the post-Conquest period, if we accept such indications as changing qualifiers and frequent use of the definite article at these dates, or if we accept that the earliest sherds of pottery that have been recovered from their cores represent the first phase of permanent occupation. Conversely, evidence for the existence of places which were later called *thorps* before c.850 is almost entirely lacking.

We have further argued, following the suggestions of others, but now reinforced by the addition of the material evidence from archaeology, that the general coherence which can be seen across the whole corpus when it comes to these questions of size, status and date, taken with the coherent and continuous geographical distribution through the southern Midlands, is indicative of a single name-type. We therefore reject as unlikely earlier attempts to differentiate sharply the *throps* of English England (that is, south and west of the line of Watling Street) from the *thorps* of the Danelaw, and we suspect that both are likely to denote much the same sorts of settlement on the ground, established during a single phase (albeit possibly a long-lasting phase) of settlement development.

It is conceded that the word *thorp* or *throp* could have been used to describe places before 800, and would have been available to those coining settlement names. It is certainly possible that early names occur among the surviving corpus, but such names are extremely difficult to isolate and the characteristics of the whole group consistently point to a later rather than earlier date. Again, we can restate that there are few physical signs of occupation before the mid-ninth century in any of those *thorps* where archaeological finds have been reported, with the exception of a single sherd of Ipswich Ware from Calthorpe NFK, a fact that only lends further support to this argument. This goes for the situation inside the Danelaw as well as outside it, and on balance it seems to us likely that the great majority of *thorp*-names in, for instance, Yorkshire, Lincolnshire and Norfolk were coined in the context of Scandinavian-speaking communities following the settlements that began in the later ninth century. If this is not the case, then the consistent degree of renaming with identifiably Norse personal names and other elements as qualifiers is extraordinary. Taken together, these various observations suggest that the *thorps* exemplify a convergence of naming-practice, if not settlement-development, between English- and Norse-speaking communities after the arrival of the latter. These deductions seem to us to be persuasive and to stand on their own, whether or not our further suggestions are accepted.

Our work has substantially added to the number of *thorps* that can be located in those English counties lying south and west of Watling Street; in the more intensively studied Danelaw counties we have only been able to offer up a few more. We might confidently predict that, as detailed local surveys continue to be undertaken, more *thorps* will be discovered, particularly among recorded medieval field and furlong names.[1] But we are equally convinced that these additions to the

---

1   Five additional *thorp*-names have in fact emerged at a late stage in the production of this book and too late to be included in the database. They bring the number of known *thorps* to 901. These are: Cockrup or Coppethrop in Roel GLO (D. Aldred and C. Dyer, 'A medieval Cotswold village: Roel, Gloucestershire', *Transactions of the Bristol and Gloucestershire Archaeological Society*, 109 (1991), pp. 139–70 at pp. 148–9, 166), a name recorded by 1400; and four minor names in Stanton, SFK: Heythorpe, Thalthorpe, Upthorpe and Cleythorpe, found in D. Dymond (ed.), *The charters of Stanton, Suffolk, c.1275–1678*, Suffolk Record Society 18 (Woodbridge, 2009).

corpus will not substantially alter the overall geographical distribution pattern of *thorps* that we have been able to present. Their core area will always remain the Midland counties of Northamptonshire, Leicestershire, Lincolnshire and Rutland, with similarly strong showings in Norfolk and the Yorkshire Ridings. Beyond these areas, *thorps* will be less numerous but will still occur, producing the impression of an attenuated tail running through the south Midlands, into the south-western counties of Gloucestershire, Wiltshire, Somerset and Dorset, and just encroaching upon east Devon. To the north, the number of *thorps* found to the west of the Pennines and into County Durham and Northumberland will, similarly, remain low.

This restricted range, as we have seen, has been accounted for in different ways. A.H. Smith believed the distribution of the English *throps* – south and west of the Danelaw line – was principally a function of settlement chronology: they were not in the south-east because the earliest Anglo-Saxon settlers of that region came from a part of the Continent where the element was not (yet) in use; they were not in the south-west because the element had gone out of fashion before the Anglo-Saxons reached that area. When it came to the north of England, Smith accounted for the relative rarity of Scandinavian *thorp*-names west of the Pennines by arguing that the term was a Danish rather than a Norwegian introduction. Fellows-Jensen has doubted this latter explanation, observing that *thorp* is found in Norway and its colonies; moreover, in her opinion, the *bȳ*-names of the north-west represent a Danish type moving across the Pennines, and so there ought to be a reason why Danish *thorp* – if that is what it is – did not spread in the same way. She concludes that *thorp* was simply not felt appropriate for the types of settlement made or occupied in the north-west. Meanwhile, with regard to the situation in southern England, we have seen that Fellows-Jensen doubts Smith's chronological explanation of distribution, and prefers to relate the string of *thorps* and *throps* to a continuity landscape, implying that they denote a communality of settlement type across the Midlands, or, in the terminology of Roberts and Wrathmell, across the 'Central Province' – that is, straddling the Danelaw divide.[2] All the indicators that we observe support this idea. Now, armed with more examples, a greater chronological precision for their foundation and a better sense of their original layouts and landscape settings than were available to previous commentators, we feel that we can move towards an explanation for this distinctive distribution and offer some thoughts about the role *thorps* played in the organisation and exploitation of the early medieval English countryside.

The key to understanding *thorps*, we propose, lies in recognising their shared landscape context. *Thorps* are commonly encountered in areas of the country where

2   B. Roberts and S. Wrathmell, *An atlas of rural settlement in England* (London, 2000).

soils good for arable farming can be found, and far more rarely, if at all, beyond these. Although the match is not perfect, this relationship between settlement and soils is readily apparent when the full distribution of *thorps* is set against this physical background, and becomes even stronger when we restrict our view to those *thorps* where a written attestation or archaeological evidence proves their existence before the end of the thirteenth century. This observation was not entirely expected: after all, previous commentators have emphasised that *thorps* occupy marginal spaces off the rich alluvial soils of valley bottoms and the loams of the valley sides, and on the clays of the Midland watersheds. The implication has always been that *thorps* tend to occupy far from prime locations; that in an empty landscape, early colonisers would choose to settle and work the vales rather than the interfluves. But, as recent surveys have begun to show, those areas away from the major river systems where *thorps* can be found have long been recognised for their arable potential. Despite the difficulties that working such heavy soils presented, the challenge was accepted and met from at least the Roman period onwards and probably back into late prehistory. This was achieved even with ploughing equipment that was far less sophisticated than that available to the farmer in the late Anglo-Saxon period. With the introduction of the heavy plough and later the mould-board, the clays of the English lowlands were eminently workable and would prove capable of producing rewardingly high yields by the end of the early Middle Ages.[3]

We are thus inevitably drawn towards the idea that arable farming may well have been the mainstay of the *thorp* economy. Indeed, in the absence of other shared landscape traits – *thorps* are found in low-lying places as well as on hilltops, for instance – we might suggest that it was either a heavy emphasis on arable farming or even total specialisation in this activity that served to define *thorps* as a group of settlements, and to differentiate them from other places, at least until the high Middle Ages. Support for this is provided in the Danelaw counties, at least, by contrasting *thorp* locations with places in -bȳ, where these two elements co-exist. Bȳs cluster on soils ideal for the keeping of dairying herds, younger cattle and flocks of sheep, but not on primary arable soils, offering the possibility that, in the early stages of these two name formations, places variously labelled -bȳ and -thorp were perhaps performing very different, but ultimately complementary, farming activities. We have also proposed, although far from conclusively, that the simple, regular layouts which characterise the early form of *thorps* may also point in this same direction. Equitable plot sizes suggesting a low level of social stratification

3   G. Astill, 'An archaeological approach to the development of agricultural technologies in medieval England', in G. Astill and J. Langdon (eds), *Medieval farming and technology: the impact of agricultural change in northwest Europe* (Leiden, 1997), pp. 193–224 at 196–204.

and the basic arrangement of toft and open croft associated with *thorps* – rather than toft and croft filled with ancillary buildings for the keeping of livestock, as found in *bȳs* – is just the kind of arrangement that we might expect in places housing a peasant population cultivating standard holdings in the surrounding fields and providing labour services or hired labour for an arable demesne. Furthermore, we have the evidence for mills in Domesday Book, where they are found in greater numbers than might have been predicted in association with *thorps* and remain relatively rare on *bȳ* holdings.

What we have, therefore, is a clearly defined regional distribution, a firm grasp on the chronology of the appearance of *thorps* in the English countryside and an understanding of the shape these settlements took. Their temporal and geographical distribution, in particular, places *thorps* in the very areas and at the very time that we understand the landscape to have been undergoing fundamental change. What is most exciting, of course, given the strong association we have between *thorps*, arable soils and the arable economy, is that we know that the primary factor driving this shift in farming practice was no less than a cereal revolution.

Thorps and the open fields

Building upon the observations of Fellows-Jensen, it occurred to us early on that there was a good match between the overall distribution of *thorps* and *throps* and the maps which show the regions where open-field agriculture is known to have been practised (Figure 7.1). In fact, in many ways the match is extraordinary. Although there are some anomalies in detail, the overall characteristics of the two distributions are strikingly similar. To reiterate once again, *thorps* are strong in the arc from Yorkshire in the north and east through Lincolnshire, Nottinghamshire, Leicestershire and Northamptonshire to the south-west Midlands; they are strong also in Norfolk. Conversely, we find them absent, or largely so, from the far south-west, the far south-east, much of the west Midlands, the north-west and Northumberland. The possibility that the type of settlement denoted by *thorp* and *throp* might in some way be related not just to arable farming generally but to a particular type of arable farming – that is, open-field agriculture – is at first sight an attractive one.

On further reflection the association becomes more interesting and, we think, more convincing. Following Fellows-Jensen and Wagner, we have argued that there is reason to see continuity of usage of the name form across the Danelaw line, and that all the indications – including the strong Norse associations of so many of the Danelaw names – point to this being a phenomenon of the later pre-Conquest period. These characteristics, established from analysis of the names,

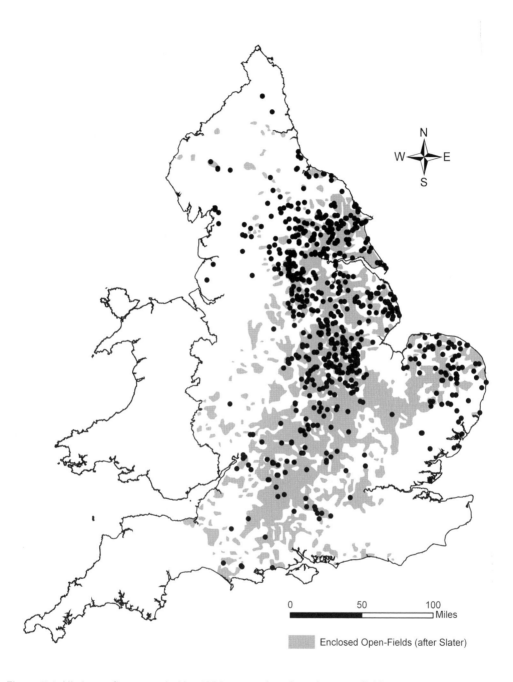

Figure 7.1 All *thorps* first recorded by 1300 mapped against the open-field core as reconstructed from enclosures of the late eighteenth and nineteenth centuries.

certainly fit well with the conclusions of archaeologists and landscape historians regarding the origins of open-field farming. This subject, of course, remains a contentious one,[4] and competing theories rather than consensus are in play. But few would quibble with the idea that this type of agriculture required the reorganisation of communities around newly laid-out arable lands, and that this process had its origins around the middle of the Anglo-Saxon period (that is, the eighth and ninth centuries) and had spread – perhaps from a core in the southern Midlands – north and south in later Anglo-Scandinavian England. Whereas we are accustomed to consider the linguistic, legal, administrative and cultural *differences* between 'Danish' and 'English' England in the ninth and tenth centuries, this fundamental agrarian upheaval is known to have affected society on both sides of the line. So, in the case of place-names, we are used to seeing maps that show elements characteristically Norse and significantly restricted to the Danelaw, but here there is a mechanism whereby terminology could have been shared across the divided country. Indeed, one might feel that the introduction and spread of open-field farming – with the attendant widespread upheaval in land tenure and settlement pattern – really *ought* to be reflected somewhere in the major pre-Conquest place-names of central England. The possibility that *thorp* may be an element in the vocabulary of that agricultural revolution is an attractive one.

Although it may be attractive, such an explanation is certainly not straightforward. For one thing, we know that the term *throp*, perhaps also as unmetathesised *thorp*, existed in England in the pre-Viking period: it is attested, as a broad equivalent to *tūn*, in glosses from the later seventh century,[5] and its earliest record in onomastic use could be as early, but the documentation is not secure. Nonetheless, there is every reason to believe that it came over with the early Anglo-Saxons, and that it is likely to have been applied to places during the earliest centuries and in non-open-field contexts. That we do not find it in surviving names that show signs of being ancient is intriguing, although it is not an isolated case: the fundamental study by Cox showed that the common habitative terms *worth* and *tūn* were, respectively, absent and poorly represented among the earliest-recorded names, and it has since become widely accepted that they came into 'fashion' in the middle to late Anglo-Saxon period, with the necessary implication that, despite being in the language, they were underexploited in the earlier period.[6] Things were perhaps rather more complicated, however: *tūns*, *worths* and *throps* may, for instance, have been settlements too small and insignificant to attract mention

---

4   Williamson, *Shaping medieval landscapes*, chapter 1 provides a good summary of the debate.

5   See Appendix 1.

6   B. Cox, 'The place-names of the earliest English records', JEPNS, 8 (1975–6), pp. 12–66 at pp. 65–6; Gelling, *Signposts*, pp. 181–3.

early on, although some of them may have survived and risen to greater prominence at a later period.[7] We have to accept that some of our *thorps* may be old despite it having been impossible so far to prove this archaeologically. Nonetheless, there is no real difficulty in imagining that certain terminology, probably in association with particular developments in settlement type, could come to prominence at certain times. The name-types, the dates of record, the absence from Anglo-Saxon local documentation and the archaeological indications all support the contention that the surviving English *throp*-names were in general more likely to have been coined after AD 800 than before. This suits the open-field hypothesis, as, quite remarkably, does further evidence from the *Upthrop* charter S 214.

We left discussion of this document at the end of Chapter 4 (above, pp. 83–4), having observed that it seems to establish the existence by AD 869 – just before the recorded Scandinavian settlements – of *thorp/throp* place-names in the Midlands. Moreover, its directional qualifier, *Upp-*, is typical of the group as a whole, suggesting that it is not wholly different in kind from the later *thorp*-names. It remains now to observe that there are further important points to be drawn from the text of the charter. Having described the boundaries, or appurtenances, of the *Upthrop* estate, it continues in Old English as follows:

> Ægþer ge etelond ge eyrðlond ge eac wudoland all hit is gemæne þara fif & twentig higda & æt Peadan beorge seondan sex æcras innlondes ægþer ge medlondes ge eyrðlondes

> The pastureland, ploughland and also woodland is all common-land of the twenty-five hides; and at *Peadan beorg* there are six acres of 'inland', [comprising] both meadow and ploughland.

This appears to give us a rare insight into tenurial arrangements involving an early recorded *thorp*; indeed, potentially the earliest-recorded *thorp*. With that in mind, two things in particular catch the eye. First, the 5-hide estate *ubi appellatur on Upþrope* 'at the place which is called *on Upthrope*' appears to be involved also in a larger, 25-hide unit. Given that the inland, or demesne land, is at *Peadan beorg*, it is perhaps likely that the larger estate went under the latter name: in any case, this appears to be a welcome indication that the *thorp* is a dependent, or at least smaller, unit within a larger structure.

More extraordinary is the second observation, relating to the form of agriculture practised on the large estate. This clearly involved a high degree of communality, in which woodland, pasture and arable were all held in common. The designation, in

---

7   This question is explored more fully in Parsons, *Pre-Viking place-names of Northamptonshire*.

particular, of arable – ploughland, *eyrðlond* – inevitably brings to mind open-field farming. This appears to offer the strongest documentary support for our hypothesis that we could possibly hope for: Old English *throp* in use in an open-field context in the second half of the ninth century.[8] *Thorps* are so relatively rare in pre-Conquest charters that it would not be surprising if we got no further indications of their landscapes from this source; it may therefore be very significant that another *thorp* estate, Adlestrop GLO, seems to have attested open-field characteristics.[9]

The next complication, however, is the accommodation of the Scandinavian element. *Thorp* in Denmark, particularly, is very frequent, and characteristic of place-names of Viking-age date. In England we have seen that *thorp* is frequently combined with Norse elements and personal names in the Danelaw, and we find every reason to suspect that many of these names are indeed coinages of the Scandinavian period. In that case, we have to consider the nature of the continuum that, we are suggesting, runs across the country. In short, if *thorp* and *throp* – to use the usual shorthand for the English form – are used in the same circumstances, for the same sort of settlement, from south-west to north-east, how does that relate to the apparent double linguistic origin? If the general hypothesis is correct it would seem either that both languages used their cognate terms for the same type of settlement (even though we are implying that the settlement type may have been new in England in the ninth century), or that one language influenced the use of the cognate in the other. In this latter case, accepting the evidence and the date of the *Upthrop* charter, we would have to suggest that, since English *throp* had a place in open-field farming before the Scandinavian settlements, it may have affected the application of Old Norse *thorp* in England.

These complexities open doors to questions that we are not prepared to tackle here. Was open-field farming independently developed in Scandinavia and Anglo-Saxon England? Could the use of *thorp* in Denmark owe anything to influence from the Danelaw? These are topics which we must leave for others to explore if they agree that our study of the English situation merits further examination. But while the relationship between English and Norse terms necessarily complicates our hypothesis, we certainly do not think that it necessarily damages it. The alternatives described in the previous paragraph are quite credible, and again, the

8   This is only one of a number of apparent late-Anglo-Saxon references to open-field farming in the pre-Conquest charters. See, e.g., D. Hooke, 'Open-field agriculture: the evidence from pre-Conquest charters of the West Midlands', in T. Rowley (ed.), *The origins of open-field agriculture* (London, 1981), pp. 39–63.

9   See M.D. Costen, 'Some evidence for new settlements and field systems in late Anglo-Saxon Somerset', in L. Abrams and J.P. Carley (eds), *The archaeology and history of Glastonbury Abbey* (Woodbridge, 1991), pp. 39–55 at p. 41. The charter is S 1548, unfortunately consisting only of undated (although evidently pre-Conquest) bounds.

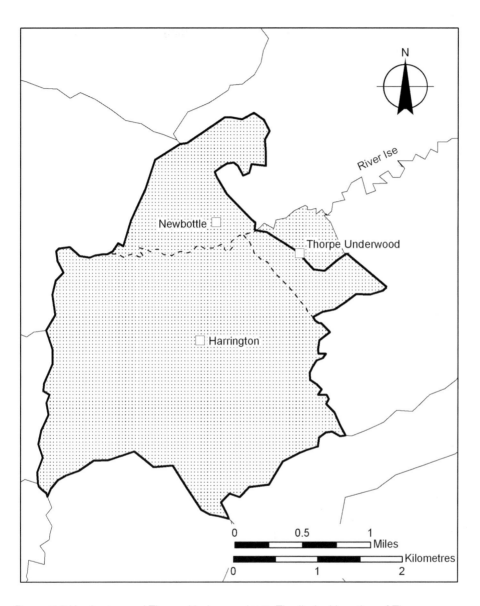

Figure 7.2 Harrington and Thorpe Underwood NTH. The liminal location of Thorpe Underwood in relation to the manor and parish boundaries of Harrington is paralleled in many other cases drawn from across those parts of the country where nucleated villages predominate.

archaeologically recognised phenomenon of the spread of open-field farming would have been a uniquely strong mechanism for the kind of linguistic influence here envisaged. Subject to a fuller understanding of the archaeology, both here and in Scandinavia, the simplest explanatory model may be this: that open-field agriculture had developed in parts of England by the middle of the ninth century; that a distinctive type of small settlement labelled a *throp* or *thorp* became associated with it; and that incoming Scandinavian settlers, from the later ninth century onwards, were among those who took up this type of farming, and with it they adopted the settlement type called a *thorp*, the term being already familiar to them, although whether it was used identically in their homeland is currently unknown.

Another important issue needs to be addressed here. If there is indeed a link with open-field farming, what kind of settlement might a *thorp* have been? What role could it have played in the reorganised landscape? There is certainly an interesting paradox here. We have seen extensive evidence to show that *thorps* were in origin small, subsidiary places; we have also seen the maps which show that – whether or not *thorps* had a functional connection with the open fields – they are found to a very large extent in the same areas as those fields. Yet the landscape of open-field farming is generally characterised as a landscape of nucleated settlements: in laying out the large common fields, it is argued, dispersed farmsteads were swept away and the community relocated into nucleated centres. *Thorps*, it appears, are typically hamlets which occur in areas of nucleated villages (Figure 7.2) – that is to say, settlement types that should not be there. How are we to make sense of this?

In the first place, the documentary and place-name evidence suggest that this is a problem that needs to be tackled, whatever the exact role of *thorps*. Two items which have already been discussed come back to mind here. One is the relatively frequent presence of very minor *thorps*, surviving generally only as field-names, in the classically open-field landscape of Leicestershire (see above, pp. 27–8). Conceivably, perhaps, these names could denote the memory of dispersed settlements that pre-date the laying-out of the common fields. But at least one was a farmstead in the thirteenth century, and others have Scandinavian qualifiers, suggesting that they had some function in or after the late ninth century. The other point worth noting is the account in the *Upthrop* charter of how 'the aforesaid little estate is embossed and bounded around by ... little properties' called Willhere's *wīc*, Cynemund's *wīc* and Ud[d]a's *wīc*. Here there is a large estate explicitly farmed in common in the ninth century, and it seems natural to associate that with the development of open-field farming. Yet the landscape is clearly still occupied by some dispersed settlements, including these *wīcs* and the *throp*. There should be enough here to make us wonder about the conflation of open-field agriculture and nucleated villages: did one require the other, and where they both developed, did they necessarily do so at the same time? The answer to both questions, of course, is no. It is quite clear from later medieval evidence for settlement form and the disposition of open fields in some parts of the Midlands that, where there was sufficient space for arable expansion and relatively little pressure from population growth, open fields could be laid out successfully without the need for total nucleation, and these fields might then be fruitfully managed and farmed by communities who continued to live in dispersed or polyfocal settlements. And there is equally unequivocal evidence that both settlements and their fields might both undergo radical reorganisation independently even after the basic pattern of farming and settlement had been established.

One intriguing possibility is that we should think not in terms of the role that *thorps* played in an *already* reorganised landscape, but rather in terms of the role that they played in that reorganisation itself. Might we be dealing here with a type of settlement that, while it came into being in association with the laying-out of the new fields, is not in origin a primary nucleation, but is rather a secondary or subsidiary or outlying hamlet? The mechanism by which the archaeologically attested pre-open-field landscape of dispersed farmsteads gave way to the landscape of nucleated villages is poorly understood.[10] Generally, however, it is thought that the move was made directly (whether quickly or slowly is incidental in this context), without passing though any intermediate stages – that is, that full dispersion gave way to full nucleation. But *thorps* may offer an alternative model. Might a first stage towards full nucleation not have been the grouping of individual farmsteads into a number of small hamlet clusters? This seems an eminently sensible course of action to follow, for one of the logistic problems that communities who nucleated and introduced open-field farming together would have faced was that this reorganisation immediately increased the distance between the farmer and his landholdings. Since inefficiencies and costs rise with distance, as simple economic models show, it is difficult to see what advantages communities saw in bringing people together in one central place and setting out extensive fields. Is it possible, therefore, that as large estates began to break up into smaller land units, and as the principal settlements within them began to nucleate, surrounding themselves with huge communal fields, they also found it helpful to establish outposts near the margins of their landholdings associated with the new field systems? The minor *thorps* in Leicestershire, for example, include several instances in which there is a correlation between *thorps* and the names of known open fields.[11] Did many of the fields, or every field, have its own

---

10 For a good survey of the historiography of nucleation see Rippon, *Beyond the village*, Chapter 1.

11 E.g. *Cawthorpe felde* in Thorpe Langton is one of the open fields of the township (EPNS LEI, 4, p. 277); similar perhaps is *le Westhorp*, one of three locational *thorps* known from the parish of Kirby Bellars, equivalent to West Field, one of the three early great fields (EPNS LEI, 3, p. 93).

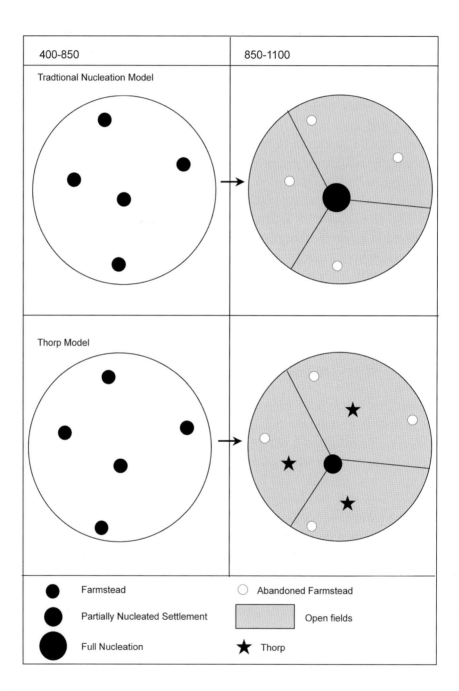

Figure 7.3. Schematic model of the proposed intermediary phase in nucleation which may be associated with the laying-out of open fields and the establishment of *thorps*, outlying settlements from where each of these new and extensive arable blocks was farmed.

thorp? Were they settlements – perhaps no more than temporary or seasonal shelters – for workers in the distant fields, for ploughmen or even perhaps slaves tied to the demesne? Is it possible that something like this is the origin of the *thorps* across the open-field landscapes of medieval England (Figure 7.3)? If so, then this connects the creation of *thorps* with another great movement of the period 850–1050, the settling of slaves on the land and the emergence of *servi casati*. In western England at this time 'ploughman' meant a landless worker, often a slave. Over time they were settled on holdings and became *gebūrs* and *enches*, terms which by the tenth and eleventh century had come to mean tenants. Certainly it was tenants holding land from and owing services to the lord that characterise the *thorp* inhabitants recorded in Domesday Book and later feudal inquiries. But might they have begun as settlements for *servi casati* with ploughing duties, only to become tenant settlements later?

Unfortunately we are hardly in a position to answer this question because few of these minor *thorp* field-names have been precisely located and none has been the subject of archaeological investigation. But it is worth considering the possibility against the indications, such as they are, of the qualifiers in the names themselves, both those of *thorps* now lost and those which survived to become identifiable settlements. We have already discussed these, and observed that they seem to have rather little to tell us about the function of *thorps* (see above pp. 53–7 and 66–8). The frequent directional terms, and indeed the frequent absence of qualifiers – simplex names – are indicative of status, not function. We have found little that clearly relates to agricultural practice: a few possible pigs, sheep and fowl on one hand, perhaps some recurrent cabbage on the other, but not much that establishes a clear pattern. In the Danelaw mills are quite common, although the relevant names are all recorded after 1200, but this at least appears to echo the Domesday evidence for mills associated with *thorps* by the end of the eleventh century. There is nothing here that speaks loudly in favour of, or against, this (or any other) hypothesis for the origin of the name-type. But if *thorps* were associated with the large open fields, it is hardly surprising that crops, which would vary and rotate, would not be fixed in the names; and if some essentially arable settlements specialised also in keeping some pigs or chickens, names like Gristhorpe YON and Cockrup GLO could be accounted for perfectly satisfactorily.

A more marked pattern, and one clearly of interest in the current context, is made by the names implying groups of youths or workers (see above, pp. 54 and 67–8), which are found on both sides of the Danelaw boundary. The clearest examples are Boythorp(e) DRB NFK YOE, Knapthorpe NTT and Swanthorpe HMP; further possible comparable instances involve ON *sveinn*, OE/ON *b(e)arn*, ME *enche*, ON *kati* and OE *(ge)būr*. It is intriguing to recall that Coates has interpreted one of these as in origin a seasonal settlement: here, certainly, is a type that *could* relate to the kind of establishments that we have suggested above. It is to be conceded, however, that those who worked the fields – if that is who they are – are denoted by rather generic terms, rather than by vocabulary clearly designating 'ploughmen'.[12] Here we may need to take refuge in the onomastic principle of overlooking the commonplace: if *thorps* were usually established for ploughmen, *servi casati*, or demesne tenants, their presence would not make them distinctive or give rise to names.

The pattern in the qualifiers that is perhaps most surprising, and might offer a challenge to the hypothesis here presented, is the recurrence – on the Danelaw side of the line – of royal associations, as in Coneythorpe YOW (see above, p. 54). This, it might be observed, is rather a surprising feature of the name-group in general, not only in the light of our hypothesis. Unless all the indications that have been discussed should be set aside, *thorps* are in origin small, relatively insignificant settlements. The repeated association with royal ownership, therefore, is presumably not a function of great worth or status; rather, it seems likely to reflect the circumstance that a number of the large estates within which *thorps* were subordinate were in royal hands. The rather frequent appearance of the king as qualifier is then perhaps directly related to the instability of compounding noted throughout this work: when it functioned entirely within a larger estate, such a settlement would probably be known simply as *Thorp*; if it survived as a unit in itself, because the larger estate was broken up or sold off, then its royal associations would naturally suggest a distinguishing qualifier. Some such explanation, in which the *thorp* is characterised as royal because it is, or was, part of a large royal estate, seems more likely than that royalty made a particular habit of acquiring these small, everyday farms. The same reasoning presumably applies

---

12 Ploughmen could have been denoted by the Old English *erthling* (EPNE, 1, p. 158). The terms given here are generally rather imprecise and generic in their applications: cf. the comments above, p. 68, on ME *enche*; however, it is worth noting that here one particular application, in the collocation *goad-inch*, does relate specifically to a 'plough-boy' (EPNS GLO, 1, p. xi). The *swān* of Swanthorpe is generally taken as a 'herdsman' or even specifically a 'swineherd'. Before we start building hypotheses on this, however, it should be noted that it is also glossed more generally as a 'labourer, peasant' (MED, s.v. *swōn*, sense (c)), while the cognate ON *sveinn* is a 'boy, servant, attendant'.

13 It might be conceded that since a fair proportion of *thorps* did grow to a reasonable size and become parishes, etc., then they could at that stage have been worthy acquisitions for rich landholders. We know that Bishopthorpe YOW was acquired by the archbishop of York in the thirteenth century, for instance, and the name was earlier simplex. Assuming that swift growth in the late Anglo-Saxon period may quite often have taken place (above, pp. 75–9), later acquisition by large landholders – royal, ecclesiastical or otherwise – could have created a number of names in this way, but would be no guide to the original settlement type.

to most of those in ecclesiastical ownership (see above, pp. 40, 54).[13]

Lastly, there remains something to say about the incidence of personal names as qualifiers. It has been shown that personal names are combined with *thorp* far more commonly in the north and east of the range than in the south and west; and, indeed, that – although it is not as simple as identifying 'English' and 'Norse' sides of a Danelaw barrier – the densest evidence for personal names as *thorp*-qualifiers is very predominantly Scandinavian in linguistic origin and early in date. While we have been at pains to stress continuity in the character and distribution of *thorps* across the country, therefore, here is a genuine point of contrast that demands some kind of explanation. In the terms of our hypothesis – that *thorps* may be bound up with the spread of open-field farming – it seems natural to suggest that there may, after all, have been something different about the way that the innovations were adopted or developed in areas that saw dense Scandinavian settlement. A high incidence of personal naming suggests a high incidence of private, individual tenure or ownership. That seems rather to strike at the heart of the communal common-field system.[14] Yet it raises intriguing and important questions: is it possible that open fields in Yorkshire and Norfolk were laid out, among Scandinavian communities, with a different kind of organisation and ethos from those that governed developments in the pre-Viking Midlands? Or is it possible that communal estates developed in much the same way in, say, the ninth century, but became widely hijacked as private property among Scandinavian communities in the tenth?[15] In either case it is intriguing, in light of the onomastic principle of overlooking the commonplace, mentioned above, that the few names which might have denoted 'common' or 'community' *thorps* are found in Yorkshire and Lincolnshire, heartlands of dense Scandinavian settlement (above, pp. 56–7).

If different types of tenure – presumably more private ownership – accounts for the large number of personal names attached to *thorps* in the areas that received more Scandinavian settlers, this is certainly not a complete explanation. It is, for instance, fascinating that, in the same Danelaw counties, later-recorded names consistently contain proportionately fewer personal names. Does private ownership become less prevalent over time? Or could it be that the *thorps* which

---

14 The problem may not be as serious as it first appears. Villages practised communal farming while the manor in which the village lay was owned by an individual. In this sense the village and the manor were two separate institutions. Place-names taking personal names might therefore be taking their cue from the manor rather than the wider community.

15 There could be some kind of parallel for this in current understandings of bȳ-names, which are often explained as settlements taken out of large older estates into individual ownership among Scandinavian-speaking communities of the ninth and tenth centuries: bȳ-names too are characterised by large numbers of Norse pers.ns as qualifiers. See Abrams and Parsons, 'Place-names', pp. 399, 404–11.

entered private ownership early became in doing so detached from their original estates, and thereby became more liable to be recorded as separate 'places'? There would therefore be a bias towards the early recording of such names, while the later recording of others need not suggest that those *thorps* were established later. We offer no definitive answers to these questions here. But we believe that progress could be made with them in detailed regional study, combining archaeological, documentary and onomastic materials following the methodology that we have used here.

We might, of course, turn this line of reasoning on its head, and point to the absence of personal names used as qualifiers with the English *throps*, particularly in the central southern Midlands, the proposed core area for the precocious development of open-field farming.[16] Does the absence of personal names in these place-names suggest that communal farming strategies overriding those of the individual had already been adopted at an early date? It would be nice to think so but it would be equally unwise to conclude so. Indeed, we have presented the counter-arguments to our hypothesis to highlight our awareness of the dangers of simple readings of the evidence.

It would be convenient, for example, to think that behind all *thorps* lies a single story; that there exists a universal explanation which accounts for, or explains away, their name, their landscape setting, their internal layout and physical arrangement, their social organisation and their economic and administrative functions. It would be neat to conclude that *thorps* are places linked exclusively to open-field farming: that the introduction of this new farming practice was aided by the development of a new settlement type, the *thorp*; that the place-name *thorp* is synonymous with this farming system; and that neither the settlements nor these extensive fields could have existed without the other. Yet, however attractive the idea that *thorps* enabled communities to overcome the logistic challenges posed by the transition from farming in severalty to farming in common, and however exciting the idea that *thorps* offer us a new way of thinking about village nucleation

16   A southern Midland core is proposed in Roberts and Wrathmell's hypothetical model for the spread of open-field farming (*Region and place*, p. 145, fig. 5.11). This is coincident with the early date of introduction that has been argued by Foard, Brown and Hall for Northamptonshire: see T. Brown and G. Foard, 'The Saxon landscape: a regional perspective', in P. Everson and T. Williamson (eds), *The archaeology of landscape* (Manchester, 1998), pp. 67–94, and D. Hall, *The open fields of Northamptonshire*, Northamptonshire Record Society publications 38 (Northampton, 1995). Other archaeological indicators also point to this area too. For instance, in the zooarchaeological record a shift from cattle to sheep in rural assemblages appears to coincide with the proposed date for the introduction of the open fields (pers. comm. Naomi Sykes), while a shift away from manuring arable with domestic refuse (presumably in favour of dunging on the hoof) has been detected in this Midland core at a time at which in other areas (non-open-field areas) manuring with homestead and farmyard materials was intensifying. See Jones, 'Signatures in the soil'.

as an incremental, phased process by which the move from full dispersal to full nucleation passed through an intermediary stage, remaining ambiguities in the evidence require us to leave space for alternative explanations.

Here we can do little more than identify areas where further clarification is needed. We know, for instance, that *thorps* found a place in the landscape of extensive estates. The *Upthrop* charter makes this explicitly clear, and it is implicit in the tenurial and judicial dependency of many Domesday *thorps* and their ecclesiastical dependency on other places. Both contain echoes of earlier estate structures. But what was their precise role within these estates? Should we see them as equivalents to berewicks and bartons, specialist cereal-producing centres, or something else? Might these *thorps* have originally practised non-open-field methods of arable cultivation? And what happened to the *thorps* as the estates were broken up? Again, we know that *thorps* continued to grow in number in the later landscape of smaller estates, of manors and of parishes. We must presume that the function they performed in these settings must have been different, if only in terms of scale, from that of those early *thorps* found in the extensive estates.

What relationship might *thorps* have had with emerging urban centres? It is difficult to ignore, for instance, the observation that, following an initial short lapse of time, the rise in the number of *thorps* marches in step with the development of towns and markets. This is an important question, particularly so since in Denmark this very relationship has been identified as a fundamental hallmark of *thorps* there. Thurston notes, for example, that '[w]hile some torps are on good land, many are in stony uplands. What they have in common is proximity to towns.'[17] We have noted in passing the apparent constellation of *thorps* around places such as York, Leicester and Peterborough, which, while sharing very different beginnings, had all become well-established towns by 1100–1200. Of course, synchronicity is one thing, but proving a causal relationship is something entirely different, and the geographical correlation is not strong. But might some *thorps* have found a role in providing grain to the growing centres? Indeed, might a small number of our corpus have been established for this very reason? The need to produce surplus for a rising non-productive population was almost certainly one of the many stimuli to the introduction of open-field farming, and, once established, market forces encouraged intensification and specialisation in animals and crops. Equally, by the beginning of the thirteenth century no rural community – *thorps* are no exception – was isolated from the forces of the urban market. So the question needs to be asked: just how influential were some towns in the early formation of our *thorps*?

17   Thurston, 'The knowable, the doable and the undiscussed', p. 665.

We must also recognise ultimately that we are dealing with a group of places that began to form in the ninth and tenth centuries, and would continue to do so well into the early modern period. We are dealing, then, with a place-name that has currency for over a millennium. There is every likelihood that, over this time, the original sense of the term or its defining features will have been lost, forgotten or become irrelevant. Certainly, by the end of the Middle Ages we already seem to pick up a transformation from something specific to something more general. For Langland and Chaucer, writing in the fourteenth century, a *thorp* had become a byword for any small rural settlement.[18] No small wonder, then, that when the full corpus is examined, some of the relationships we have uncovered – in particular, the link between soil types and these places – becomes weaker. Over time, the sense that *thorps* were places specifically engaged in arable farming appears to be lost. Thereafter *thorp* becomes a useful term to be applied to any or all rural settlements irrespective of their form, status or function, particularly in landscapes where *thorp* was a dominant element of the existing naming pattern.

Such, then, are the problems of dealing with such a large and varied group of places. There will always be exceptions to rules, and there will almost always be many ways by which they came into being, rather than just one. That said, we believe that the history of many *thorps*, perhaps the greater majority of them, may well be closely entwined with the story of the open fields of England. These small, dependent and seemingly unimportant – some might say irrelevant – places, we suggest, played a pivotal role in the cereal revolution of the early medieval period and the consequent reorganisation of the English landscape in the two centuries either side of the Norman Conquest. *Thorps* were born out of these transformations of farming practices and settlement patterns from the late ninth century onwards. But *thorps*, both as places and as communities, were not simply witnesses to these changes in the landscape: rather, they were active participants in them. What are *thorps*? They are places which may have helped to alter indelibly the face of the English countryside.

18   OED, *Thorp*.

Appendix 1

Throp in Anglo-Saxon glosses

The word appears in five Anglo-Saxon glossaries, although four of them ultimately derive the relevant item from a single source, which rather reduces the witness-count. The exception appears the most straightforward instance. A list copied in the first half of the eleventh century contains the gloss 'fundus, þrop',[1] where *fundus* is a term defined by Lewis and Short's *Latin Dictionary* as 'a piece of land, a farm, estate'. This clearly sits within the range of senses we might expect for *throp/thorp*.

The other group of glosses seems more challenging. Here *throp* appears in association with Lat *compitum*, which primarily means 'cross-roads'. In one instance it is additionally combined with OE *thing-stōw* 'meeting-place'. These senses are rather different from what is generally suggested by Germanic cognates and later English evidence, but they have been admitted into the dictionary definitions of *throp*, have been sought in some place-names and have coloured discussions of the Germanic term's ultimate etymology.[2] Closer inspection of the glosses, however, suggests that it is not at all certain that either 'cross-roads' or 'meeting-place' was ever a straightforward translation of OE *throp*.

Glosses and glossaries are notoriously hazardous guides to English vocabulary.[3] Equivalents to Latin words were added to manuscripts, sometimes in the context of a continuous Latin text, sometimes in lists already removed from

---

1   L. Kindschi, 'The Latin–Old English glossaries in Plantin-Moretus MS 32 and British Museum MS Additional 32,246', PhD dissertation (Stanford University, 1955), p. 139, line 1. For the manuscript see N.R. Ker, *Catalogue of manuscripts containing Anglo-Saxon* (Oxford, 1957), no. 2. The relevant section of glossary is Ker's item d.

2   DEPN, for instance, s.n. Throphill NTB, suggests that 'A better etymology for Thropton NTB is given by the meaning "cross-roads" evidenced for *þrop*.' EPNE, 2, p. 207, argues that an etymological connection with Lat *turba* 'crowd' is supported by the equation in the glosses with *thing-stōw*.

3   See, for instance, the various studies collected in P. Lendinara, *Anglo-Saxon glosses and glossaries* (Aldershot, 1999), including, e.g., 'Misunderstanding a gloss, past and present', pp. 87–98.

their context. Glosses were extracted, copied and recopied, reordered, compared, rationalised and sometimes simply mistaken. In consequence, stages of transmission need to be reconstructed, as far as possible, for any gloss to be properly understood. In the case of the *compitum* gloss, this transmission can be partly recovered. Three practically identical witnesses establish the form of an entry in a late-seventh-century collection of glosses:[4]

'conpetum, tuun uel ðrop' (Erfurt)
'conpetum, tuun, þrop' (Corpus II)
'conpetum, tun, þrop' (Cleopatra I)

A fourth witness elaborates on the same original gloss:

'competum .i. uilla, *uel* þingstow, *uel* þrop' (Harley)

Pheifer notes that this last glossary, in British Library MS Harley 3376, is characterised by 'the practice of combining material from different sources in a single interpretation', and by 'the compiler's habit of translating Old English interpretations into Latin, which then precedes or replaces them'.[5] These features presumably account both for the introduction of *thing-stōw* into our item (of which more below), and for the replacement of OE *tūn* by Lat *villa*.

Whether *tūn* in the original, or *villa* in the Harley translation, the inclusion of another term beside *throp* is a detail of the gloss which is clearly of great importance. For it is not enough to say that *throp* in this complex is given as an equivalent to Lat *compitum* 'cross-roads'. Rather, *throp* and *tūn* were together originally associated with *compitum*. Since *tūn* is an enclosure and settlement term – the semantics of which are fairly well understood and do not encompass 'cross-roads' – it is necessary to question how the original glossator understood the Latin word: this will inevitably have implications for our understanding of *throp* in the context.

The matter would be easier to judge if the ultimate source of *compitum* in the glossaries were apparent. Unfortunately it is not known for certain, although Pheifer makes a plausible guess at a passage from the prologue to Orosius's

---

4   The group is treated by J.D. Pheifer, *Old English glosses in the Épinal-Erfurt Glossary* (Oxford, 1974), pp. xxi–xl, with details of the manuscripts, editions, etc. The relevant gloss in his edition of the Erfurt glossary is p. 17, no. 307. The absence of the item from the oldest manuscript of the group, Épinal, is not suspicious since the centrefold of its first quire, containing much of C–E, is lost. For further discussion of the seventh-century origins of the underlying glossary see Pheifer, 'Early Anglo-Saxon glossaries and the school of Canterbury', *Anglo-Saxon England*, 16 (1987), pp. 17–44.

5   Pheifer, *Old English glosses*, p. xxxvi.

History, a source which is well represented elsewhere in the same glossaries.[6] In the prologue to his work, Orosius uses the Latin word in the following context:[7]

> qui alieni a ciuitate Dei ex locorum agrestium conpitis et pagis pagani uocantur

> those who, alienated from the kingdom of God, are called 'pagans', from the conpitis and pagis of rural places

Certainly, if this were the source of the original gloss it is easy to see how terms for rural settlements might have been provided for the Latin words which actually mean 'cross-roads' and, perhaps, 'districts' respectively. Indeed, in this context throp and tūn, straightforwardly denoting small, agrarian settlements, look rather more appropriate than a term meaning 'cross-roads'.

Orosius's choice of Latin word is not so surprising, however, in the light of examination of its usage elsewhere. A passage from Isidore of Seville's early-seventh-century Etymologies makes clear a further development in the application of compitum:[8]

> Conpita sunt ubi usus est conventus fieri rusticorum; et dicta conpita quod loca multa in agris eodem conpetant; et quo convenitur a rusticis.

> Compita are places where gatherings of country people are customarily made, and they are called compita because many regions in the country meet (competant) there, and there country people assemble.

Isidore correctly relates the word to the verb competere 'to meet, come together'. Although the primary sense of the noun would appear to be simply 'junction, cross-roads', subsequent development of these junctions as meeting-places for the rural community is readily comprehensible, and this usage was presumably in Orosius's mind when he wrote his passage.

---

6 For the suggestion, see Pheifer, Old English glosses, p. 139 (note on gloss 307). For the contribution of Orosius to the glossaries, ibid., pp. xlvi–xlviii; also Pheifer, 'Early Anglo-Saxon glossaries', pp. 26–8.

7 C. Zangemeister (ed.), Pauli Orosii Historiarum Adversum Paganos Libri VII (Vienna, 1882), p. 3. For a French translation see M.-P. Arnaud-Lindet, Orose: Histoires (contre les païens) (Paris, 1990–), vol. 1, p. 8; she gives 'ceux qui ... sont appelés païens d'après les carrefours ruraux et les cantons paysans'. This passage from the prologue is not represented in the ninth-century Old English translation of Orosius.

8 Isidore, Etymologiarum sive Originum, ed. W.M. Lindsey, 2 vols (Oxford, 1911), 2, Book XV, chapter 2, section 15. Translation adapted from: S.A. Barney et al. (eds and tr.), The etymologies of Isidore of Seville (Cambridge, 2006), p. 306.

On various counts, then, it is unlikely that the Anglo-Saxon who glossed *compitum* with *tūn* or *throp* was searching for words that meant 'cross-roads'. Had that been the intention then *tūn*, at least, would surely not have been chosen. And if the source of the Latin word was Orosius's text, or something similar, then 'cross-roads' is not really the operative sense. In a context where the author is describing the rural haunts of unsophisticated people, *compitum* may easily have been misunderstood, or partially understood, as referring to small rural settlements. Alternatively, it may have been taken more appropriately as 'meeting-place': there is, after all, the Harley gloss *thing-stōw*, which gets associated with *compitum* here. Perhaps there is greater substance to the notion that OE *throp* could itself carry the meaning 'meeting-place'?

Again, however, on examination this does not seem likely. First, that original association with *tūn* counts against this interpretation of the gloss-complex just as it counted against the 'cross-roads' interpretation: *tūn* is surely not an obvious equivalent for 'meeting-place' either. Second, there is the negative evidence offered by the names of England's hundreds and wapentakes, which tend to be called after their meeting-places. There are therefore numerous instances of *thing-stōw*, *mōt-stōw*, etc., as well as many names derived from mounds, trees and stones.[9] Not a single hundred-name contains *thorp/throp*, however, which might have been expected if this term had a special association with meeting-places. And third, it is possible to explain away Harley's *thing-stōw* once more as a characteristic 'accident' of glossary compilation. It has already been noted that Harley tends to translate some of its English glosses into Latin, but this is only one aspect of a very complex and rather muddled compilation. The glossary takes numerous previous lists of glosses, evidently including one that contained the 'conpetum, tun, þrop' item, and combines, rationalises or confuses them in various ways.[10] Thus *compitum* (in singular, plural and variant spellings) is glossed four separate times; three times the 'cross-roads' sense is rendered in different ways, the other instance is the item we have seen:[11]

> competum .i. uilla . uel þingstow . uel þrop .

It may not be beyond the bounds of possibility that the compiler inserted thing-

9   O.S. Anderson, *The English hundred-names*, 3 vols (Lund, 1934–9), 3, pp. 159–61.

10 R.T. Oliphant, *The Harley Latin–Old English glossary* (The Hague, 1966), pp. 12–19; cf. Pheifer's comments, quoted above.

11 This is Oliphant's no. C1283; the 'cross-roads' sense (e.g. 'competis ... wega gelaetum') is found in his glosses C1281, C1282 and C1350. It should be noted that Oliphant's edition is not reliable in detail (cf. the review in *Anglia* 86 (1968), pp. 495–500), but the readings of the first three glosses are confirmed by the earlier edition in T. Wright and R.P. Wülcker, *Anglo-Saxon and Old English vocabularies*, 2 vols (London, 1884), 1, p. 207, nos 10–12.

stōw into this gloss as a close equivalent for both *compitum* and *throp* (although presumably not *villa*), but in the context of combination and conflation it does not seem likely. Much more probable is that the original 'conpetum, tun, þrop' gloss has been altered by the translation of *tūn* and the addition of another gloss, probably derived from another list in which *compitum* was translated by *thing-stōw*. Many of the various sources of the Harley glossary can be traced elsewhere, but the precise source here again eludes us, if it was indeed an earlier glossary in which *compitum* was equated with *thing-stōw*. We do, however, have something closely similar. In the same eleventh-century glossary that has 'fundus, þorp' is the item:[12]

> competa, ceorla samnung, uel gemotstow.

That is to say, OE *ceorla samnung*, a 'gathering of farmers', or *gemōt-stōw* 'meeting-place'. For once there is no doubt about this gloss's origins, because it is found in a discrete batch that clearly derives from terms explained in Book XV of Isidore's *Etymologies*: in other words, it comes directly from the passage about assembly-places for rural people cited above. Isidore's work was much read and glossed in Anglo-Saxon England, and it is not unlikely that *thing-stōw* was originally a gloss added to another manuscript in exactly this same context. From there it may perhaps have been combined in the Harley glossary with the 'conpetum … þrop' item by a rather unthinking process of conflation: if *compitum* meant *throp* in one list, but *thing-stōw* in another, then the instinct to include both together may have been simply mechanical. But the conflation need not have been so thoughtless. It is possible – perhaps likely – that various stages of compilation are reflected in the final form of the glossary. If in this case the translation of *tūn* to *villa* came first then it is not beyond the bounds of possibility to suppose that the subsequent insertion of *thing-stōw* resulted from a rationalisation along the following lines: Lat *compitum* can be equated with Lat *villa*; that is to say, in English terms, it might be either *thing-stōw* (= *compitum* on the authority of Isidore) or *throp* (perceived here as a gloss on *villa*). If this interpretation – which has the merit of respecting the sense of the Lat *vel … vel* 'either … or' – were correct, then the connection between *thing-stōw* and *throp* would be anything but direct and straightforward.

In conclusion, there are reasons to doubt whether *throp* was ever understood as 'meeting-place'; and it is still less likely that it was intentionally equated with 'cross-roads'. Nothing outside this complex of glosses, in English or in cognate languages, gives clear support to either of these senses. The semantic progression 'cross-roads' > 'meeting-place' > 'hamlet, settlement' would be straightforward,

---

12 Kindschi, 'Latin–Old English glossaries', p. 135, line 10.

of course, and Lat *compitum* clearly encompasses the first two of these stages. *Throp* could, conceivably, share the semantic range of the Latin word, and extend it to encompass the sense 'hamlet'. There is, however, no real evidence for this extended sequence: these glosses are not transparent in their implications, and if anything they tend to suggest – especially in the explicit pairing of *throp* with *tūn* – that the intended sense here, as in place-names and later records of English, is basically '(small, rural) settlement'.

As an afterword, it could be suggested that the gloss with which we started ('fundus, þrop') actually provides the greatest challenge to our expectations. Like the 'competa, ceorla samnung' gloss, this certainly has its origins in Isidore's *Etymologies*. It comes from a passage which reads:[13]

> Fundus dictus quod eo fundatur vel stabiliatur patrimonium. Fundus autem et urbanem aedificium et rusticum intellegendum est.
>
> An 'estate' (*fundus*) is so called because the family's patrimony is founded (*fundare*) and established on it. Further, an estate should be taken as both one's urban and rural property.

This definition follows a sequence of types of settlement (Lat *vicus, urbs, casa, castrum*, etc.) and if the word was glossed in the context of Isidore's explanatory text, then the choice of *throp* as an equivalent for *fundus* 'estate', with the almost abstract force of 'property', would be surprising and thought-provoking. *Fundus* can also denote a single farm in Latin, but it is clearly not used that way here by Isidore. On the other hand, however, there are inconsistencies in the implications of different glosses in this collection. While the example we have seen, 'compita, ceorla samnung, uel gemotstow', must surely have been added in the context of the whole text, as the verbal and conceptual correspondences show, other items from Isidore seem to be taken out of context: Kindschi gives the example of *tramites* (literally 'paths, tracks'), glossed *waeterweg* 'water-way', where the lemma clearly derives from a section of Book XIV of the *Etymologies* in which there are no watery implications.[14] It may be, then, that although the lemma was derived from Isidore, *fundus* was here glossed out of context.

---

13   Isidore, *Etymologiarum*, ed. Lindsey, 2, Book XV, chapter 13, section 4; Barney *et al.* (eds and tr.), *The etymologies of Isidore*, p. 314.
14   Kindschi, 'Latin–Old English glossaries', p. 8.

Appendix 2

Thorps first recorded before 1300 AD

This appendix is divided into three sections. The first two list the names found within and outside the line of the Danelaw, as defined above, pp. 28–32. Note that there are entries in both sections for four 'border' counties: Bedfordshire, Buckinghamshire, Essex and Northamptonshire. Lastly comes a notice of the only *thorp* that cannot be attributed to one side or the other: by chance, this is the earliest secure instance, and plays an important part in our argument.

Under each name are given brief details of the location, the earliest spelling(s), the etymology that we have preferred, and bibliographical references. Clearly this is very abbreviated: for the problems, possibilities and nuances of the etymologies, reference should be made to the cited literature, and in some cases to discussion in our text. Note in particular that comment in this Appendix is generally restricted to the etymology of the earliest record: as discussed above, *thorps* often gain, lose or change qualifying elements, and while this is partly illustrated in the forms cited here, for reasons of space the details are not discussed. In a number of cases there are also problems of identification and of precise location: again, for the details the bibliographical references need to be chased up. Grid references are sometimes approximate, intended to be appropriate for the scale of map used in this study but not necessarily for closer regional work.

i. Danelaw

Bedfordshire
Souldrop (Souldrop) SP 9861. *Sultrop* 1196, *Sultorp* 1198
   EPNS BED & HNT, pp. 42–3, DEPN, p. 431, CDEPN, p. 560. OE *sulh* 'plough, furrow, valley'

Buckinghamshire
Castle Thorpe (Castle Thorpe) SP 7944. *Castelthorpe* 1252, *Throp* 1255
   EPNS BUC, p. 14, DEPN, p. 469, CDEPN, p. 119. Old French/Middle English *castel*

Cambridgeshire
le Thorp (Cambridge) TL 4458. *(le) Thorp* 1296–9
   EPNS CAM, p. 347. Simplex

Cumberland
Thorpe (Greystoke) NY 4431. *Thorp* 1279
   EPNS CUM, 1, p. 198, SSNNW, p. 59. Simplex

Derbyshire
Boythorpe (Chesterfield) SK 3769. *Buitorp* 1086, *Boytorp* 1185
   EPNS DRB, 2, p. 234, SSNEM, pp. 104–5, DEPN, p. 57. OE **boia* 'boy'
Hackenthorpe (Beighton) SK 4183. *Hacentorpe* 1200–18
   EPNS DRB, 2, p. 210, SSNEM, p. 127, DEPN, p. 209. ON pers.n. *Hákon*
Harlesthorpe (Clowne) SK 4975. *Tharlestropp* 1216–72 (17th), *Tharlesthorp* 1319
   EPNS DRB, 2, p. 238, SSNEM, p. 127. ON pers.n. *Thóraldr*
Ingmanthorpe (Brampton) SK 3373. *Ingemanthorp* 13th
   EPNS DRB, 2, p. 221, SSNEM, p. 128. ON pers.n. *Ingimundr* or *Ingimann*
Jordanthorpe (Norton) SK 3681. *Jurdanethorp ante* 1290
   EPNS DRB, 2, p. 284, SSNEM, p. 128. PostC pers.n. *Jourdain*
Netherthorpe (Staveley) SK 4474. *Netherthorp* 1216–72
   EPNS DRB, 2, p. 302, SSNEM, p. 130. OE *neothera*/ON *nethri* 'lower'
Netherthorpe (Killamarsh) SK 4780. *Netherthorpe* 1299
   EPNS DRB, 2, p. 274. OE *neothera*/ON *nethri* 'lower'
Northops (Ault Hucknall) SK 4765. *Nerthorp* 1257, *Northorp* 13th
   EPNS DRB, 2, p. 269. OE/ON *north* 'north'
Oakerthorpe (South Wingfield) SK 3854. *Ulkerthorpe* 1175, *Ulkerthorpe* 1154–89
   EPNS DRB, 2, pp. 335–6, SSNEM, p. 130, DEPN, p. 347. ON pers.n. *Úlfkell*
Thorpe (Thorpe) SK 1550. *Torp* 1086
   EPNS DRB, 2, p. 407, SSNEM, p. 118 (no. 1), DEPN, p. 469, CDEPN, p. 611.
   Simplex
Waterthorpe (Beighton) SK 4382. *Walterthorpe* 1276
   EPNS DRB, 2, p. 210, SSNEM, p. 133, CDEPN, p. 655. PostC pers.n. *Walter*
Westhorpe (Sawley and Wilsthorpe) SK 4731. *Westorp* 1188
   EPNS DRB, 2, pp. 499–500. OE *west*/ON *vestr* 'west'
Williamthorpe (N. Wingfield) SK 4366. *Wilelmestorp* 1086
   EPNS DRB, 2, pp. 333–4, SSNEM, p. 121. PostC pers.n. *Willelm*
Wilsthorpe (Sawley and Wilsthorpe) SK 4733. *Wiuelestorp* 1169
   EPNS DRB, 2, p. 500, SSNEM, p. 134, DEPN, p. 521. Uncertain
Woodthorpe (Holmesfield) SK 3178. *Vodethorp* c.1280
   EPNS DRB, 2, p. 265, SSNEM, p. 134. OE *wudu* 'wood'

Woodthorpe (Staveley) SK 4574. *Woesthorp* 1154–89, *Wodesthorp* 1264
  EPNS DRB, 2, p. 303, SSNEM, p. 134, DEPN, p. 532, CDEPN, p. 697. OE *wudu*
  'wood'
Woodthorpe (Woodthorpe) SK 3764. *Wodethorp* 1258
  EPNS DRB, 2, p. 337, SSNEM, p. 134. OE *wudu* 'wood'

Durham
Fulthorpe (Grindon) NZ 4124. *Fultorp* 12th
  EPNS DUR, 1, pp. 87–8, Watts, *County Durham place-names*, p. 47. OE *ful* 'foul,
  dirty'
Little Thorpe (Easington) NZ 4242. *Thorep* c.1040 (12th)
  Watts, *County Durham place-names*, p. 72, DEPN, p. 469. Simplex
Thorpe Bulmer (Hart) NZ 4535. *villata de (Nesebite) Thorp(e)* 1242–3
  EPNS DUR, 1, p. 101, Watts, *County Durham place-names*, p. 125, DEPN, p. 469.
  Simplex/place-name
Thorpe Thewles (Grindon) NZ 4023. *Torp* c.1144–9, *Thorpp' Thewles* 1265
  EPNS DUR, 1, pp. 88–9, Watts, *County Durham place-names*, p. 125, DEPN, p. 469,
  CDEPN, p. 612. Simplex
Threlthorp (Castle Eden) NZ 4237. *Threlthorp* c.1170
  Watts, 'Scandinavian settlement-names', p. 26. ON *thræll* 'slave'

Essex
Thorpe-le-Soken (Thorpe-le-Soken) TM 1822. *Torp(eia)* 1119–1202, *Torpf* 1179
  EPNS ESX, pp. 352–3, DEPN, p. 469, CDEPN, p. 612. Simplex

Huntingdonshire
Ellington Thorpe (Ellington) TL 1571. *Sybethorp* 1227, *Elyngton cum Sibethorp* 1286
  EPNS BED & HNT, pp. 239–40. ON or OE pers.n
Upthorpe (Spaldwick) TL 1272. *Upthorp(e)* 1260
  EPNS BED & HNT, p. 248. OE/ON *upp* 'up, above'

Lancashire
Cracanethorp (Lancaster) SD 5364. *Cracanethorp* 1267–8
  Ekwall, *Lancashire*, p. 247, SSNNW, p. 202, DEPN, p. 127, CDEPN, p. 164.
  Uncertain
Gawthorpe Hall (Whalley) SD 8034. *Gouthorp'* 1256 (15th), *Goukethorp* 1324
  Ekwall, *Lancashire*, p. 83, SSNNW, p. 57, DEPN, p. 194, CDEPN, p. 248. ON *gaukr*
  'cuckoo'
Thorp (Croston) SD 4720. *Torp* 1177
  Ekwall, *Lancashire*, p. 137, SSNNW, p. 59. Simplex

Thorp (Halsall) SD 4003. *Thorp* ante 1190
    Ekwall, *Lancashire*, p. 119, SSNNW, p. 59. Simplex
Thorpe (Prestwich with Oldham) SD 9108. *Thorp* 1260
    Ekwall, *Lancashire*, p. 52, SSNNW, p. 59. Simplex

Leicestershire
Barkby Thorpe (Barkby Thorpe) SK 6309. *Thorp* c.1130
    EPNS LEI, 3, p. 29, SSNEM, p. 118 (no. 3). Simplex
Beckingthorpe (Bottesford) SK 8039. *Beclingthorp* 1272–1307
    EPNS LEI, 2, p. 22, SSNEM, pp. 123–4, Cox, *Leicestershire and Rutland place-names*, p. 9. ON pers.n.?
Boothorpe (Ashby Woulds) SK 3117. *Bortrod* 1086, *Bocthorp* c.1130, *Bothorp'* 1242
    SSNEM, p. 104, Cox, *Dict. LEI & RUT*, p. 13, DEPN, p. 52. Uncertain
Brandestorp SK 5302. *Brandestorp* 1086
    SSNEM, p. 105, Cox, 'Place-names of Leicestershire and Rutland', p. 112. ON pers.n. *Brandr*
Brasthorp (Ashby de la Zouche) SK 3518. *Brastorp* 1286
    SSNEM, p. 124, Cox, 'Place-names of Leicestershire and Rutland', p. 338. ON pers.n.?
Bromkinsthorpe (Leicester) SK 5605. *Brunechinestorp* 1086
    EPNS LEI, 1, p. 218, SSNEM, p. 105, Cox, *Dict. LEI & RUT*, p. 16. OE pers.n. *Brūncyng*
Brunestanestorp (unlocated in Goscote hundred). *Brunstanestorp* c.1055 (13th), *Brunestanestorp* 1086
    SSNEM, p. 105, Cox, 'Place-names of Leicestershire and Rutland', p. 111. OE pers.n. *Brūnstān*
Bruntingthorpe (Bruntingthorpe) SP 6090. *Brandinestor* 1086, *Brentingestorp'* 1199, *Brantingthorp* 1236
    SSNEM, p. 105, Cox, *Dict. LEI & RUT*, p. 17, DEPN, p. 71. OE pers.n.?
Catthorpe (Catthorpe) SP 5578. *Torp* 1086
    SSNEM, p. 119 (no. 24), Cox, *Dict. LEI & RUT*, p. 22, DEPN, p. 91, CDEPN, p. 120. Simplex
Countesthorpe (Countesthorpe) SP 5895. *Torp* 1156 (14th), *Thorp* 1276
    SSNEM, p. 132 (no. 6), Cox, *Dict. LEI & RUT*, p. 28, DEPN, p. 125, CDEPN, p. 161. Simplex
Donisthorpe (Donisthorpe) SK 3114. *Dvrandestorp* 1086, *Durantestorp* c.1130
    SSNEM, p. 108, Cox, *Dict. LEI & RUT*, p. 31, EPNS DRB, 3, p. 651, DEPN, p. 147, CDEPN, p. 190. PostC pers.n. *Durand*
Easthorpe (Bottesford) SK 7938. *Estthorp* c.1240
    EPNS LEI, 2, p. 33, SSNEM, p. 125, Cox, *Dict. LEI & RUT*, p. 33. OE *ēast* 'east'

Edmondthorpe (Edmondthorpe) SK 8517. *Edmerestorp* 1086, *Torp* 1094–1123,
  Edmeresthorp 1344
  SSNEM, p. 108, Cox, *Dict. LEI & RUT*, p. 34, DEPN, p. 161, CDEPN, p. 209. OE
  pers.n. Ēadmǣr
Elmesthorpe (Elmesthorpe) SP 4696. *Ailmerestorp* 1199; also a *Torp* 1086 here?
  SSNEM, pp. 125–6, Cox, *Dict. LEI & RUT*, p. 34, DEPN, p. 164, CDEPN, p. 213.
  Simplex?; then OE pers.n. Æthelmǣr
Esthorp (Kirby Bellars) SK 7118. *le Esthorp* 1272–1307 (15th), *Estthorpleys* post 1250
  (15th)
  EPNS LEI 3, p. 89. OE ēast 'east'
Franethorp (Owston and Newbold) SK 7609. *Franethorp* m.13th
  SSNEM, p. 126, Cox, 'Place-names of Leicestershire and Rutland', p. 246. ON
  pers.n. *Fráni or *Frǽni
Garthorpe (Garthorpe) SK 8320. *Garthorp* c.1130
  EPNS LEI, 2, pp. 149–50, SSNEM, pp. 109–10, Cox, *Dict. LEI & RUT*, p. 39, DEPN,
  p. 193, CDEPN, p. 247. Probably OE gāra 'gore'
Godtorp (Somerby) SK 8110. *Godtorp* 1086, *Gillethorp* c.1130
  EPNS LEI, 2, p. 226, SSNEM, p. 110. OE gōd or ON góthr 'good'
Huberetorp (Osgathorpe) SK 4320. *Huberetorp* c.1200
  SSNEM, p. 128, Cox, 'Place-names of Leicestershire and Rutland', p. 390. PostC
  pers.n.?
Keythorpe (Tugby and Keythorpe) SK 7600. *Caitorp* 1086
  EPNS LEI, 3, p. 259, SSNEM, p. 112, Cox, *Dict. LEI & RUT*, p. 56, DEPN, p. 275.
  ON pers.n.?
Leesthorpe (Pickwell) SK 7913. *Lvvestorp* 1086
  EPNS LEI, 2, pp. 238–9, SSNEM, p. 113, Cox, *Dict. LEI & RUT*, p. 61, DEPN, p. 294.
  OE pers.n. Lēof or Lēofhēah
Littlethorpe (Narborough) SP 5496. *Torp* 1086
  SSNEM, p. 119 (no. 27), Cox, *Dict. LEI & RUT*, p. 64, DEPN, p. 469. Simplex
Lubbesthorpe (Lubbesthorpe) SK 5401. *Lupestorp* 1086
  SSNEM, p. 113, Cox, *Dict. LEI & RUT*, p. 65, DEPN, p. 306. OE pers.n. *Lubb
Midulthorp (Kirby Bellars) SK 7217. *middilthorpleys* m.13th (15th), *le Midulthorp* 1400
  (15th)
  EPNS LEI, 3, p. 91. OE middel 'middle'
Netherthorp (Little Dalby) SK 7714. *Netherthorp* 13th (1404), *Torpmilnemeduwe* 1271
  (15th)
  EPNS LEI, 2, p. 87. OE neothera/ON nethri 'lower'
Northorp (Hathern) SK 5022. *Northorp* 1276
  Wagner, *Studies*, p. 162. OE/ON north 'north'
Northorp (Thurmaston) SK 6109. *Northorp* 1298

EPNS LEI, 3, p. 242. OE/ON *north* 'north'

Oakthorpe (Oakthorpe) SK 3213. *Achetorp* 1086

SSNEM, p. 114, Cox, *Dict. LEI & RUT*, p. 75, EPNS DRB 3, pp. 650–1, DEPN, p. 347, CDEPN, p. 448. Uncertain

Oddestorp (Medbourne) SP 8093. *Oddestorp* 13th

EPNS LEI, 4, p. 195. ON pers.n. *Oddr*

Osgathorpe (Osgathorpe) SK 4219. *Osgodtorp* 1086

SSNEM, pp. 114–15, Cox, *Dict. LEI & RUT*, pp. 77–8, DEPN, p. 352, CDEPN, pp. 453–4. ON pers.n. *Ásgautr*

Othorpe (Slawston) SP 7795. *Actorp* 1086

SSNEM, p. 114, Cox, *Dict. LEI & RUT*, p. 78, DEPN, p. 352. Uncertain

Primethorpe (Broughton Astley) SP 5293. *Torp* 1086

SSNEM, p. 119 (no. 31), Cox, *Dict. LEI & RUT*, p. 82, DEPN, p. 374, CDEPN, p. 483. Simplex

Redmyldthorp (Redmile) SK 7935. *Redmylthorp* 1252

EPNS LEI, 2, pp. 196–7, SSNEM, pp. 130–1. Place-name Redmile

Ringlethorpe (Scalford) SK 7723. *Ricoltorp* 1086, *Ringolfestorp* c.1130

EPNS LEI, 2, pp. 208–9, SSNEM, pp. 115–16, Cox, *Dict. LEI & RUT*, p. 85. Pers.n., uncertain language

Shelthorpe (Loughborough) SK 5418. *Serlesthorp* 1284

SSNEM, p. 131, Cox, *Dict. LEI & RUT*, p. 92. PostC pers.n. Serlo

Sowtorp' (Great Bowden) SP 7488. *Sowtorp'* post 1250

EPNS LEI, 4, p. 183. OE/ON *sūth(r)* 'south'

Thorp (Croxton Kerrial) SK 8329. *thorp* 1272–1307; cf. *Thorpdalebec* e.13th

EPNS LEI, 2, p. 109. Simplex

Thorp on le Toftis (Belgrave) SK 5907. *Thorp on le Toftis* 1278

EPNS LEI, 3, pp. 52–3. Simplex

Thorpe Acre (Loughborough) SK 5120. *Torp* 1086

SSNEM, p. 118 (no. 7), Cox, *Dict. LEI & RUT*, p. 104, DEPN, p. 469, CDEPN, p. 611. Simplex

Thorpe Arnold (Waltham) SK 7620. *Torp* 1086

EPNS LEI, 2, pp. 277–8, SSNEM, p. 118 (no. 8), Cox, *Dict. LEI & RUT*, p. 104, DEPN, p. 469, CDEPN, p. 611. Simplex

Thorpe Langton (Thorpe Langton) SP 7492. *Torp* 1086

SSNEM, p. 119 (no. 13), Cox, *Dict. LEI & RUT*, p. 104, DEPN, p. 469, CDEPN, p. 612. Simplex

Thorpe Satchville (Thorpe Satchville) SK 7311. *Thorp* c.1130

EPNS LEI, 3, pp. 263–4, SSNEM, p. 119 (no. 18), Cox, *Dict. LEI & RUT*, p. 104, DEPN, p. 469, CDEPN, p. 612. Simplex

Ullesthorpe (Ullesthorpe) SP 5087. *Vlestorp* 1086

SSNEM, p. 120, Cox, *Dict. LEI & RUT*, p. 108, DEPN, p. 486, CDEPN, p. 636. ON pers.n. Úlfr

Westhorp (Coston) SK 8422. *Westhorp* 1268

Wagner, *Studies*, p. 191. OE *west*/ON *vestr* 'west'

Westhorp (Garthorpe) SK 8321. *Westhorp* 1268

    EPNS LEI, 2, p. 155. OE *west*/ON *vestr* 'west'

Westthorpe (Bottesford) SK 8038. *Westorp'* 1249

    EPNS LEI, 2, p. 23. OE *west*/ON *vestr* 'west'

Wifeles Ðorpe (Breedon on the Hill) SK 4022. *Wifeles Ðorpe* 972 (13th)

    SSNEM, p. 121, Cox, 'Place-names of Leicestershire and Rutland', p. 350. Uncertain

Woodthorpe (Loughborough) SK 5417. *Torp* 1236, *Wudetorp* 1253, *Torpmontford* 13th

    SSNEM, p. 133 (no. 13), Cox, *Dict. LEI & RUT*, p. 116, CDEPN, p. 697. Simplex

Lincolnshire

Ackthorpe (South Elkington) TF 3089. *Achetorp* 1154–89 (14th)

    SSNEM, p. 122, Cameron, *Dict. LIN*, p. 1. ON pers.n.?

Addlethorpe (Addlethorpe) TF 5469. *Arduluetorp, Herdertorp* 1086

    SSNEM, p. 101, Cameron, *Dict. LIN*, p. 1, DEPN, p. 3, CDEPN, p. 4. OE pers.n. *Eardwulf*

Aisthorpe (Aisthorpe) SK 9480. *Estorp, Æstorp* 1086, *Esttorp* 1115

    SSNEM, p. 101, Cameron, *Dict. LIN*, p. 1, DEPN, p. 4, CDEPN, p. 5. OE *ēast* 'east'

Althorpe (Keadrby with Althorpe) SE 8309. *Aletorp* 1086, *Aletorp* 1067–9 (12th)

    SSNEM, pp. 101–2, Cameron, *Dict. LIN*, p. 2, DEPN, p. 8, CDEPN, p. 11. ON pers.n. Áli or Alli

Authorpe (Authorpe) TF 4080. *Agetorp* 1086

    SSNEM, p. 102, Cameron, *Dict. LIN*, p. 7, DEPN, p. 19, CDEPN, p. 27. ON pers.n. Ag(h)i

Authorpe (Mumby) TF 5373. *Aghetorp* c.1115

    SSNEM, p. 102, Cameron, *Dict. LIN*, p. 7, DEPN, p. 19, CDEPN, p. 27. ON pers.n. Ag(h)i

Avethorpe (Aslackby) TF 0629. *Avetorp* 1086

    SSNEM, p. 102, Cameron, *Dict. LIN*, p. 8. ON pers.n. Afi

Bainthorpe (Baumber) TF 2375. *Baintorp* 13th (14th)

    SSNEM, p. 123. River-name Bain

Banthorpe (Braceborough) TF 0611. *Barnetorp* 1086

    SSNEM, p. 102, Cameron, *Dict. LIN*, p. 9. ON pers.n.?

Bassingthorpe (Bitchfield) SK 9628. *Torp* 1086

    SSNEM, p. 119 (no. 22), Cameron, *Dict. LIN*, p. 11, DEPN, p. 30, CDEPN, p. 41. Simplex

Birthorpe (Billingborough) TF 1033. *Berchetorp* 1086, *Birkethorp* 1192
  SSNEM, p. 103, Cameron, *Dict. LIN*, p. 15, DEPN, p. 45. ON *birki* 'birch copse'
Biscathorpe (Biscathorpe) TF 2384. *Biscopetorp* 1086
  SSNEM, pp. 103–4, Cameron, *Dict. LIN*, p. 15, DEPN, p. 45. OE *biscop*/ON *biskup* 'bishop'
Bonthorpe (Willoughby with Sloothby) TF 4872. *Brvnetorp* 1086, *Burnetorp* c.1115, *Bruntorp* 1212
  SSNEM, p. 104, Cameron, *Dict. LIN*, p. 16, DEPN, p. 52. ON pers.n.?
Bowthorpe (Toft with Lound and Manthorpe) TF 0615. *Bergestorp* 1086, *Buretorp* 1201, *Bourthorp* 1323
  SSNEM, p. 104. Uncertain
Bredestorp TF 0116. *Bredestorp* 1086, *Breidestorp* c.1100
  SSNEM, p. 105, SPNLY, p. 64. ON pers.n. *Breiðr*
Buslingthorpe (Buslingthorpe) TF 0885. *Esetorp* 1086, *Esatorp* c.1115, *Buslingthorpa* 12th
  SSNEM, p. 105, Cameron, *Dict. LIN*, p. 24, DEPN, p. 78. OE/ON pers.n.?
Calcethorpe (Calcethorpe) TF 2488. *Torp* 1086, *Cheilestorp* c.1115
  SSNEM, p. 119 (no. 23), Cameron, *Dict. LIN*, p. 27, DEPN, p. 81. Simplex
Casthorpe (Barrowby) SK 8635. *Kaschingetorp* 1086, *Chaschintorp* 1086
  SSNEM, p. 106, Cameron, *Dict. LIN*, p. 29, DEPN, p. 89, SPNLY, pp. 162–3. Pers.n.; uncertain language
Castlethorpe (Broughton) SE 9807. *Castorp* 1086, *Cheistorp* c.1115
  EPNS LIN, 1, pp. 28–9, SSNEM, p. 106, Cameron, *Dict. LIN*, p. 29, DEPN, p. 89. ON pers.n.?
Cawthorpe (Bourne) TF 0922. *Caletorp* 1086
  SSNEM, p. 106, Cameron, *Dict. LIN*, p. 30, DEPN, p. 92. ON pers.n.? Cf. above, p. 56
Cawthorpe (Little Cawthorpe) TF 3583. *Calethorp* c.1150, *Carletorp* 1205, *Calthorp* 1241
  SSNEM, p. 124, Cameron, *Dict. LIN*, p. 30, DEPN, p. 92. ON pers.n.? Cf. above, p. 56
Cawthorpe (Covenham St Bartholomew) TF 3395. *Caletorp* c.1115, *Calthorp* 1100–15 (13th)
  EPNS LIN, 4, p. 6, SSNEM, p. 106, DEPN, p. 92. ON pers.n.? Cf. above, p. 56
Caythorpe (Caythorpe) SK 9348. *Catorp* 1086, *Carltorp* 1086, *Cattorp* 1190
  SSNEM, pp. 106–7, Cameron, *Dict. LIN*, p. 30, DEPN, p. 92, CDEPN, p. 122. ON pers.n.? Cf. above, p. 65, n. 12
Claythorpe (Belleau) TF 4179. *Clactorp* 1086, *Clactorp* 1202
  SSNEM, p. 107, Cameron, *Dict. LIN*, p. 30, DEPN, p. 110. ON pers.n.?
Counthorpe (Castle Bytham) TF 0020. *Cudetorp* 1086, *Cunctorp* 1191, *Cunitorp* 1219
  SSNEM, p. 107, Cameron, *Dict. LIN*, pp. 33–4, DEPN, p. 125. Uncertain

Culverthorpe (Culverthorpe) TF 0240. *Torp* 1086
   SSNEM, p. 119 (no. 25), Cameron, *Dict. LIN*, p. 36, DEPN, p. 136, CDEPN, p. 175.
   Simplex

Derrythorpe (Keadrby with Althorpe) SE 8208. *Dudingthorp'* c.1184 (15th), *Dodithorp'*
   1263
   SSNEM, p. 125, Cameron, *Dict. LIN*, p. 38, DEPN, p. 142, CDEPN, pp. 184–5. OE
   pers.n. *Dodding

Dexthorpe (Dalby) TF 4071. *Dristorp* 1086, *Drextorp* c.1180, *Draaistorp'* 1208
   SSNEM, pp. 107–8, Cameron, *Dict. LIN*, p. 388, DEPN, p. 143. ON pers.n.?

Dunsthorpe (Old Somerby) SK 9235. *Dunetorp* 1086, *Dunesthorp* 1173–4, *Dunnestorp'*
   1231
   SSNEM, p. 108. OE pers.n. *Dunn*

Dunsthorpe (Hameringham) TF 3068. *Dunstorp* 1154–89
   SSNEM, p. 125. OE pers.n. *Dunn*

Easthorpe Court (Wigtoft) TF 2636. *esttorph'* c.1190 (13th)
   SSNEM, p. 125. OE *ēast* 'east'

Elsthorpe (Edenham) TF 0523. *Aiglestorp* 1086, *Eylestorp'* 1212, *Eylesthorp* 1242–3
   SSNEM, p. 108, Cameron, *Dict. LIN*, p. 41, DEPN, p. 165. OE or PostC pers.n

Ewerby Thorpe (Ewerby) TF 1347. *Oustorp* 1086, *Oustorp* c.1160, *Torp* 1219
   SSNEM, pp. 108–9, Cameron, *Dict. LIN*, p. 42, DEPN, p. 170. ON *austr* 'east'

Fanthorpe (Louth) TF 3289. *Falmethorp* 1212
   SSNEM, p. 126, Cameron, *Dict. LIN*, p. 43, DEPN, p. 173. Uncertain

Farlesthorpe (Farlesthorpe) TF 4774. *Farlestorp* 1160–75
   SSNEM, p. 126, Cameron, *Dict. LIN*, p. 43, DEPN, p. 174, CDEPN, p. 224. ON
   pers.n. *Faraldr* or *Farúlfr*

Fenthorpe (Leake) TF 4249. *Fenthorp'* e.13th (14th)
   SSNEM, p. 126. OE *fenn* 'fen'

Friesthorpe (Friesthorpe) TF 0683. *Frisetorp* 1086, *Frisatorp* c.1115
   SSNEM, p. 109, Cameron, *Dict. LIN*, p. 46, DEPN, p. 188, CDEPN, p. 241. OE/ON
   Frīsa/Frīsir 'Frisians'

Gainsthorpe (Hibaldstow) SE 9501. *Gamelstorp* 1086, *Gainestorp* 1156–7, *Gamelestorp*
   1179–80
   EPNS LIN, 1, p. 70, SSNEM, p. 109, Cameron, *Dict. LIN*, p. 49, DEPN, p. 191. ON
   pers.n. *Gamall*

Ganthorpe (Gt Ponton and Stoke Rochford) SK 9229. *Germuntorp* 1086
   SSNEM, p. 109, DEPN, p. 192, SPNLY, p. 99. ON/PostC pers.n

Garthorpe (Garthorpe) SE 8419. *Gerulftorp* 1086
   SSNEM, p. 109, Cameron, *Dict. LIN*, p. 49, DEPN, p. 193, CDEPN, p. 247.
   ON/PostC pers.n

Grainthorpe (Grainthorpe) TF 3896. *Germundstorp* 1086

SSNEM, p. 109, Cameron, *Dict. LIN*, p. 52, DEPN, p. 202, CDEPN, p. 258. ON/PostC pers.n

Grimblethorpe (Gayton le Wold) TF 2386. *Grimchiltorp* c.1115
SSNEM, pp. 110–11, Cameron, *Dict. LIN*, p. 54, DEPN, p. 205. ON pers.n. *Grímkell*

Grimsthorpe (Edenham) TF 0423. *Grimestorpe* 1166
SSNEM, p. 127, Cameron, *Dict. LIN*, p. 54, DEPN, p. 206, CDEPN, p. 263. ON pers.n. *Grímr*

Gunthorpe (Owston) SK 8096. *Gunetorp* c.1200
SSNEM, p. 127, Cameron, *Dict. LIN*, p. 55, DEPN, p. 208. ON pers.n. *Gunni*

Hanthorpe (Morton) TF 0824. *Hermodestorp* 1086
SSNEM, p. 111, Cameron, *Dict. LIN*, p. 58, DEPN, p. 217, CDEPN, p. 277. ON pers.n. *Hermóthr*

Hasthorpe (Willoughby in the Marsh) TF 4869. *Haroldestorp* 1086
SSNEM, p. 111, Cameron, *Dict. LIN*, p. 60, DEPN, p. 224. ON pers.n. *Haraldr*

Hawthorpe (Irnham) TF 0427. *Auuartorp* 1086
SSNEM, p. 111, Cameron, *Dict. LIN*, p. 61, DEPN, p. 227. ON pers.n. *Hávarthr*

Helethorpe (Rand) TF 1079. *Helghetorp* 1212
SSNEM, p. 128, SPNLY, p. 138. ON pers.n. *Helgi*

Hogsthorpe (Hogsthorpe) TF 5372. *Hocgestorp* 1173–82, *Hoggestorp* 1195
SSNEM, p. 128, Cameron, *Dict. LIN*, p. 64, DEPN, p. 244, CDEPN, p. 308. OE pers.n.?

Kettleby Thorpe (Bigby) TA 0407. *Torp* 1086
EPNS LIN, 2, pp. 49–50, SSNEM, p. 118 (no. 4), Cameron, *Dict. LIN*, p. 73, DEPN, p. 274. Simplex

Kettlethorpe (Kettlethorpe) SK 8475. *Ketlethorp'* c.1225 (14th)
SSNEM, p. 128, Cameron, *Dict. LIN*, p. 73, DEPN, p. 274, CDEPN, p. 343. ON pers.n. *Ketill*

Kingthorpe (Apley) TF 1375. *Chinetorp* 1086
SSNEM, p. 112, Cameron, *Dict. LIN*, p. 74, DEPN, p. 278. OE *cyne*- 'royal'

Langton Thorpe (Woodhall) TF 2268. *Torp* 1086
SSNEM, p. 118 (no. 5). Simplex

Laysingthorpe (Scremby) TF 4467. *Laisingtorp* 1208
SSNEM, p. 129, SPNLY, p. 186. ON pers.n.?

Laythorpe (Kirkby la Thorpe) TF 0945. *Ledulvetorp* 1086
SSNEM, p. 113, Cameron, *Dict. LIN*, p. 79. ON pers.n. *Leithúlfr*

Lobthorpe (N. Witham) SK 9520. *Lopintorp* 1086
SSNEM, p. 113, Cameron, *Dict. LIN*, p. 81, DEPN, p. 302. ON pers.n.?

Londonthorpe (Londonthorpe) SK 9537. *Lundertorp* 1086
SSNEM, p. 113, Cameron, *Dict. LIN*, p. 81, DEPN, p. 303, CDEPN, p. 379. ON *lundr* 'grove'

Mablethorpe (Mablethorpe) TF 5085. *Malbertorp* 1086
  SSNEM, p. 114, Cameron, *Dict.* LIN, p. 85, DEPN, p. 310, CDEPN, p. 392. PostC
  pers.n. *Malbert*

Manthorpe (Toft) TF 0716. *æt Mannethorp* c.1067 (12th), *Mannetorp* 1086
  SSNEM, p. 114, Cameron, *Dict.* LIN, p. 86, DEPN, p. 313, CDEPN, p. 396.
  Uncertain. See above, p. 57, n. 64

Manthorpe (Belton) SK 9339. *Mannetorp* 1185
  SSNEM, p. 129, Cameron, *Dict.* LIN, p. 86, DEPN, p. 313, CDEPN, p. 396.
  Uncertain. See above, p. 57, n. 64

Mawthorpe (Willoughby in the Marsh) TF 4673. *Malthorp* 1242–3, *Mauthorp* 1251
  SSNEM, p. 129, Cameron, *Dict.* LIN, p. 87, DEPN, p. 318. ON pers.n.?

Millthorpe (Pointon) TF 1131. *Milnetorp'* late 12th, *Milnetorp* 1202
  SSNEM, pp. 129–30, Cameron, *Dict.* LIN, p. 88, DEPN, p. 326. OE *myln*

Northorpe (Halton Holgate) TF 4365. *Northorp'* 1295
  Cameron, *Dict.* LIN, pp. 92–3. OE/ON *north* 'north'

Northorpe (Northorpe) SK 8996. *Đorp* 1061–66 (12th), *Torp* 1086
  SSNEM, p. 119 (no. 29a), Cameron, *Dict.* LIN, p. 93, DEPN, p. 344, CDEPN, p. 442.
  Simplex

Northorpe (Thurlby) TF 0917. *Nortorp* 1202
  Cameron, *Dict.* LIN, pp. 92–3, CDEPN, p. 442. OE/ON *north* 'north'

Obthorpe (Thurlby) TF 0915. *Opestorp* 1086, *Obthorp'* 1075 (14th)
  SSNEM, p. 114, Cameron, *Dict.* LIN, p. 94. OE or ON pers.n

Raventhorpe (Holme) SE 9308. *Ragnaldtorp* 1067 (12th), *Rageneltorp* 1086
  EPNS LIN, 6, pp. 75–6, SSNEM, p. 115, Cameron, *Dict.* LIN, p. 101, DEPN, p. 382.
  ON pers.n. *Ragnaldr*

Ringsthorpe (Barkston) SK 9241. *Riggestorp* 13th, *Ringstorp* 1316
  SSNEM, p. 131, SPNLY, pp. 226–7. Uncertain

Sausthorpe (Sausthorpe) TF 3869. *Saustorp* 1175, *Saltorp* 1154–89
  SSNEM, p. 131, Cameron, *Dict.* LIN, p. 106, DEPN, p. 405, CDEPN, p. 529. ON
  pers.n.?

Scotterthorpe (Scotter) SE 8701. *Scalkestorpe* 1067–9 (12th), *Scaltorp* 1086
  SSNEM, p. 116, Cameron, *Dict.* LIN, p. 107, DEPN, p. 408, CDEPN, p. 532. ON
  pers.n.?

Scottlethorpe (Edenham) TF 0521. *Scachertorp* 1086, *Scotelthorp* c.1150
  SSNEM, p. 116, Cameron, *Dict.* LIN, p. 107, DEPN, p. 408. Uncertain

Scremthorpe (Bratoft) TF 4964. *Scremtorp* 1212, *Scripinthorp* 1281
  SSNEM, p. 131, DEPN, p. 409. Uncertain

Scunthorpe (Scunthorpe) SE 8910. *Escumetorp* 1086
  EPNS LIN, 1, pp. 59–60, SSNEM, p. 117, Cameron, *Dict.* LIN, p. 108, DEPN, p. 409,
  CDEPN, p. 533. ON pers.n. *Skúma*

Shillingthorpe Hall (Braceborough) TF 0711. *Scheldintorp* 1193
    SSNEM, p. 131, Cameron, *Dict. LIN*, p. 109, DEPN, p. 417. ON pers.n.?
Southorpe (Northorpe) SK 8895. *altero Torp* 1086
    SSNEM, p. 119 (no. 29b), Cameron, *Dict. LIN*, p. 114, DEPN, p. 432. Simplex
Southorpe (Edenham) TF 0622. *Sudtorp* 1086
    SSNEM, p. 117, DEPN, p. 432. OE/ON *sūth(r)* 'south'
Southorpe (Gayton le Wold) TF 2485. *Suthorp* 1150–60
    SSNEM, p. 132. OE/ON *sūth(r)* 'south'
Springthorpe (Springthorpe) SK 8789. *Springetorp* 1086
    SSNEM, p. 117, Cameron, *Dict. LIN*, p. 115, DEPN, p. 435, CDEPN, p. 565. OE
    spring 'spring' or 'copse'
Stragglethorpe (Brant Broughton) SK 9152. *Stragerthorp'* late 12th, *Tragetorp* 1212,
    Stragerthorp 1242
    SSNEM, p. 132, Cameron, *Dict. LIN*, p. 118, DEPN, p. 449, CDEPN, p. 584. PostC
    pers.n.?
Swinethorpe (Eagle) SK 8769. *Suenestorp* 1181, *Sueinestorp* 1196
    SSNEM, p. 132, Cameron, *Dict. LIN*, p. 122, DEPN, p. 457. ON pers.n.?
Swinthorpe (Snelland) TF 0680. *Sonetorp* 1086
    SSNEM, pp. 117–18, Cameron, *Dict. LIN*, p. 122, DEPN, p. 457. ON pers.n. Súni
Tattershall Thorpe (Tattershall Thorpe) TF 2159. *Torp* 1086
    SSNEM, p. 118 (no. 6), Cameron, *Dict. LIN*, p. 123, CDEPN, p. 613. Simplex
Theddlethorpe (Theddlethorpe) TF 4688. *Tedlagestorp* 1086
    SSNEM, p. 118, Cameron, *Dict. LIN*, p. 124, DEPN, p. 456, CDEPN, p. 607. OE or
    ON pers.n
Thoresthorpe (Saleby) TF 4577. *Thuorstorp* 1086
    SSNEM, p. 118, Cameron, *Dict. LIN*, p. 125, DEPN, p. 466. ON pers.n. Thórir
Thorpe (Trusthorpe) TF 4982. *Fugelestorp* 1210
    SSNEM, pp. 126–7, Cameron, *Dict. LIN*, p. 126, CDEPN, p. 611. OE or ON pers.n.?
Thorpe in the Fallows (Thorpe in the Fallows) SK 9080. *Torp* 1086, *Turuluestorp*
    c.1115
    SSNEM, p. 118 (no. 10), Cameron, *Dict. LIN*, p. 126, DEPN, p. 469, CDEPN, p. 612.
    Simplex
Thorpe Latimer (Helpringham) TF 1339. *Torp* 1199–1214, *Torp* 1203
    SSNEM, p. 132 (no. 1), Cameron, *Dict. LIN*, p. 126, DEPN, p. 469. Simplex
Thorpe le Vale (Ludford Magna) TF 2090. *Fruntorp'* 1160–70, *Thorp* 1335
    SSNEM, p. 133, Cameron, *Dict. LIN*, pp. 126–7, DEPN, p. 469. Uncertain
Thorpe on the Hill (Thorpe on the Hill) SK 9065. *Torp* 1086
    SSNEM, p. 119 (no. 12), Cameron, *Dict. LIN*, p. 126, DEPN, p. 469, CDEPN, p. 612.
    Simplex
Thorpe Parva (Westborough) SK 8544. *Parua Thorp* 13th, *Thorp* 1316

SSNEM, p. 132 (no. 2). Simplex

Thorpe St Peter (Thorpe St Peter) TF 4861. *Torp* 1086

  SSNEM, p. 119 (no. 17), Cameron, *Dict. LIN*, p. 126, DEPN, p. 469, CDEPN, p. 612. Simplex

Thorpe Tilney (Timberland) TF 1157. *Torp* 1170

  SSNEM, p. 132 (no. 3), Cameron, *Dict. LIN*, p. 127, DEPN, p. 469. Simplex

Thorpfeld (Bishop Norton) SK 9892. *Thorpfeld* post 1240, *thorpfeld* 1348–9

  EPNS LIN, 6, p. 198. Qualifier suggesting lost simplex

Torp (Low Langton) TF 1576. *Torp* 1086

  SSNEM, p. 118 (no. 2). Simplex

Towthorpe (Londonthorpe) SK 9238. *Tuuetorp* 1086

  SSNEM, p. 120, SPNLY, pp. 285–6. ON pers.n. *Tófi*

Trusthorpe (Trusthorpe) TF 5183. *Druistorp* 1086, *Struttorp'* 1196

  SSNEM, p. 120, Cameron, *Dict. LIN*, pp. 129–30, DEPN, p. 481, CDEPN, p. 630. PostC pers.n.?

Upperthorpe (Haxey) SE 7500. *Hubaldestorp* 1086, *Ouerthorp* 1331

  SSNEM, pp. 120–1, Cameron, *Dict. LIN*, p. 131, DEPN, p. 487. OE or PostC pers.n

Westhorpe (Somerby) SK 9633. *Westorp* 1086

  SSNEM, p. 121. OE *west*/ON *vestr* 'west'

Willingthorpe (Lincoln) SK 9772. *Willigtorp* 1126

  EPNS LIN, 1, p. 46, SSNEM, p. 134. OE *wilign* 'willow'

Wilsthorpe (Braceborough) TF 0913. *Wiuelestorp* 1086

  SSNEM, p. 121, Cameron, *Dict. LIN*, p. 140, DEPN, p. 521, CDEPN, p. 682. Uncertain

Winthorpe (Winthorpe) TF 5665. *Winetorp* 1154–89, *Wintorp* 1175–81

  SSNEM, p. 134, Cameron, *Dict. LIN*, p. 141, DEPN, p. 525, CDEPN, p. 688. OE pers.n. *Wine*

Woodthorpe (Woodthorpe) TF 4380. *Endretorp* 1086, *Wdetorp* 1147, *Wudetorp* 1181–2

  SSNEM, p. 121, Cameron, *Dict. LIN*, p. 143, DEPN, p. 532. ON pers.n.?

Woolsthorpe (Woolsthorpe) SK 8334. *Ulestanestorp* 1086

  SSNEM, pp. 121–2, Cameron, *Dict. LIN*, p. 132, DEPN, p. 533. OE pers.n. *Wulfstān*

Woolsthorpe (Colsterworth) SK 9224. *Wolestorp* 1185

  SSNEM, pp. 134–5, Cameron, *Dict. LIN*, p. 143, DEPN, p. 533. OE pers.n.?

Yaddlethorpe (Bottesford) SE 8806. *Iadulftorp* 1086

  EPNS LIN, 6, p. 23, SSNEM, p. 122, Cameron, *Dict. LIN*, p. 146 (addendum), DEPN, p. 542, CDEPN, p. 708. OE pers.n. *Ēadwulf*

Yawthorpe (Corringham) SK 8992. *Iolestorp* 1086

  SSNEM, p. 122, Cameron, *Dict. LIN*, p. 146, DEPN, p. 543. ON pers.n. *Jóli*

Norfolk

Alethorpe (Alethorpe) TF 9431. *Alatorp* 1086
  DEPN, p. 6, SPNN, p. 13. ON pers.n. *Áli*

Algarsthorpe (Great Melton) TG 1408. *Eskeresthorp* c.1050 (13th), *Asgarsthorp* 1279
  SPNN, p. 43. ON pers.n. *Ásgeirr*

Althorpe (Billockby) TG 4213. *Althorpe* c.1300
  EPNS NFK, 2, p. 49. Perhaps OE *ald* 'old'

Appethorp (unlocated). *Appethorp* 1086
  SPNN, p. 17. ON pers.n. *Api*

Ashwellthorpe (Ashwellthorpe) TM 1497. *at Thorp* c.1050 (13th), *Torp* 1086, *Aissewellethorp* 1254
  DEPN, p. 16, CDEPN, p. 23. Simplex

Baconsthorpe (Baconsthorpe). TG 1236. *Torp* 1086, *Bacunestorp* 1203
  EPNS NFK, 3, p. 54; cf. DEPN, p. 21, CDEPN, p. 30. Simplex

Baconsthorpe Farm (in Shropham hundred) TM 0495. *Baconstorp* 1086
  DB, *Norfolk*, 4, 46; cf. DEPN, p. 21, CDEPN, p. 30. PostC pers.n. (surname) *Bacun*

Bagthorpe (Bagthorpe) TF 7932. *Bachestorp* 1086, *Bagetorp* 1198
  DEPN, p. 23, SPNN, pp. 93–4, CDEPN, p. 32. ON or OE pers.n

Besthorpe (Besthorpe) TM 0595. *Besthorp* 1086
  DEPN, p. 40, Fellows-Jensen, 'East Anglia', pp. 52–3, CDEPN, p. 53. ON pers.n.?

Bowthorpe (Bowthorpe) TG 1709. *Boethorp, Bowethorp* 1086
  DEPN, p. 56, CDEPN, p. 75, SPNN, p. 97. OE *boga*/ON *bogi* 'bow, bend'

Boythorp (Bacton) TG 3333. *Boytorp* 1183
  EPNS NFK, 2, p. 138. OE **boia* 'boy'

Broomsthorpe (Broomsthorpe) TF 8528. *Brunestor* 1086, *Brunestorp* 1198
  DEPN, p. 69. OE pers.n. *Brūn*

Burnham Thorpe (Burnham Thorpe) TF 8541. *Bruneham torp* 1086, *Brunhamtorp* 1199
  DEPN, p. 76, CDEPN, p. 613. Place-name

Calthorpe (Calthorpe) TG 1831. *Caletorp* 1086
  EPNS NFK, 3, pp. 68–9, DEPN, p. 83, SPNN, p. 244, CDEPN, p. 111. ON pers.n.? Cf. above, p. 56

Carboistorp (unlocated). *Carboistorp* 1086
  SPNN, p. 248, Fellows-Jensen, 'East Anglia', p. 54. ON pers.n.?

Clakesthorp (Matlask) TG 1534. *Clakesthorp* 1300
  EPNS NFK, 3, p. 23. ON pers.n. *Klakkr*

Cleythorpe (Cockley Cley) TF 7903. *Cleietorpa* 1086
  DB, *Norfolk*, 21, 14. Place-name

Clipestorp (Bale) TG 0136. *Clipestorp* 1198
  EPNS NFK, 3, p. 112, SPNN, p. 268. ON pers.n. *Klyppr*

Cockthorpe (Cockthorpe) TF 9842. *Torp* 1086, *Coketorp* 1254
    DEPN, p. 115, CDEPN, p. 148. Simplex

Crownthorpe (Crownthorpe) TG 0803. *Congrethorp* 1086
    DEPN, p. 133, CDEPN, p. 172. Uncertain

Custthorpe TF 7813. *Culestorpa* 1086
    DB, *Norfolk*, 22, 7. Uncertain

Dikethorp (Dykebeck) TG 0901. *Dikethorp, In hidichetorp* 1086
    Fellows-Jensen, 'East Anglia', p. 54. Uncertain

Edingthorpe (Edingthorpe) TG 3233. *Ædidestorp* 1177
    EPNS NFK, 2, pp. 153–4, DEPN, p. 160, CDEPN, p. 209. OE (fem.) pers.n. Ēadgȳth

Felthorpe (Felthorpe) TG 1617. *Felet(h)orp* 1086
    DEPN, p. 177, CDEPN, p. 228. OE pers.n.?

Flockthorpe (Hardingham) TG 0304. *Flokethorp* 1086
    DEPN, p. 182, SPNN, p. 123. ON pers.n. Flóki

Fodderstone (in Clacklose hundred) TF 6509. *Photestorp* 1086
    DB, *Norfolk*, 15, 2, SPNN, pp. 125–6. OE or ON pers.n.?

Freethorpe (Freethorpe) TG 4005. *Frietorp* 1086
    DEPN, p. 187, SPNN, p. 127, Fellows-Jensen, 'East Anglia', p. 54, CDEPN, p. 240. ON pers.n.?

Gasthorpe (Gasthorpe) TL 9881. *Gadesthorp* 1086
    DEPN, p. 193, CDEPN, p. 247, SPNN, p. 128. ON pers.n. Gaddr

Gayton Thorpe (Gayton Thorpe) TF 7418. *Torp* 1086, *Aylswiththorp* 1316, *Geytonthorp* 1401–2
    DEPN, p. 194, CDEPN, p. 613. Simplex

Glosthorpe (Ashwicken) TF 6918. *Glorestorp* 1086
    DEPN, p. 199, Fellows-Jensen, 'East Anglia', p. 54. OE or ON pers.n

Gowthorpe (Swardeston) TG 2002. *Goutestorp'* 1198
    SPNN, p. 133. ON pers.n. Gauti

Gunthorpe (Gunthorpe) TG 0134. *Gunatorp* 1086
    EPNS NFK, 3, pp. 125–6, DEPN, p. 208, SPNN, p. 165, CDEPN, p. 266. ON pers.n. Gunni

Hardgrimestorp (Gunthorpe) TG 0135. *Hardgrimestorp* 13th
    EPNS NFK, 3, p. 126, SPNN, p. 197. ON or Anglo-Scand. pers.n

Honingham Thorpe (Honingham) TG 1111. *Thorp* 1086
    DB, *Norfolk*, 4, 9. Simplex

Ingoldisthorpe (Ingoldisthorpe) TF 6832. *In evlvesthorp, Torp* 1086, *Inguluesthorp* 1101–7 (14th)
    DEPN, p. 265, CDEPN, p. 332, SPNN, p. 229. ON pers.n. Ingólfr

Kinesthorpe (Buxton) TG 2322. *Kinestorp* 1199
    EPNS NFK, 3, p. 67. OE pers.n.?

Morningthorpe (Morningthorpe) TM 2192. *Torp, Maringatorp* 1086
  DEPN, p. 469, CDEPN, p. 422. Lost place-name *Marings?* See above, p. 45, n. 26
Pensthorpe (Pensthorpe) TF 9429. *Penestorpa* 1086, *Pengestorp* 1254
  DEPN, pp. 362–3. Uncertain
Pockthorpe (Pockthorpe) TG 2308. *Poketorp* 1203
  EPNS NFK, 1, p. 20. OE *pūca* 'goblin'
Poketorp (Filby) TG 4613. *at Thorpe* c.1020–50 (13th), *Poketorp* 1202
  EPNS NFK, 2, p. 9. Simplex
Rainthorpe Hall (Newton Flotman) TM 2097. *Rainestorp* 1086
  SPNN, p. 206. ON pers.n.?
Saxlingham Thorpe (Saxlingham Thorpe) TM 2197. *Saxlinghamtorp* 1254,
  Saxlyngham Thorp 1291
  DEPN, p. 406, CDEPN, p. 529. Place-name *Saxlingham*
Saxthorpe (Saxthorpe) TG 1130. *Saxthorp* 1086
  EPNS NFK, 3, p. 98, DEPN, p. 406, CDEPN, p. 530, SPNN, p. 323. ON pers.n. *Saxi*
Sculthorpe (Sculthorpe) TF 8931. *Sculatorpa* 1086
  DEPN, p. 409, CDEPN, p. 533, SPNN, p. 337. ON pers.n. *Skúli*
Smalethorpes (Hevingham) TG 1921. *Smalethorpes* 1198
  EPNS NFK, 3, p. 85. OE *smæl* 'narrow, small'
Swainsthorpe (Swainsthorpe) TG 2100. *Sueinestorp, Torp* 1086
  DEPN, p. 455, SPNN, p. 356, CDEPN, p. 593. ON pers.n. *Sveinn*
Themelthorpe (Themelthorpe) TG 0523. *Timeltorp* 1203
  DEPN, p. 465, SPNN, p. 432, CDEPN, p. 607. Uncertain
Thorpe (Shipdham) TF 9708. *Torp* 1086
  DB, *Norfolk*, 15, 17. Simplex
Thorpe Abbots (Thorpe Abbots) TM 2079. *T(h)orp* 1086
  DEPN, p. 469, CDEPN, p. 611. Simplex
Thorpe Market (Thorpe Market) TG 2435. *Torp* 1086
  EPNS NFK, 3, p. 42, DEPN, p. 469, CDEPN, p. 612. Simplex
Thorpe next Haddiscoe (Thorpe next Haddiscoe) TM 4398. *Torpe* 1254
  DEPN, p. 469, CDEPN, p. 611. Simplex
Thorpe Parva (Thorpe Parva) TM 1679. *Torp* 1086
  DEPN, p. 469. Simplex
Thorpe St Andrew (Thorpe St Andrew) TG 2709. *T(h)orp* 1086
  DEPN, p. 469, CDEPN, p. 612. Simplex
Thorpgate (Felmingham) TG 2529. *Thorpgate* 1269
  EPNS NFK, 2, p. 159. Qualifier, with ON *gata* 'road'
Thorpland (in Gallow hundred) TF 9332. *Torpaland* 1086
  DEPN, p. 469. Qualifier, with OE/ON *land* 'land'
Thorpland (Wallington) TF 6108. *Torpelanda* 1086, *Torp* 1086

DB, *Norfolk*, 13, 6. Simplex, and qualifier, with OE/ON *land* 'land'

Toketorp (unlocated in Forehoe hundred). *Toketorp, Tochestorp* 1086

SPNN, p. 371. ON pers.n. *Tóki*

Torp (unlocated in Loddon hundred). *Torp* 1086

DB, *Norfolk*, 12, 26. Simplex

Weasenham Thorpe (Weasenham) TF 8421. *Wesinhamthorp* 1291

DEPN, p. 503. Place-name Weasenham

Northamptonshire

Althorp (Althorp) SP 6865. *Olletorp* 1086, *Holtrop* 12th, *Holthorpe* 1300

EPNS NTH, pp. 78–9, SSNEM, p. 102, DEPN, p. 8. OE pers.n.?

Apethorpe (Apethorpe) TL 0295. *Patorp* 1086, *Apethorp'* 12th

EPNS NTH, p. 198, SSNEM, p. 102, DEPN, p. 11, CDEPN, p. 15. ON pers.n. *Api*

Crowthorp (Oundle) TL 0388. *Crowethorp* 12th

EPNS NTH, p. 214, SSNEM, p. 124. OE *crāwe* 'crow'

Deenethorpe (Deenethorpe) SP 9592. *Trop* 1235, *Deenthorp* 1246

EPNS NTH, pp. 163–4, SSNEM, p. 133 (no. 7), DEPN, p. 141, CDEPN, p. 182. Simplex

Dogsthorpe (Peterborough) TF 1901. *Dodesthorpe* 12th (s.a. 963), *Doddestorp* c.1115

EPNS NTH, p. 226, SSNEM, p. 108, DEPN, p. 147. OE pers.n. *Dodd*

Dowthorpe (Earls Barton) SP 8563. *Widetorp* 1086, *Barton Thorp* 1261

EPNS NTH, p. 138, SSNEM, p. 108. Uncertain

Eaglethorpe (Warmington) TL 0791. *Ekelthorpgrene* 1297

EPNS NTH, pp. 215–16, SSNEM, p. 125. OE pers.n.?

Finnesthorp (unlocated). *Fastulf aet Finnesthorpe* c.971–984 (12th)

SPNN, pp. 122–3. ON pers.n. *Finnr*

Glassthorpe (Floore) SP 6661. *Clachestorp* 1086, *Clachetorp* 12th, *Clakestorp* 1178

EPNS NTH, p. 83, SSNEM, p. 107, DEPN, p. 197. ON pers.n.?

Gunthorpe (Paston) TF 1802. *Gunetorp* 1130

EPNS NTH, p. 236, SSNEM, p. 111, DEPN, p. 208. ON pers.n. *Gunni*

Hothorpe (Hothorpe) SP 6685. *Vdetorpe* 1086

EPNS NTH, p. 115, SSNEM, pp. 111–12, DEPN, p. 252. Uncertain

Kingsthorpe (Kingsthorpe) SP 7563. *Torp* 1086, *Kingestorp* 1190

EPNS NTH, p. 133, SSNEM, p. 119 (no. 26), DEPN, p. 277, CDEPN, p. 347. Simplex

Kingsthorpe (Polebrook) TL 0885. *Chingestorp* 1086

EPNS NTH, p. 215, SSNEM, p. 112, DEPN, p. 277. OE *cyning* 'king'

Longthorpe (Peterborough) TL 1698. *æt Þeorp* c.971–84 (12th), *Torp* 1086

EPNS NTH, p. 227, SSNEM, p. 119 (no. 28), CDEPN, p. 381. Simplex

Ravensthorpe (Ravensthorpe) SP 6670. *Ravenestorp* 1086

EPNS NTH, p. 87, SSNEM, p. 115, DEPN, p. 382, CDEPN, p. 493. ON or OE pers.n

Rothersthorpe (Rothersthorpe) SP 7156. *Torp* 1086, *Trop'* 12th

    EPNS NTH, pp. 151–2, SSNEM, p. 119 (no. 32), DEPN, p. 393, CDEPN, p. 509. Simplex

Southorpe (Southorpe) TF 0803. *Sudtorp* 1086

    EPNS NTH, p. 242, SSNEM, p. 117, DEPN, p. 432, CDEPN, p. 562. OE/ON *sūth(r)* 'south'

Thorpe Lubbenham (Thorpe Lubbenham) SP 7086. *Torp* 1086

    EPNS NTH, p. 122, SSNEM, p. 119 (no. 14), DEPN, p. 469. Simplex

Thorpe Malsor (Thorpe Malsor) SP 8379. *Alidetorp* 1086, *Thorp'* 12th

    EPNS NTH, p. 122, SSNEM, pp. 119–20, DEPN, p. 469, CDEPN, p. 612. OE pers.n.?

Thorpe Underwood (Harrington) SP 7881. *alia Thorp'* 12th

    EPNS NTH, p. 114, SSNEM, p. 119 (no. 19), DEPN, p. 469. Simplex

Thorpe Waterville (Thorpe Achurch) TL 0281. *Torpe* 12th

    EPNS NTH, p. 219, SSNEM, p. 119 (no. 21), DEPN, p. 469, CDEPN, p. 613. Simplex

Torpel (Ufford) TF 1105. *Torpell'* 1131

    EPNS NTH, pp. 244–5, SSNEM, p. 133 (no. 14). Simplex (with Anglo-Norman diminutive suffix)

Upthorp (Benefield) SP 9889. *Upthorp* c.1220

    EPNS NTH, p. 212. OE/ON *upp* 'up, above'

Wigsthorpe (Lilford cum Wigsthorpe) TL 0482. *Wykingethorp* 1232

    EPNS NTH, p. 185, SSNEM, p. 134, DEPN, p. 518, CDEPN, p. 679. ON pers.n.?

Wilby Thorp (Wilby) SP 8666. *Wylebythorp* 1251

    EPNS NTH, p. 141, SSNEM, p. 134. Place-name Wilby

Wothorpe (Wothorpe) TF 0305. *Writhorp* 11th (13th), *Writorp* 1086

    EPNS NTH, p. 247, SSNEM, p. 122, DEPN, p. 536. OE *wrīth* 'shoot, bush, thicket'

Nottinghamshire

Aldethorpp (Caunton) SK 7460. *Aldethorpp* 13th

    EPNS NTT, p. 291. OE *ald* 'old'

Algarthorpe (Basford) SK 5542. *Thorp* c.1200, *Algerthorpp'* 1276

    EPNS NTT, p. 138, SSNEM, p. 132 (no. 4). Simplex

Alwoldestorp (Caythorpe) SK 6845. *Alwoldestorp* 1086

    SSNEM, p. 102. OE pers.n. *Ælfweald* or *Æthelweald*

Besthorpe (Besthorpe) SK 8264. *Bestorp* 1147

    EPNS NTT, p. 201, SSNEM, p. 103, DEPN, p. 40, CDEPN, p. 53. OE *bēos* 'bent-grass'

Besthorpe (Caunton) SK 7360. *Bestorp* 1086

    EPNS NTT, pp. 183–4, SSNEM, p. 103, DEPN, p. 35. OE *bēos* 'bent-grass'

Bilsthorpe (Bilsthorpe) SK 6560. *Bildestorp* 1086

EPNS NTT, p. 45, SSNEM, p. 103, DEPN, p. 43, CDEPN, p. 57. ON pers.n.?

Caythorpe (Caythorpe) SK 6846. *Cathorp* c.1170
    EPNS NTT, pp. 159–60, SSNEM, p. 124, DEPN, p. 92, CDEPN, p. 122. ON pers.n.?
    See above, p. 65, n. 12

Costhorpe (Carlton in Lindrick) SK 5886. *Cossardtorp* 1195
    EPNS NTT, p. 72, SSNEM, p. 124. PostC pers.n. (surname) *Cossard*

Danethorpe (North Collingham) SK 8457. *Dordentorp* 1086, *Berlesthorp'* c.1200,
    Dornestorp 1232
    EPNS NTT, p. 203, SSNEM, p. 107. OE pers.n.?

Easthorpe (Southwell) SK 7053. *Estorp* 1227
    EPNS NTT, p. 176, SSNEM, p. 125. OE *ēast* 'east'

Fleecethorpe (Hodsock) SK 6283. *Flikesthorp'* c.1200
    EPNS NTT, p. 82, SSNEM, p. 126. ON pers.n. *Flík* or *Flikkr*

Garbythorpe (Barton in Fabis) SK 5232. *Karberthorp* 1280
    EPNS NTT, p. 244, SSNEM, p. 127. PostC pers.n.?

Gleadthorpe (Warsop) SK 5970. *Gletorp* 1086, *Gledethorp* 1154–89
    EPNS NTT, p. 102, SSNEM, p. 110, DEPN, p. 198. Uncertain

Grassthorpe (Grassthorpe) SK 7967. *Grestorp* 1086
    EPNS NTT, p. 186, SSNEM, p. 110, DEPN, p. 203, CDEPN, p. 259. OE or ON *gres*
    'grass'

Gunthorpe (Gunthorpe) SK 6744. *Gulnetorp, Gunnetorp* 1086
    EPNS NTT, p. 167, SSNEM, p. 111, DEPN, p. 208, CDEPN, p. 266. ON pers.n. *Gunni*
    or *Gunnhildr*

Habblesthorpe (North Leverton) SK 7882. *Happelesthorp* 1153–4 (14th),
    Happelesthorp 1267
    EPNS NTT, pp. 34–5, SSNEM, p. 127, DEPN, p. 208, CDEPN, p. 268. OE pers.n.?

Knapthorpe (Caunton) SK 7458. *Chenapetorp* 1086
    EPNS NTT, p. 184, SSNEM, p. 112. ?OE *cnapa* 'boy'

Mattersey Thorpe (Mattersey) SK 6889. *Thorp* 1298
    EPNS NTT, pp. 86–7, SSNEM, p. 133 (no. 8). Simplex

Middlethorpe (Caunton) SK 7558. *Torpa* c.1150, *Middelthorp'* 1260
    EPNS NTT, p. 184, SSNEM, p. 133 (no. 9). Simplex

Milnthorpe (Norton) SK 5771. *Milnethorp* 1227
    EPNS NTT, p. 88, SSNEM, p. 130. OE *myln* 'mill'

Newthorpe (Greasley) SK 4846. *Neutorp* 1086
    EPNS NTT, p. 146, SSNEM, p. 114, DEPN, p. 341. OE *nīwe* 'new'

Odestorp (East Retford) SK 7080. *Odestorp* 1086
    SSNEM, p. 114. ON pers.n.?

Osmanthorpe (Edingley) SK 6756. *Osuuitorp* 1086, *Osmundorp* c.1175
    EPNS NTT, p. 161, SSNEM, p. 115. OE pers.n. *Oswīg*, then *Osmund*

Owthorpe (Owthorpe) SK 6733. *Ovetorp* 1086
> EPNS NTT, p. 238, SSNEM, p. 115, DEPN, p. 355, CDEPN, p. 458. OE or ON pers.n

Perlethorpe (Perlethorpe) SK 6470. *Torp* 1086
> EPNS NTT, p. 91, SSNEM, p. 119 (no. 30), DEPN, p. 363, CDEPN, p. 469. Simplex

Scroppen þorp (Scrooby) SK 6590. *to scroppen thorpe* 958 (14th)
> EPNS NTT, p. 96, SSNEM, p. 116. Uncertain

Sibthorpe (Sibthorpe) SK 7645. *Sibetorp* 1086
> EPNS NTT, p. 216, SSNEM, p. 117, DEPN, p. 421, CDEPN, p. 550. OE or ON pers.n

Staythorpe (Staythorpe) SK 7554. *Startorp* 1086
> EPNS NTT, p. 196, SSNEM, p. 117, DEPN, p. 440, CDEPN, p. 573. Uncertain

Sternthorpe (Sutton on Trent) SK 7966. *Sternethorp* 1203
> EPNS NTT, p. 196, SSNEM, p. 132. Uncertain

Thorpe by Newark (Thorpe by Newark) SK 7649. *Torp* 1086
> EPNS NTT, p. 218, SSNEM, p. 119 (no. 16), DEPN, p. 469, CDEPN, p. 611. Simplex

Thorpe in the Glebe (Thorpe in the Glebe) SK 6025. *Torp* 1086, *Bochardistorp* 1235
> EPNS NTT, p. 257, SSNEM, p. 119 (no. 11), DEPN, p. 469. Simplex

West Thorpe (Willoughby in the Wolds) SK 6325. *Westorp'* 1226
> EPNS NTT, p. 259, SSNEM, p. 133. OE *west*/ON *vestr* 'west'

Westethorp (Kinoulton) SK 6730. *Westethorp* 1250
> EPNS NTT, p. 291. OE *west*/ON *vestr* 'west'

Westhorpe (Southwell) SK 6853. *Westorp'* 1268
> EPNS NTT, p. 176, SSNEM, p. 133. OE *west*/ON *vestr* 'west'

Winthorpe (Winthorpe) SK 8156. *Wimuntorp* 1086
> EPNS NTT, pp. 208–9, SSNEM, p. 121, DEPN, p. 525, CDEPN, p. 688. OE or ON pers.n

Woolsthorpe (Lowdham) SK 6546. *Ulvestorp* c.1200
> EPNS NTT, p. 172, SSNEM, pp. 134–5. ON pers.n.?

Rutland

Alesthorp (Burley) SK 8911. *Alestanestorp* 1086, *Alestanthorp* 1282
> EPNS RUT, p. 11, SSNEM, p. 101, Cox, Dict. LEI & RUT, p. 119. OE pers.n. *Ealhstān*

Barleythorpe (Barleythorpe) SK 8409. *Thorp juxta Ocham* c.1200, *Bolaresthorp* 1203
> EPNS RUT, pp. 64–5, SSNEM, p. 132 (no. 5), CDEPN, p. 36. Simplex

Belmesthorpe (Ryhall) TF 0410. *Beolmesðorp* 1042–55 (12th), *Belmestorp* 1086
> EPNS RUT, p. 161, SSNEM, p. 103, DEPN, p. 36, CDEPN, p. 49. OE pers.n. *Beornhelm*

Fregsthorp (Ketton) SK 9904. *Frygisthorp'* 1300–20
> EPNS RUT, p. 150, SSNEM, p. 126. ON pers.n.?

Gunthorpe (Gunthorpe) SK 8605. *Gunetorp'* 1200

EPNS RUT, p. 89, SSNEM, p. 127, DEPN, p. 208. ON pers.n. *Gunni*

Ingthorpe (Tinwell) SK 9908. *Ingelthorp* 1189 (14th), *Ingetorp* 1203
    EPNS RUT, pp. 167–8, SSNEM, p. 128, DEPN, p. 265. ON pers.n.?

Kilthorpe (Ketton) SK 9803. *Ketelistorp* c.1250
    EPNS RUT, p. 151, SSNEM, p. 128. ON pers.n. *Ketill*

Martinsthorpe (Martinsthorpe) SK 8604. *Martinestorp'* 1206
    EPNS RUT, pp. 199–200, SSNEM, p. 129, DEPN, p. 317. Lat pers.n. (PostC type, but perhaps an earlier bearer: see discussion in EPNS RUT)

Sculthorpe (North Luffenham) SK 9203. *Sculetorp* 1086
    EPNS RUT, p. 257, SSNEM, p. 257, Cox, *Dict. LEI & RUT*, p. 137. ON pers.n. *Skúli*

Thorpe by Water (Thorpe by Water) SP 8996. *Torp* 1086
    EPNS RUT, pp. 302–3, SSNEM, p. 119 (no. 20), Cox, *Dict. LEI & RUT*, p. 139, DEPN, p. 469, CDEPN, p. 612. Simplex

Tolethorpe (Little Casterton) TF 0210. *Toltorp* 1086
    EPNS RUT, pp. 134–5, SSNEM, p. 120, DEPN, p. 476. ON pers.n. *Tóli*

Westhorpe (Wing) SK 8903. *Westhorp* 1296
    EPNS RUT, pp. 228–9, SSNEM, p. 133. OE *west*/ON *vestr* 'west'

Staffordshire

Thorpe Constantine (Thorpe Constantine) SK 2608. *Torp* 1086
    SSNEM, p. 118 (no. 9), Horovitz, *Place-names of Staffordshire*, p. 535, DEPN, p. 469, CDEPN, p. 612. Simplex

Suffolk

Akethorp (Lowestoft) TM 5493. *Aketorp* 1086, *Akethorp* 1207
    Baron, 'Place-names of East Suffolk', p. 15, SPNN, p. 4, Fellows-Jensen, 'East Anglia', p. 54. ON pers.n. *Áki*

Blackthorpe (Rougham) TL 9162. *Blakethorpe* c.1187
    EPNS collection. OE *blæc* 'black'

Clachestorp (unidentified in Loes hundred). *Clachestorp* 1086
    DB, Suffolk, 6, 274. ON pers.n. *Klakkr*

Godrichestorp (Thorndon) TM 1469. *Godrichestorp* 1195
    Baron, 'Place-names of East Suffolk', p. 77. OE pers.n. *Godrīc*

Gotesthorpe (unlocated). *Gotesthorpe* 1280, *Goudestorp* n.d., *Gasthorp* 1335
    Lindkvist, *Middle-English place-names*, p. 143. ON pers.n. *Gautr*

Ixworth Thorpe (Ixworth Thorpe) TL 9172. *Torp* 1086
    DEPN, p. 268, CDEPN, p. 613. Simplex

Redfaresthorp (unlocated). *at Redfaresþorpe* 978–1016 (13th)
    Robertson, *Anglo-Saxon charters*, no. 73. ON pers.n.?

Thorp (Heveningham) TM 3473. *Torp* 1086

DB, *Suffolk*, 32, 21. Simplex

Thorp (Pakenham) TL 9267. *T(h)orp* c.1186–8 (13th)
  Davis, *Kalendar of Abbot Samson*, pp. 4, 10. Simplex

Thorp Hall (Dallinghoo) TM 2654. *Torp* 1086
  Baron, 'Place-names of East Suffolk', p. 153. Simplex

Thorpe (Aldringham with Thorpe) TM 4760. *Torp* 1086
  Baron, 'Place-names of East Suffolk', p. 30, CDEPN, p. 612. Simplex

Thorpe (Stoke Ash) TM 1170. *Torp* c.1230 (13th), *Thorp in Stok'* c.1250 (13th)
  Brown, *Eye Priory* 1, nos 213, 254. Simplex

Thorpe Common (Trimley St Martin) TM 2737. *Torp(a)* 1086
  DEPN, p. 469, Baron, 'Place-names of East Suffolk', p. 168. Simplex

Thorpe Hall (Ashfield) TM 2162. *Torp* 1086
  Baron, 'Place-names of East Suffolk', p. 137. Simplex

Thorpe Hall (Hasketon) TM 2350. *Thorp* 1251, *?Torp* 1086
  Baron, 'Place-names of East Suffolk', p. 144, Arnott, *Deben Valley*, p. 9. Simplex

Thorpe Morieux (Thorpe Morieux) TL 9472. *æt Þorpæ* 962–91 (11th), *Torp* 1086
  DEPN, p. 469, CDEPN, p. 612. Simplex

Thorplond (Rushmere) TM 4987. *Thorplond* c.1190–1228 (14th)
  Harper-Bill, *Blythburgh Priory* 2, no. 386. Qualifier, with OE/ON *land* 'land'

Torp (Erwarton) TM 2134. *Torp* 1086
  Laverton, *Shotley Peninsula*, pp. 86–7. Simplex

Torpe (unlocated in Stow hundred). *Torpe* 1086
  DB, *Suffolk*, 31, 47. Simplex

Westhorpe (Westhorpe) TM 0469. *Westtorp* 1086
  Baron, 'Place-names of East Suffolk', pp. 78–9, DEPN, p. 508, CDEPN, p. 665. OE *west*/ON *vestr* 'west'

Westmorland

Clawthorpe (Burton) SD 5376. *Clerthorp* 1220–46, *Clerkthorp* 1260
  EPNS WML, 1, p. 58, SSNNW, p. 202, DEPN, p. 110. PostC pers.n.?

Crackenthorpe (Appleby St Michael) NY 6622. *Cracanthorp* 1185–99
  EPNS WML, 2, p. 101, SSNNW, p. 202, DEPN, p. 127, CDEPN, p. 164. Uncertain

Crackenthorpe (Beetham) SD 4979. *Crakintorp* 1254
  EPNS WML, 1, p. 68, SSNNW, p. 202, DEPN, p. 127, CDEPN, p. 164. Uncertain

Hackthorpe (Lowther) NY 5223. *Hacatorp* c.1150
  EPNS WML, 2, p. 182, SSNNW, p. 57, DEPN, p. 209, CDEPN, p. 268. ON pers.n.?

Melkinthorpe (Lowther) NY 5224. *Melcanetorp* c.1150
  EPNS WML, 2, p. 183, SSNNW, p. 58, DEPN, p. 320, CDEPN, p. 406. OIrish or OWelsh pers.n

Milnthorpe (Heversham) SD 4981. *Milntorp* 1272
EPNS WML, I, p. 95, SSNNW, p. 204, DEPN, p. 326, CDEPN, p. 414. OE *myln* 'mill'

Yorkshire, East Riding

Allerthorpe (Thornton) SE 7847. *Aluuarestorp* 1086
EPNS YOE, p. 184, SSNY, p. 54, DEPN, p. 6, CDEPN, p. 9. OE or ON pers.n

Arnestorp (Goxhill ?) TA 1844. *Arnestorp* 1086
SSNY, p. 54, SPNLY, p. 11. ON pers. n. *Arn*

Austhorp (unlocated). *Austhorp* 1285
EPNS YOE, p. 328. ON *austr* 'east'

Babthorpe (Hemingbrough) SE 6730. *Babetorp* 1086
EPNS YOE, p. 258, SSNY, p. 55, DEPN, p. 21. Pers.n.; uncertain language

Barthorpe Bottoms (Acklam) SE 7861. *Barchertorp* 1086
EPNS YOE, p. 148, SSNY, p. 55, DEPN, p. 28. ON pers.n. *Bǫrkr*

Belthorpe House (Bishop Wilton) SE 7955. *Torp, Balchetorp* 1086
EPNS YOE, p. 175, SSNY, p. 55, DEPN, p. 36. ON pers.n. *Belgr*

Bowthorpe (Hemingbrough) SE 6831. *Boletorp* 1086
EPNS YOE, p. 261, SSNY, p. 55, DEPN, p. 56. Uncertain

Boythorpe (Foxholes) TA 0173. *Buitorp* 1086
EPNS YOE, p. 115, SSNY, p. 55, DEPN, p. 57. OE **boia* 'boy'

Brantingham Thorpe (Brantingham) SE 9429. *Toschetorp* 1086, *Thorpe juxta Brantyngham* 1379
EPNS YOE, p. 222, SSNY, p. 70. ON pers.n.?

Bugthorpe (Bugthorpe) SE 7757. *Bughetorp* 1086
EPNS YOE, p. 149, SSNY, p. 56, DEPN, p. 73, CDEPN, p. 98. ON pers.n. *Buggi*

Burythorpe (Burythorpe) SE 7965. *Berguetorp* 1086
EPNS YOE, pp. 142–3, SSNY, p. 56, DEPN, p. 78, CDEPN, p. 105. ON (fem.) pers.n. *Bjǫ*

Caythorpe (Rudston) TA 0968. *Caretorp* 1086
EPNS YOE, p. 99, SSNY, p. 56, DEPN, p. 92. ON pers.n. *Kári*

Chetelestorp (Thornton ?) SE 7644. *Chetelestorp* 1086
SSNY, p. 61 (no. 3), SPNLY, p. 167. ON pers.n. *Ketill*

Chetelstorp (Escrick) SE 6342. *Chetelstorp* 1086
SSNY, p. 61 (no. 2), SPNLY, p. 167. ON pers.n. *Ketill*

Clementhorpe (York) SE 6052. *Clementesthorp* 1070–80 (14th)
EPNS YOE, p. 284. Saint's name

Colestainthorpe (Wressell ?) SE 7132. *Colestainthorpe* 1249
SPNLY, p. 179, Lindkvist, *Middle-English place-names*, p. 68. ON pers.n. **Kolsteinn*

Crachetorp (Hessle) TA 0327. *Crachetorp* 1086
   SSNY, p. 56. ON pers.n.?
Danthorpe Hall (Humbleton) TA 2234. *Danetorp* 1086
   EPNS YOE, p. 53, SSNY, p. 57, DEPN, p. 139. ON *Danir* 'Danes'
Dowthorpe Hall (Swine) TA 1637. *Duuetorp* 1086
   EPNS YOE, pp. 47–8, SSNY, p. 57, SPNLY, p. 73, DEPN, p. 150. ON pers.n.?
Easthorpe (Londesborough) SE 8646. *Estorp* 1086
   EPNS YOE, p. 232, SSNY, p. 57, DEPN, p. 157. OE *ēast* 'east'
Eddlethorpe (Westow) SE 7565. *Eduardestorp, Guduualestorp* 1086
   EPNS YOE, p. 144, SSNY, p. 57, DEPN, p. 160. OE pers.n. *Ēadweard* or *Ēadweald*
Enthorpe (Lund) SE 9647. *Emethorp* 1276
   EPNS YOE, p. 163. Uncertain
Everthorpe (North Cave) SE 8932. *Evertorp* 1086, *Yverthorp* 1190–1214
   EPNS YOE, p. 225, SSNY, p. 58, DEPN, p. 170. ON *efri* 'upper'
Foggathorpe (Bubwith) SE 7537. *Fulcartorp* 1086
   EPNS YOE, p. 240, SSNY, p. 58, DEPN, p. 183, CDEPN, pp. 234–5. ON or PostC pers.n
Fornetorp (Thwing ?) TA 0570. *Fornetorp* 1086
   SSNY, p. 58. ON pers.n.?
Fowthorpe (Hunmanby) TA 0977. *Foletorp* 12th
   EPNS YOE, p. 110, SPNLY, p. 84. ON pers.n. Foli
Fraisthorpe (Carnaby) TA 1465. *Frestinthorp* 1086
   EPNS YOE, p. 87, SSNY, p. 58, DEPN, p. 186, CDEPN, p. 239. ON pers.n. *Freistingr* or *Freysteinn*
Fridaythorpe (Fridaythorpe) SE 8759. *Fridagstorp* 1086
   EPNS YOE, p. 129, SSNY, p. 58, DEPN, p. 188, CDEPN, p. 241. Pers.n., uncertain language
Gowthorpe (Bishop Wilton) SE 7656. *Gheuetorp* 1086, *Goukthorp* 1235
   EPNS YOE, p. 176, SSNY, p. 59, DEPN, p. 202. ON *gaukr* 'cuckoo'
Gowthorpe Lane (Blacktoft) SE 8423. *Gouthorpe* 1295
   EPNS YOE, p. 244. ON *gaukr* 'cuckoo'
Gribthorpe (Bubwith) SE 7136. *Gripetorp* 1086
   EPNS YOE, p. 240, SSNY, p. 59, DEPN, p. 205. ON pers.n. *Grípr* or *Grípi*
Grimestorp (Hemingbrough) SE 6631. *Grimestorp* 1133
   EPNS YOE, p. 258, SPNLY, p. 354. ON pers.n. *Grímr*
Grimthorpe (Great Givendale) SE 8153. *Grimtorp* 1086, *Thorpe* 1120–9
   EPNS YOE, p. 178, SSNY, p. 59. ON pers.n. *Grímr*
Hagthorpe (Hemingbrough) SE 6731. *Achetorp* 1086
   EPNS YOE, p. 258, SSNY, p. 59. ON pers.n. *Haki*
Haisthorpe (Burton Agnes) TA 1364. *Aschiltorp* 1086, *Haschelthorp* 1190

EPNS YOE, p. 89, SSNY, p. 59, DEPN, p. 211, CDEPN, p. 270. ON pers.n. Hǫskuldr or Áskell

Harlthorpe (Bubwith) SE 7137. *Herlesthorp* 1150–60
  EPNS YOE, p. 241, SPNLY, pp. 139–40, DEPN, p. 220, CDEPN, p. 280. ON pers.n.?

Harpethorp (unlocated). *Harpethorp* 1246
  EPNS YOE, p. 328. Uncertain

Helperthorpe (Helperthorpe) SE 9570. *Elpetorp* 1086, *Helperthorp* 1160–70
  EPNS YOE, pp. 123–4, SSNY, p. 60, DEPN, p. 232, CDEPN, p. 295. ON (fem.) pers.n. Hjalp

Hilderthorpe (Bridlington) TA 1867. *Hilgertorp* 1086
  EPNS YOE, pp. 102–3, SSNY, p. 60, DEPN, p. 239, CDEPN, p. 304. ON or PostC pers.n

Ianulfestorp (Dunnington ?) SE 6752. *Ianulfestorp* 1086
  EPNS YOE, p. 181, SSNY, p. 60. OE or ON pers.n

Kelleythorpe (Great Driffield) TA 0357. *Calgestorp* 1086, *Kelingtorp* 1180–90
  EPNS YOE, p. 155, SSNY, p. 61, DEPN, p. 270. ON pers.n. *Kelling*

Kennythorpe (Langton) SE 7866. *Cheretorp* 1086, *Kenerthorp* 12th
  EPNS YOE, p. 141, SSNY, p. 61, DEPN, p. 272, CDEPN, p. 340. OE pers.n.?

Kettlethorpe (North Cave) SE 8832. *Torp* 1086, *Ketolthorp* 1285
  EPNS YOE, p. 225, SSNY, p. 69 (no. 29), DEPN, p. 274. Simplex

Langthorpe Hall (Swine) TA 1335. *Lambetorp* 1086
  EPNS YOE, p. 48, SSNY, p. 62. ON pers.n.?

Layerthorpe (York) SE 6053. *Legeraþorp* 1070–80 (14th), *Layrthorp* 1161–74
  EPNS YOE, p. 292. Uncertain

Lowthorpe (Lowthorpe) TA 0860. *Loghetorp* 1086
  EPNS YOE, p. 93, SSNY, p. 62, DEPN, p. 306, CDEPN, p. 384. ON pers.n. *Lági* or *Logi*

Menethorpe (Westow) SE 7667. *Mennistorp* 1086, *Meningthorp* 1219
  EPNS YOE, p. 145, SSNY, p. 63, DEPN, p. 321. ON pers.n. **Menning*

Menthorpe (Hemingbrough) SE 7034. *Menethorp* 12th
  EPNS YOE, p. 261, SPNLY, p. 195, DEPN, p. 322. ON pers.n.? Cf. above, p. 57, n. 64

Mowthorpe (Kirby Grindalythe) SE 9067. *Muletorp* 1086
  EPNS YOE, p. 125, SSNY, p. 63. OE or ON pers.n

Northorpe (Hornsea) TA 2047. *Nortorp* 1198
  EPNS YOE, p. 65. OE/ON north(r) 'north'

Northorpe (Easington) TA 3919. *Torp* 1086
  SSNY, p. 69 (no. 34). Simplex

Ousethorpe (Pocklington) SE 8050. *Torp* 1086, *Ulvethorp* 1190–1215
  EPNS YOE, p. 181, SSNY, pp. 69–70 (no. 36), DEPN, p. 355. Simplex

Owsthorpe (Eastrington) SE 8330. *Duuestorp* 1086, *Hausthorp* 1285
    EPNS YOE, p. 247, SSNY, p. 57, DEPN, p. 355. ON pers.n.? Then ON *austr* 'east'
Painsthorpe (Kirby Underdale) SE 8058. *Torfe* 1086, *Painesthorp* 1088–93
    EPNS YOE, p. 131, SSNY, p. 70 (no. 37), DEPN, p. 357. Simplex
Pennythorpe Plantation (Howden) SE 7429. *Pinelthorpe* 1199
    EPNS YOE, p. 254. Uncertain
Pensthorpe (Welwick) TA 3421. *Peningestorp* 1200
    EPNS YOE, pp. 22–3. OE pers.n.?
Pockthorpe (Nafferton) TA 0559. *Pochetorp* 1086
    EPNS YOE, p. 95, SSNY, p. 64, DEPN, p. 369. OE *pūca* 'goblin'
Raisthorpe (Wharram Percy) SE 8564. *Redrestorp* 1086
    EPNS YOE, p. 132, SSNY, p. 64, DEPN, p. 379. ON pers.n. *(H)reitharr*
Raventhorpe (Cherry Burton) SE 9942. *Ragheneltorp* 1086, *Rauenesthorp* 1199–1216
    EPNS YOE, p. 191, SSNY, p. 65. ON (fem.) pers.n. *Ragnhildr*
Ricstorp (Muston ?) TA 0979. *Ricstorp* 1086
    SSNY, p. 65. Uncertain
Rudetorp (Market Weighton) SE 8443. *Rudetorp* 1086
    EPNS YOE, p. 229, SSNY, p. 65. ?ON *ruth* 'clearing'
Scagglethorpe (Settrington) SE 8373. *Scachetorp* 1086
    EPNS YOE, p. 139, SSNY, p. 66, DEPN, p. 406, CDEPN, p. 530. Uncertain
Scardiztorp (Skirpenbeck ?) SE 7457. *Scardiztorp* 1086
    SSNY, pp. 66–7. Uncertain
Southorpe (Hornsea) TA 2048. *Torp* 1086, *Suththorp'* 1249–69
    EPNS YOE, p. 65, SSNY, p. 70 (no. 40). Simplex
Steintorp (Etton ?) SE 9843. *Steintorp* 1086
    SSNY, p. 67. ON *steinn* 'stone'
Sunthorpe (Kilnsea) TA 4116. *Suntorp* 1187–1207, *Suinthorp* 1238
    EPNS YOE, pp. 16–17. ?OE/ON *swīn/svín* 'swine'. See above, p. 55
Swaythorpe (Kilham) TA 0664. *Suauetorp* 1086
    EPNS YOE, pp. 97–8, SSNY, p. 68, CDEPN, p. 594. ON pers.n. *Sváfi*
Tharlesthorpe (Patrington) TA 3122. *Toruelestorp* 1086, *Toraldestorp* 1190–1193
    EPNS YOE, p. 25, SSNY, p. 68. ON pers.n. *Thóraldr*
Thornthorpe (Burythorpe) SE 7964. *Torgrimestorp* 1086
    EPNS YOE, p. 143, SSNY, p. 68, DEPN, p. 468. ON pers.n. *Thorgrímr*
Thorpe (Lockington) SE 9947. *Torp* 1086, *Gunmundetorp'* 1200, *Wymundethorp* 1247
    EPNS YOE, p. 162, SSNY, p. 68 (no. 2). Simplex
Thorpe Bassett (Thorpe Bassett) SE 8673. *Torp* 1086, *Thorp Bassett* 1267
    EPNS YOE, p. 137, SSNY, p. 69 (no. 15), DEPN, p. 469, CDEPN, p. 612. Simplex
Thorpe Garth (AlDRBrough) TA 2438. *Thorp in Aldeburgh* 1180–97, *Torp* 12th
    EPNS YOE, p. 60. Simplex

Thorpe Hall (Rudston) TA 0967. *Torp* 1086
    EPNS YOE, p. 99, SSNY, p. 68 (no. 1). Simplex
Thorpe Hill (Welwick) TA 3422. *on þorp, be westan þorp* 1033 (14th), *Torp* 1086
    EPNS YOE, p. 23, SSNY, p. 69 (no. 11). Simplex
Thorpe le Street (Market Weighton) SE 8343. *Torp* 1086
    EPNS YOE, p. 229, SSNY, p. 69 (no. 25), DEPN, p. 469, CDEPN, p. 612. Simplex
Thorpe Lidget (Howden) SE 7428. *Ðorp* 959 (12th)
    EPNS YOE, p. 255, SSNY, p. 69 (no. 22). Simplex
Tibthorpe (Kirkburn) SE 9855. *Tibetorp* 1086
    EPNS YOE, p. 167, SSNY, p. 70, DEPN, p. 472, CDEPN, p. 616. OE or ON pers.n
Torp (Tibthorpe ?) SE 9655. *Torp* 1086
    SSNY, p. 68 (no. 6). Simplex
Towthorpe (Londesborough) SE 8645. *Toletorp* 1086
    EPNS YOE, p. 232, SSNY, p. 70. ON pers.n. *Tóli*
Towthorpe (Wharram Percy) SE 9062. *Touetorp* 1086
    EPNS YOE, p. 134, SSNY, p. 70, DEPN, p. 479. ON pers.n. *Tófi*
Vlchiltorp (Sledmere ?) SE 9364. *Vlchiltorp* 1086
SSNY, p. 71, SPNLY, p. 326. ON pers.n. *Úlfkell*
Vluesthorp (unlocated). *Vluesthorp* 13th
    EPNS YOE, p. 328, SPNLY, p. 322. ON pers.n. *Úlfr*
Vmfraithorp (unlocated). *Vmfraithorp* 1199
    EPNS YOE, p. 328. PostC pers.n. *Hunfrid* > *Humfrey*
Weaverthorpe (Weaverthorpe) SE 9670. *Wifretorp* 1086
    EPNS YOE, pp. 122–3, SSNY, p. 71, DEPN, p. 503, CDEPN, p. 658. OE or ON pers.n
Wilsthorpe (Carnaby) TA 1766. *Wiflestorp* 1086
    EPNS YOE, p. 88, SSNY, p. 71, DEPN, p. 521. Uncertain
Youlthorpe (Bishop Wilton) SE 7655. *Aiulftorp* 1086, *Jolletorp* 1166
    EPNS YOE, pp. 175–6, SSNY, p. 71, DEPN, p. 545, CDEPN, p. 712. ON pers.n.
    Eyjulfr

Yorkshire, North Riding
Agglethorpe (Coverham) SE 0886. *Aculestorp* 1086
    EPNS YON, p. 254, SSNY, p. 54, DEPN, p. 4, CDEPN, p. 4. OE pers.n. *Ācwulf*
Allerthorpe Hall (Pickhill) NZ 4802. *Herleuestorp* 1086
    EPNS YON, p. 225, SSNY, p. 54, DEPN, p. 6. ON pers.n. *Herleifr*
Arnodestorp (Hinderwell ?) NZ 7916. *Arnodestorp* 1086
    EPNS YON, p. 161, SSNY, p. 54. PostC pers.n.?
Carthorpe (Burneston) SE 3184. *Caretorp* 1086
    EPNS YON, p. 226, SSNY, p. 56, DEPN, p. 88, CDEPN, p. 118. ON pers.n. *Kári*
Coneysthorpe (Barton le Street) SE 7171. *Coningistorp* 1086

EPNS YON, p. 48, SSNY, p. 56, DEPN, p. 120, CDEPN, p. 154. ON *konungr* 'king'

Easthorpe (Appleton le Street) SE 7373. *Estorp* 1086, *Jarpethorp* 1201

    EPNS YON, p. 46, SSNY, p. 57, SPNLY, p. 155. OE *ēast* 'east'

Ellenthorpe Hall (Kirby Hill) SE 4267. *Adelingestorp* 1086

    EPNS YON, pp. 179–80, SSNY, p. 57, DEPN, p. 163. OE *ætheling* 'prince'

Etersthorpe (Cayton) TA 0683. *Eterstorp* 1086

    EPNS YON, p. 104, SSNY, p. 58. ON pers.n.?

Fornthorpe (Dalby) SE 6371. *Fornetorp* 1086, *Fornthorp* 1301

    EPNS YON, p. 30, SSNY, p. 58. ON pers.n.?

Fyling Thorpe (Fylingdales) SE 9199. *Prestethorpe* 1280

    EPNS YON, p. 117, CDEPN, p. 244. OE *prēost* 'priest'

Ganthorpe (Terrington) SE 6770. *Gameltorp* 1086, *Galmestorp* 1169

    EPNS YON, p. 34, SSNY, p. 58, DEPN, p. 192, CDEPN, p. 246. ON pers.n. *Galmr*

Gristhorpe (Cayton) TA 0583. *Grisetorp* 1086

    EPNS YON, p. 104, SSNY, p. 59, DEPN, p. 206, CDEPN, p. 264. ON pers.n.? See above, p. 55

Howthorpe (Hovingham) SE 6675. *Holtorp* 1086

    EPNS YON, p. 50, SSNY, p. 60, DEPN, p. 254. OE/ON *hol(r)* 'hollow'

Hundulfthorpe (North Kilvington ?) SE 4286. *Hundulftorp* 1086

    SSNY, p. 60, SPNLY, p. 145. ON pers.n. *Hundúlfr*

Kettlethorpe (Thornton Dale) SE 8286. *Chetelestorp* 1086

    EPNS YON, p. 89, SSNY, p. 61 (no. 1). ON pers.n. *Ketill*

Kilton Thorpe (Skelton) NZ 7018. *Torp* 1086, *Thorpkilton* 1406

    EPNS YON, p. 143, SSNY, p. 69 (no. 9). Simplex

Kingthorpe House (Pickering) SE 7984. *Chinetorp* 1086

    EPNS YON, p. 83, SSNY, pp. 61–2, DEPN, p. 278. OE *cyne-* 'royal'

Langthorpe (Kirby Hill) SE 3969. *Torp* 1086, *Langleithorp* 1157

    EPNS YON, p. 180, SSNY, p. 69 (no. 30), DEPN, p. 287, CDEPN, p. 361. Simplex

Laysthorpe (Stonegrave) SE 6577. *Lechestorp* 1086

    EPNS YON, p. 54, SSNY, p. 62, DEPN, p. 291. ON pers.n. *Leikr*

Leidtorp (Thornton Dale ?) SE 8383. *Leidtorp, Liedtorp* 1086

    SSNY, p. 62. Uncertain

Linthorpe (Middlesborough) NZ 5118. *Levingtorp* c.1138

    EPNS YON, pp. 161–2, DEPN, p. 299. OE pers.n. *Lēofa* or *Lēofing*

Mowthorpe (Terrington) SE 6771. *Muletorp* 1086

    EPNS YON, p. 35, SSNY, p. 63, DEPN, p. 333. ON pers.n.?

Nunthorpe (Great Ayton) NZ 5415. *Torp* 1086, *Nunnethorpe* 1301

    EPNS YON, p. 166, SSNY, p. 69 (no. 35), DEPN, p. 346, CDEPN, pp. 445–6. Simplex

Pinchinthorpe (Guisborough) NZ 6216. *Torp, Oustorp* 1086, *Pinzunthorp* c.1195–1210

EPNS YON, p. 152, SSNY, pp. 54 & 70 (no. 39), DEPN, p. 367. Simplex; also ON *austr* 'east'

Ravensthorpe Manor (Felixkirk) SE 4987. *Rauenstorp* 1086
  EPNS YON, p. 198, SSNY, p. 64, DEPN, p. 382. ON pers.n.?

Roberthorpe (Cayton) TA 0784. *Rodebestorp, Roudeluestorp* 1086
  EPNS YON, p. 104, SSNY, p. 65. Pers.n., uncertain language

Roskelthorp (Loftus) NZ 7118. *Roscheltorp* 1086
  EPNS YON, p. 141, SSNY, p. 65. ON pers.n. (H)*rosskell*

Scawthorpe (Cayton) TA 0685. *Scagestorp* 1086
  EPNS YON, p. 105, SSNY, p. 66. ON pers.n. *Skagi*

Sevenetorp (Pickhill ?) SE 3483. *Sevenetorp* 1086
  SSNY, p. 67. Uncertain. See above, p. 54

Swarthorpe (Masham) SE 2280. *Siwartorp* 1086
  EPNS YON, pp. 231–2, SSNY, p. 68. ON or OE pers.n

Tholthorpe (Alne) SE 4965. *Turulfestorp* 1086; cf. *Þurulfestune* 972–92 (11th), referring to the same place or to the estate upon which it was dependent? It may be *Thorp* in the same charter
  EPNS YON, pp. 21–2, SSNY, pp. 68 & 130, DEPN, p. 466, CDEPN, p. 608. ON pers.n. *Thórólfr*

Thorp Perrow (Well) SE 2681. *Torp* 1086
  EPNS YON, p. 229, SSNY, p. 69 (no. 13), DEPN, p. 469, CDEPN, p. 612. Simplex

Thorp Row House (Hornby) SE 2293. *Torp* 1086
  SSNY, p. 68 (no. 4). Simplex

Thorpe Hall (Wycliffe) NZ 1114. *Torp* 1086
  EPNS YON, p. 301, SSNY, p. 68 (no. 3), CDEPN, p. 612. Simplex

Thorpe Hill (Bossall ?) SE 7160. *Torp* 1086
  SSNY, p. 69 (no. 19), CDEPN, p. 612. Simplex

Thorpe le Willows (Coxwold) SE 5377. *Torp* 1086
  EPNS YON, p. 193, SSNY, p. 69 (no. 27), DEPN, p. 469, CDEPN, p. 612. Simplex

Thorpe under Stone (Catterick) NZ 1400. *Torp* 1187
  EPNS YON, p. 245, DEPN, p. 469. Simplex

Thorpefield (Thirsk) SE 4280. ?*Torp* 1086, *Petithorp juxta Thresk* c.1142, *campo de Thorp* 1243
  EPNS YON, p. 187, SSNY, p. 69 (no. 16), CDEPN, p. 613. Simplex

Thorpfield (unlocated). *Torp* 1086
  SSNY, p. 69 (no. 17). Simplex

Torp (Holme ?). *Torp* 1086
  SSNY, p. 69 (no. 8). Simplex

Torp (Sutton on the Forest ?) SE 5864. *Torp* 1086
  SSNY, p. 68 (no. 7). Simplex

Towthorpe (Huntington) SE 6359. *Touetorp* 1086
    EPNS YON, p. 13, SSNY, p. 70, DEPN, p. 479, CDEPN, p. 625. ON pers.n. *Tófi*
Ugthorpe (Lythe) NZ 7911. *Ugetorp* 1086
    EPNS YON, p. 138, SSNY, p. 70, DEPN, p. 485, CDEPN, p. 635. ON pers.n. *Uggi*
Waruelestorp (Alne ?) SE 5264. *Waruelestorp* 1086
    SSNY, p. 71. OE pers.n.?
Wiganthorpe (Terrington) SE 6870. *Wichingastorp* 1086
    EPNS YON, p. 35, SSNY, p. 71, DEPN, p. 517. ON pers.n.?

Yorkshire, West Riding
Addlethorpe (Spofforth) SE 3650. *Ardulfestorp* 1086
    EPNS YOW, 5, p. 33, SSNY, p. 53, DEPN, p. 3. OE pers.n. *Eardwulf*
Ailsitorp (Royston) SE 3808. *Ailsitorp* 12th, *Aylsithrop* 1350
    EPNS YOW, 1, p. 282. OE pers.n. *Æthelsige*
Alverthorpe (Wakefield) SE 3321. *Alvelthorp* 1199 (13th)
    EPNS YOW, 2, p. 166, DEPN, p. 8. OE pers.n.?
Armthorpe (Armthorpe) SE 6205. *Ernulfestorp, Einulvestorp* 1086
    EPNS YOW, 1, pp. 37–8, SSNY, p. 54, DEPN, p. 13, CDEPN, p. 18. OE or ON pers.n
Austhorpe (Whitkirk) SE 3733. *Ossetorp* 1086, *Oustorp* c.1180
    EPNS YOW, 4, p. 115, SSNY, p. 54, DEPN, p. 19. ON *austr* 'east'
Barnthorpe (Barnburgh) SE 4803. *Bernolftorp ante* 1158
    EPNS YOW, 1, p. 81, SPNLY, pp. 55–6. OE or ON pers.n
Bishopthorpe (Bishopthorpe) SE 5947. *Thorp, Badetorpes* 1086, *Biscupthorp* 1275
    EPNS YOW, 4, p. 225, SSNY, p. 55, DEPN, p. 46, CDEPN, p. 60. Simplex
Borygthorp (Warmfield) SE 3918. *Borygthorpgrene* 12th
    EPNS YOW, 2, p. 116. Uncertain
Bullerthorpe House (Swillington) SE 3830. *Bullokesthorp* 1251, *Bullokthorp* 1334–7
    EPNS YOW, 4, p. 94. OE pers.n.?
Buslingthorpe (Leeds) SE 3033. *Buselingtorpe* 1258
    EPNS YOW, 4, p. 128. PostC pers.n. *Buselin*
Bustardthorpe (Acomb) SE 5849. *Thorp juxta Eboracum* e.12th, *Thorp quae tenuit Osbertus*
    Bustard 12th, *Bustardestorp* 1234
    EPNS YOW, 4, p. 229. Simplex
Canonthorpe (Aston cum Aughton) SK 4685. *Canuntorp'* 1164–81
    EPNS YOW, 1, p. 159. OFr/ME *cano(u)n* 'canon'
Caretorp (Long Preston) SD 8052. *Caretorp* 1086
    EPNS YOW, VI, p. 164, SSNY, p. 56. ON pers.n. *Kári*
Chapelthorpe (Sandal Magna) SE 3116. *Schapelthorpe* 1285
    EPNS YOW, 2, p. 102, DEPN, p. 95. OFr/ME *chapel*
Choksthorpe (Royston) SE 3608. *Choksthorpe* 13th

EPNS YOW, 1, p. 275. Uncertain

Coneythorpe (Goldsborough) SE 3959. *Cunnigestorp'* 1200, *Cunningesthorp* 1201
  EPNS YOW, 5, p. 15, DEPN, p. 120. ON *konungr* 'king'

Copmanthorpe (York St Mary Bishophill Junior) SE 5646. *Copeman Torp* 1086
  EPNS YOW, 4, p. 227, SSNY, p. 56, DEPN, p. 121, CDEPN, p. 157. ON *kaup-mann*
  'merchant'

Cowthorpe (Cowthorpe) SE 4252. *Coletorp* 1086
  EPNS YOW, 5, p. 22, SSNY, p. 57, DEPN, p. 127. OE or ON pers.n

Edderthorpe (Darfield) SE 4104. *Edricthorp* 1208
  EPNS YOW, 1, p. 95. OE pers.n. Ēadrīc

Eilrichetorp (Maltby) SK 5292. *Eilrichetorp* 1147
  EPNS YOW, 1, p. 139. OE pers.n. Æthelrīc

Ellenthorpe (Gisburn) SD 8351. *Eluuinetorp* 1086
  EPNS YOW, 6, p. 174, SSNY, p. 57. OE pers.n. Æthelwine

Gawthorpe (Dewsbury) SE 2820. *Goukethorpe* 1274–1307
  EPNS YOW, 2, p. 188, DEPN, p. 194. ON *gaukr* 'cuckoo'

Gawthorpe (Kirkheaton) SE 2015. *Gou[c]thorp* 1297
  EPNS YOW, 2, p. 230, DEPN, p. 194. ON *gaukr* 'cuckoo'

Gawthorpe Hall (Sandal Magna) SE 3216. *Guketorp* 1252
  EPNS YOW, 2, p. 102–3. ON *gaukr* 'cuckoo'

Gawthorpe Hall (Harewood) SE 3245. *Gaukethorp* 12th
  EPNS YOW, 4, p. 181. ON *gaukr* 'cuckoo'

Gelsthorpe (Whixley) SE 4458. *Gaylesthorp* 1226
  EPNS YOW, 5, p. 10, SPNLY, p. 98. ON pers.n. Geilir

Goldthorpe (Bolton upon Dearne) SE 4604. *Goldetorp* 1086
  EPNS YOW, 1, pp. 83–4, SSNY, p. 59, DEPN, p. 200, CDEPN, p. 255. OE pers.n.
  Golda

Gowthorpe (Selby) SE 6132. *regia strata de Goukethorp* 12th
  EPNS YOW, 4, p. 33, SPNLY, p. 97. ON *gaukr* 'cuckoo'

Grewelthorpe (Kirkby Malzeard) SE 2376. *Torp* 1086, *Torp Gruel* 12th, *Naurethorp*
  c.1150
  EPNS YOW, 5, p. 206, SSNY, p. 69 (no. 28), DEPN, p. 205, CDEPN, p. 262. Simplex

Grimesthorpe (Sheffield) SK 3591. *Grimestorp* 1297
  EPNS YOW, 1, pp. 210–11, SSNY, p. 59, CDEPN, p. 263. ON pers.n. Grímr

Grimethorpe (Felkirk) SE 4110. *Grimestorp* late 12th
  EPNS YOW, 1, p. 268, SPNLY, p. 106, DEPN, p. 205, CDEPN, p. 263. ON pers.n.
  Grímr

Herringthorpe (Rotherham) SK 4393. *Henrithorp* 1194–9, *Heringthorp* 1307–27
  EPNS YOW, 1, pp. 185–6, SPNLY, pp. 147–8. PostC pers.n. Henri *(de Hareng)*

Hexthorpe (Doncaster) SE 5501. *Hestorp* 1086, *Hexthorp* 1246

EPNS *YOW*, 1, p. 27, SSNY, p. 60, DEPN, pp. 237–8. ON pers.n. *Heggr*

Hollingthorpe (Sandal Magna) SE 3215. *Holynthorp* 1297
 EPNS *YOW*, 2, p. 103. OE *holegn* 'holly'

Ingerthorpe (Ripon) SE 2866. *Ingeringthorp* 1154–81, *Ingeridtorp* 1162
 EPNS *YOW*, 5, p. 178, SPNLY, p. 151, DEPN, p. 264. ON (fem.) pers.n. *Ingiríthr*

Ingmanthorpe (Kirk Deighton) SE 3950. *Germundstorp* 1086, *Indegkemanethorp* 1204–9, *Yngmanthorp* 1285
 EPNS *YOW*, 5, p. 24, SSNY, pp. 60–1, DEPN, p. 265. ON pers.n. *Geirmundr*

Ingthorpe Grange (Martons Both) SD 9050. *Ucnetorp* 1086, *Unkethorpe* late 12th
 EPNS *YOW*, 6, p. 40, SSNY, p. 61. ON pers.n.?

Kettlethorpe Hall (Sandal Magna) SE 3115. *Ketelesthorp* 1242
 EPNS *YOW*, 2, p. 103, SPNLY, p. 167. ON pers.n. *Ketill*

Kirkthorpe (Warmfield) SE 3721. *Torp* 1135–40, *Kirketorp* c.1254
 EPNS *YOW*, 2, p. 117. Simplex

Leventhorp (Bradford) SE 1033. *Lewynthorp* 1216–72, *Lowinthorph* c.1240–6
 EPNS *YOW*, 3, p. 272. OE pers.n. *Lēofwine*

Leventhorpe Hall (Swillington) SE 3831. *Lewintorp* 1210–25
 EPNS *YOW*, 4, p. 94. OE pers.n. *Lēofwine*

Littlethorpe (Ripon) SE 3269. *Torp'* 1086
 EPNS *YOW*, 5, pp. 173–4, SSNY, p. 69 (no. 31), CDEPN, p. 376. Simplex

Lower Thorpe (AlmonDRBury) SE 1615. *Thorpe* late 13th
 EPNS *YOW*, 2, p. 258. Simplex

Middlethorpe (York St Mary Bishophill Senior) SE 5948. *Torp* 1086, *Thorp* c.1150, *Thorp Mauteby* 1237
 EPNS *YOW*, 4, p. 226, SSNY, p. 69 (no. 32). Simplex

Middlethorpe (Selby) SE 6133. *Midelthorp* 1297
 EPNS *YOW* 4, p. 33, DEPN, p. 324. OE *middel* 'middle'

Milnthorpe (Sandal Magna) SE 3418. *Milnethorp* 1297
 EPNS *YOW*, 2, p. 107, DEPN, p. 326. OE *myln* 'mill'

Milnthorpe (Thurnscoe) SE 4505. *Milnethorpe* 13th
 EPNS *YOW*, 1, p. 92. OE *myln* 'mill'

Milnthorpe (Darfield) SE 3603. *Milnethorpe* late 13th
 EPNS *YOW*, 1, p. 297. OE *myln* 'mill'

Minsthorpe (South Kirkby) SE 4812. *Manestorp* 1086, *Menetorp* 1166
 EPNS *YOW*, 2, p. 37, SSNY, p. 63. OE (ge)*mǣne* 'common' or (ge)*mǣnnes* 'community'

Moorthorpe (South Kirkby) SE 4510. *Torp* 1086, *Morthorp* 1246
 EPNS *YOW*, 2, p. 41, SSNY, p. 69 (no. 33). Simplex

Nether Thorpe (Thorpe Salvin) SK 5280. *Netherthorp* 13th
 EPNS *YOW* 1, p. 151. OE *neothera*/ON *nethri* 'lower'

Newthorpe (Sherburn in Elmet) SE 4632. *on Niwan Þorp* c.1020
    EPNS YOW, 4, p. 60, SSNY, p. 63, DEPN, p. 341, CDEPN, p. 436. OE *nīwe* 'new'
Northorpe (Mirfield) SE 2020. *del Norththorpe* 1297, *Northorp* 13th
    EPNS YOW, 2, p. 198. OE/ON *north(r)* 'north'
Oglethorpe Hall (Bramham) SE 4343. *Ocelestorp* 1086, *Oglestorp* 1086
    EPNS YOW, 4, pp. 83–4, SSNY, pp. 63–4, DEPN, p. 349. ON pers.n. *Oddkell*
Okynthorp (Darton) SE 3108. *Okynthorp* 1272–1307
    EPNS YOW, 1, p. 317. OE *ācen* 'oaken'
Osgathorpe House (Sheffield) SK 3590. *Osgottorp* 12th, *Hosgerthorp* 1260
    EPNS YOW, 1, p. 211, SSNY, p. 64. OE or ON pers.n
Osmondthorpe (Whitkirk) SE 3333. *Osmundthorp* 1155
    EPNS YOW, 4, p. 120, SPNLY, pp. 34–5, DEPN, p. 352. OE pers.n. *Ōsmund*
Ouchthorpe (Wakefield) SE 3224. *Uchethorpe* 1274
    EPNS YOW, 2, p. 157. ?OFr *houche* 'garden'
Painthorpe (Sandal Magna) SE 3117. *Paynesthorp* 1203
    EPNS YOW, 2, p. 104. PostC pers.n. *Pein* (< *Paganus*)
Pallathorpe (Bolton Percy) SE 5241. *Torp* 1086, *Thorpkime* 1251, *Paddocthorpe* 1285
    EPNS YOW, 4, p. 222, SSNY, p. 70 (no. 38). Simplex
Priest Thorpe (Bingley) SE 1039. *Presthorpe* 1156–85
    EPNS YOW, 4, p. 164. OE *prēost* 'priest'
Priesthorpe (Calverley) SE 2136. *Prestorp* c.1250
    EPNS YOW, 3, p. 225. OE *prēost* 'priest'
Renathorpe Hall (Sheffield) SK 3588. *Raynaldthorp* 1286
    EPNS YOW, 1, p. 212, SPNLY, p. 213. ON or PostC pers.n
Roberthorpe (Wakefield) SE 3320. *Robertthorpe* 1277
    EPNS YOW, 2, p. 168. PostC pers.n. *Ro(d)bert*
Rogerthorpe (Badsworth) SE 4714. *Rogartorp* 1086, *Thorp* 1177–93, *Torp Rogeri* 1121–7
    EPNS YOW, 2, p. 97, SSNY, p. 65. PostC pers.n. *Roger*
Scagglethorpe (Moor Monkton) SE 5056. *Scachertorp* 1086, *Scakelthorp* 1202–8
    EPNS YOW, 4, p. 259, SSNY, p. 66, DEPN, p. 406. Uncertain
Scosthrop (Arncliffe) SD 8959. *Scotorp* 1086, *Scozthorp* 1240–65
    EPNS YOW, 6, pp. 142–3, SSNY, p. 67, DEPN, p. 408. ON pers.n.?
Scotton Thorpe (Farnham) SE 3259. *Torp* 1086
    EPNS YOW, 5, p. 92, SSNY, p. 69 (no. 10). Simplex
Skelmanthorpe (Emley) SE 2310. *Scelmertorp* 1086
    EPNS YOW, 2, pp. 221–2, SSNY, p. 67, DEPN, p. 424, CDEPN, p. 552–3. ON pers.n. **Skjaldmarr*
Skinnerthorpe (Sheffield) SK 3593. *Schinartorp* 1297
    EPNS YOW, 1, p. 213, SSNY, p. 67. ON pers.n.?
Skinthorpe (Sprotbrough) SE 5403. *Scinestorp* 1086

EPNS *YOW*, 1, pp. 65–6, SSNY, p. 67. ON pers.n. *Skinnr* or *Skinni*

Snapethorpe (Wakefield) SE 3119. *Sneipetorp* 1156

EPNS *YOW*, 2, p. 155. ON pers.n. *Sneypir*

Stokethorp (Giggleswick) SD 8263. *Stokethorp* 13th

EPNS *YOW*, 6, p. 152. OE *stoc* 'outlying farm', perhaps as a place-name in itself

Streetthorpe (Kirk Sandall) SE 6108. *Stirestorp* 1086

EPNS *YOW*, 1, p. 22, SSNY, p. 67. ON pers.n. *Styrr*

Thorp (Monk Fryston) SE 5029. *Thorp* 1109–12

EPNS *YOW*, 4, p. 43. Simplex

Thorp (Halifax) SE 1226. *Thorp* 13th

EPNS *YOW*, 3, p. 83. Simplex

Thorp Arch (Thorp Arch) SE 4345. *Torp* 1086

EPNS *YOW*, 4, pp. 244–5, SSNY, p. 69 (no. 12), DEPN, p. 469, CDEPN, p. 611. Simplex

Thorp Garths (Weston) SE 1748. *le Thorp* 13th

EPNS *YOW*, 5, p. 62. Simplex

Thorpe (Burnsall) SE 0161. *Torp* 1086

EPNS *YOW*, 6, p. 96, SSNY, p. 68 (no. 5), CDEPN, p. 611. Simplex

Thorpe (Otley) SE 1641. *Hughthorp buttes* 1281, *Thorp* 1294

EPNS *YOW*, 4, p. 200. PostC pers.n. *Hugo*

Thorpe Audlin (Badsworth) SE 4715. *Torp* 1086

EPNS *YOW*, 2, p. 97, SSNY, p. 69 (no. 14), DEPN, p. 469, CDEPN, p. 611. Simplex

Thorpe Dichton (Kirk Deighton) SE 3951. *Thorpe Dichton* 1267

EPNS *YOW*, 5, p. 25. Place-name Deighton

Thorpe Hall (Selby) SE 6131. *Thorpe* 12th, *Westhorp'* 13th, *Thorp' Seleby* 1279–81

EPNS *YOW*, 4, p. 34, SSNY, p. 70 (no. 41), CDEPN, p. 612. Simplex

Thorpe Hesley (Rotherham) SK 3796. *Torp* 1086

EPNS *YOW*, 1, p. 187, SSNY, p. 69 (no. 18), CDEPN, p. 612. Simplex

Thorpe Hill (Little Ouseburn) SE 4460. *Torp* 1086

EPNS *YOW*, 5, p. 7, SSNY, p. 69 (no. 20). Simplex

Thorpe in Balne (Barnby upon Don) SE 5911. *Thorp* 1150

EPNS *YOW*, 1, p. 19, DEPN, p. 469, CDEPN, p. 612. Simplex

Thorpe on the Hill (Rothwell) SE 3126. *Torp* 1086, *Thorp othe Hull* 1309

EPNS *YOW*, 2, p. 149, SSNY, p. 69 (no. 21), DEPN, p. 469. Simplex

Thorpe Salvin (Thorpe Salvin) SK 5281. *Torp* 1086, *Thorpe Saluayn* 1255, *Richenildtorp* 1276

EPNS *YOW*, 1, p. 151, SSNY, p. 69 (no. 23), DEPN, p. 469, CDEPN, p. 612. Simplex

Thorpe Stapleton (Whitkirk) SE 3430. *Torp* 1086

EPNS *YOW*, 4, p. 123, SSNY, p. 69 (no. 24), DEPN, p. 469. Simplex

Thorpe Underwood (Little Ouseburn) SE 4659. *Tuadestorp* 1086, *?Torp* 1086, *Thorp*

1175–94

EPNS *YOW*, 5, pp. 5–6, SSNY, p. 68, DEPN, p. 469, CDEPN, pp. 612–13. ON pers.n. Thóraldr

Thorpe Willoughby (Brayton) SE 5731. *twegen þorpas* c.1020, *Torp* 1086
EPNS *YOW*, 4, pp. 30–1, SSNY, p. 69 (no. 26), DEPN, p. 469, CDEPN, p. 613. Simplex

Thorpes (Emley) SE 2311. *Torp* 12th
EPNS *YOW*, 2, p. 222. Simplex

Throapham (Dinnington St Johns) SK 5287. *Trapun* 1086, *Thropon* 1352
EPNS *YOW*, 1, pp. 144–5. Simplex? See above, pp. 80–1

Thrope House (Kirkby Malzeard) SE 1272. *Trope* 1198, *Trope* 1457, *Thorp* 1485
EPNS *YOW*, 5, pp. 203–4. Simplex? See above, pp. 80–1

Ulvesthorpe (Calverley) SE 2232. *Uluisthorp* 1189–99
EPNS *YOW*, 3, p. 237, SPNLY, p. 322. ON pers.n. Úlfr

Wildthorpe (Sprotbrough) SE 5402. *Widuntorp* 1086, *Wilthorp* 1303
EPNS *YOW*, 1, p. 66, SSNY, p. 71. OE *wilde* 'wild'

Wilstrop (Kirk Hammerton) SE 4854. *Wiulestorp* 1086, *Wyvelesthorp* 1118–50
EPNS *YOW*, 4, p. 259, SSNY, p. 71, DEPN, p. 521. Uncertain

Wilthorpe (Silkstone) SE 3406. *Wilthorp* 1202, *Wildethorp* 1495
EPNS *YOW*, 1, p. 304. OE *wilde* 'wild'

Woodthorpe (Sandal Magna) SE 3419. *le Wodethorpe* 1252
EPNS *YOW*, 2, p. 109. OE *wudu* 'wood'

Woodthorpe Hall (Handsworth) SK 4186. *Wodetorp* 13th
EPNS *YOW*, 1, p. 166. OE *wudu* 'wood'

Wrenthorpe (Wakefield) SE 3225. *Wirintorp* 1221, *Wyfrunthorp* 1260
EPNS *YOW*, 2, p. 157, DEPN, p. 538. OE (fem.) pers.n. *Wīfrūn

Uncertain county

Brinkesthorp (perhaps LEI). *Brikem'estorp* 1214, *Brinkesthorp* 1253, *Bringestorpe* 1624
Wagner, *Studies*, p. 195. OE pers.n.?

Theogendethorp (perhaps YOW). *æt Þeogendeþorpe* 1002–4 (11th)
Sawyer, *Burton Abbey*, no. 29. Uncertain

ii. England outside the Danelaw

Bedfordshire

Thrup End (Lidlington) SP 9939. *Trop* 1276, *Thorp or Thruppe End* 1637
EPNS BED & HNT, pp. 78–9. Simplex

Berkshire

Colthrop (Thatcham) SU 5167. *Colethrop'* 1220

EPNS BRK, 1, p. 188, DEPN, p. 115. OE pers.n. *Cola*

Thrupp (Great Faringdon) SU 2895. *la Thorpe* 1241, *Le Throp* 1401–2
EPNS BRK, 2, p. 367, DEPN, p. 471. Simplex

Thrupp (Radley) SU 5298. (*uiculum nomine ad*) *Tropam ante* 1170 (c.1200) *la Trope* c.1180 (13th)
EPNS BRK, 2, p. 456, DEPN, p. 471. Simplex

Buckinghamshire

Bigstrup Fm (Haddenham) SP 7408. *Bichestrope* 1161–3, *Bikelestorp* 1179
EPNS BUC, p. 161. OE pers.n. **Biccel* (but see above, pp. 72–3)

Eythrope (Waddesdon) SP 7416. *Edropa Ricardi* 1167, *Etrop* 1220
EPNS BUC, pp. 139–40, DEPN, p. 172. OE *ēa* 'river' or *ēg* 'island'

Helsthorpe (Wingrave) SP 8618. *Helpestorp* 1086, *Helpestrope* 1086
EPNS BUC, pp. 88–9. OE pers.n. *Help* or *Helphere*

Katestrop (Amersham) SU 9697. *Katestrop* 12th, *Castropmede* 13th
Wagner, *Studies*, p. 25. ON pers.n.? See above, p. 65

Sedrup (Hartwell) SP 7912. *Surop'* 1236, *Suthrop* 1241
EPNS BUC, p. 163. OE *sūth* 'south'

Dorset

Throop (Affpuddle) SY 8093. *Pidele la Trop'* 1237, *Thrope* 1268
EPNS DOR, 1, p. 290. Simplex

Throop (Tolpuddle) SY 7994. *Trop* 1280, *Throop* 1795
EPNS DOR, 1, p. 332. Simplex. Occasionally with 'west'

Throop Dairy House (Maiden Newton) SY 5997. *la Thrope* 1268
Mills, *Dorset Place-Names*, p. 144. Simplex

Essex

Easthorpe (Easthorpe) TL 9121. *Estorp* 1086
EPNS ESX, p. 388, DEPN, p. 157. OE *ēast*

Gestingthorpe (Gestingthorpe) TL 8138. *æt Gyrstlingaþorpe* 975–1016, *Ghestingetorp* 1086
EPNS ESX, p. 430, CDEPN, p. 249 DEPN, p. 195. Uncertain (see above, pp. 71–2)

Littlethorpe (Southchurch) TQ 9186. *Torpeiam* 1086, *Thorpe Paulyn* 1238, *Northtorp* 1221
EPNS ESX, p. 201. Simplex, with later affixes

Thorpehall Fm (Southchurch) TQ 9187. *Thorp* 1086, *Southorpe* 1275
EPNS ESX, p. 201. Simplex, with later affix

Westropps (Gestingthorpe) TL 8238. *Westrorp* [sic] 1274, *Westtorp* 1285
EPNS ESX, p. 628. OE *west* 'west'

Gloucestershire

Adlestrop (Adlestrop) SP 2427. *Tedestrop* 1086, *Tatlestrope* ?11th (12th)
    EPNS *GLO*, 1, pp. 211–12, DEPN, p. 3, CDEPN, p. 4. OE pers.n. *Tætel*

Brookthorpe (Brookthorpe) SO 8312. *Brostorp* 1086, *Brocht(h)rop* 1096–1112
    EPNS *GLO*, 2, p. 161, DEPN, p. 69, CDEPN, p. 93. OE *brōc* 'brook'

Cockrup Farm (Coln St Aldwyn) SP 1406. *Cocthorpe* 1266
    EPNS *GLO*, 1, p. 30. OE *cocc* 'cock' or OE pers.n

Colethrop (Haresfield) SO 8110. *Colethrop* 1248
    EPNS *GLO*, 2, p. 183. ME surname *Cole* (family name of 13th-century tenant)

Hatherop (Hatherop) SP 1505. *Etherop(e)*, *Hadrop* 1086, *Haethrop* 1139–48
    EPNS *GLO*, 1, pp. 36–7, DEPN, p. 224, CDEPN, p. 286. Uncertain

Pindrup Farm (Coln Rogers) SP 0809. *Pynthrop* 1266
    EPNS *GLO*, 1, p. 165. Uncertain

Puckrup (Twyning) SO 8936. *Pokethrop'* 1287
    EPNS *GLO*, 2, p. 71. OE *pūca* 'goblin'

Southrop (Southrop) SP 2003. *Sudthropa* c.1140, *Suthþrop* 12th
    EPNS *GLO*, 1, pp. 45–6, DEPN, p. 432, CDEPN, p. 562. OE *sūth* 'south'

Thropp (Winchcomb) SP 0228. *Throp(e)* 12th, la *Trop* 1256
    EPNS *GLO*, 2, p. 35. Simplex

Thrupp (Thrupp) SO 8703. *Trop'* 1261
    EPNS *GLO*, 1, p. 140, DEPN, p. 471, CDEPN, p. 614. Simplex

Upthorpe (Cam) ST 7499. *Upthrop* 1199–1216, *Upthrop* 1212
    EPNS *GLO*, 2, p. 217. OE *upp* 'up, high'

Westrip Farm (Cherington) ST 9098. *Westrop(pe)* 1272
    EPNS *GLO*, 1, p. 90, DEPN, p. 509. OE *west* 'west'

Williamstrip Park (Coln St Aldwyn) SP 1405. *Hetrop* 1086, *Williamsthorpe* 1287
    EPNS *GLO*, 1, p. 30, DEPN, p. 520. ?OE *hēah* 'high'; then PostC pers.n. *William* (1086 tenant)

Woolstrop (Quedgeley) SO 8114. *Wiuelestorp* 1216, *Wlvrichtrop* 1220
    EPNS *GLO*, 2, p. 188. OE pers.n. *Wulfrīc*. Earliest form here?

Hampshire

Athelardestrop (Sherborne St John) SU 6255. *Athelardestrop* 1259
    Gover, 'Hampshire place-names', p. 249. OE pers.n. *Æthelheard*

Eastrop (Eastrop) SU 6451. *Estrope* 1086
    Coates, *Place-Names of Hampshire*, p. 70. OE *ēast* 'east'

Eastrop Farm (Up Nateley) SU 6951. *Esthrope* 1100–35, *Natteleges Estrop* 1249
    Gover, 'Hampshire place-names', p. 127, OE *ēast* 'east'

Edmondsthorpe (Kingsclere) SU 5258. *Ædmundestorp* 1167

Coates, *Place-names of Hampshire*, p. 31. OE pers.n. Ēadmund

Ibthorpe (Hurstbourne Tarrant) SU 3853. *Ebbedrope* 1236, *Ybethrop* 1269

Coates, *Place-names of Hampshire*, p. 99, CDEPN, p. 328. OE pers.n. *Ibba*

la Trope (Pamber) SU 6158. *la Trope* 1203

Gover, 'Hampshire place-names', p. 251. Simplex

Southrope (Herriard) SU 6645. *Sudtrop(e)* 1164, *Suttropa* 1167

Gover, 'Hampshire place-names', p. 133, CDEPN, p. 562. OE *sūth* 'south'

Swanthorpe House (Crondall) SU 7948. *Swanethorp* 1233, *Swandrop* 1248

Coates, *Place-names of Hampshire* p. 159, DEPN, p. 455. OE *swān* 'herdsman' (see above, pp. 67–8)

Throop (Holdenhurst) SZ 1492. *la Throup* 12th

Coates, *Place-names of Hampshire*, p. 162, Mills, *Dorset place-names*, p. 144, DEPN, p. 470. Simplex

Hertfordshire

*Throp (Wheathampstead) TL 1714. Cf. *Thropfeld, Thropmulle, Thropmanland* 1272–1341

EPNS HRT, pp. 259–60. Qualifiers indicating lost simplex

Northamptonshire

Abthorpe (Abthorpe) SP 6446. *Abetrop* 1190

EPNS NTH, pp. 89–90, SSNEM, p. 122, DEPN, p. 1, CDEPN, p. 2. OE pers.n. *Abba*

Astrop (King's Sutton) SP 5036. *Estrop* 1200

EPNS NTH, p. 58, SSNEM, p. 125, DEPN, p. 18, CDEPN, p. 25. OE *ēast* 'east'

Milthorpe (Weedon Lois) SP 5946. *Middiltrop* c.1200

EPNS NTH, p. 45, SSNEM, p. 130. OE *middel* 'middle'

Overthorpe (Middleton Cheney) SP 4840. *Trop* 1235, *Thorp near Charwell* 1299

EPNS NTH, p. 55, SSNEM, p. 133 (no. 10). Simplex

Thorpe Mandeville (Thorpe Mandeville) SP 5346. *Torp* 1086

EPNS NTH, pp. 61–2, SSNEM, p. 119 (no. 15), DEPN, p. 469, CDEPN, p. 612. Simplex

Thrupp (Norton) SP 6065. *æt Þrope* 956–1002, *Torp* 1086

EPNS NTH, pp. 27–8, SSNEM, p. 119 (no. 33), DEPN, p. 471. Simplex

Westhorp (Byfield) SP 5153. *Westorp* 1086

EPNS NTH, p. 33, SSNEM, p. 121. OE *west* 'west'

Westhorp (Marston St Lawrence) SP 5442. *Westhrop* 1219

EPNS NTH, p. 55, SSNEM, p. 133. OE *west* 'west'

Northumberland

Throphill (Mitford) NZ 1385. *Trophil* 1166, *Throphill* c.1250

EPNS NTB & DUR, p. 197, DEPN, p. 471, CDEPN, p. 614. Qualifier with OE *hyll*
'hill'. See above, p. 80

Thropton (Rothbury) NU 0202. *Tropton* 1176
    EPNS NTB & DUR, p. 197, DEPN, p. 471, CDEPN, p. 614. Qualifier with OE *tūn*
    'farm, estate, village'. See above, p. 80

Oxfordshire

Astrop Farm (Brize Norton) SP 3007. *Estrope* 1086
    EPNS OXF, 2, p. 307. OE *ēast* 'east'

Calthorpe House (Banbury) SP 4541. *Cotthrop* 1278–9, *Co(rt)thrope* 1285, *Colthrop*
    1285
    EPNS OXF, 2, pp. 412–13, DEPN, p. 83. ?OE *col* 'charcoal'

Cokethorpe Park (Hardwick with Yelford) SP 3806. *Soctrop* 1226, *Cocthrop* 1278–9,
    Coketrope 1285
    EPNS OXF, 2, p. 324, DEPN, p. 115. ?OE *cocc* 'cock' or OE pers.n

Dunthorp (Heythrop) SP 3528. *Dvnetorp* 1086
    EPNS OXF, 2, p. 272, DEPN, p. 154, EPNE 1, p. 139. OE *dūn* 'hill' or OE pers.n

Heythrop (Heythrop) SP 3527. *Edrope* 1086, *Heðrop* 11th
    EPNS OXF, 2, pp. 271–2, DEPN, p. 238, CDEPN, p. 302. OE *hēah* 'high'

Neithrop (Banbury) SP 4540. *Ethrop* 1224, *Nethrop* 1278–9, *Hethethrop* 1285
    EPNS OXF, 2, p. 413, DEPN, p. 337. ?OE *neothera* 'lower'

Sititrop (Shipton on Cherwell) SP 4816. *Sititrop* 1217–30 (13th)
    EPNS OXF, 2, p. 282. Uncertain

Thrupp (Thrupp) SP 4616. *Trop* 1086
    EPNS OXF, 2, p. 292, DEPN, p. 471, CDEPN, p. 614. Simplex

Tythrop House (Kingsey) SP 7406. *Duchitorp* 1086, *Teutropa* 1199, *Twithrope* 1205
    EPNS OXF, 1, p. 112, DEPN, p. 484. Uncertain

Somerset

Eastrip (Bruton) ST 6834. *Estrope* 1086
DEPN, p. 158. OE *ēast* 'east'

Surrey

Thorpe (Thorpe) TQ 0168. *Torp* 1086; also *in loco qui dicitur Thorpe* 672–4 (13th): see
    above, pp. 69–70
    EPNS SUR, p. 134, DEPN, p. 469, CDEPN, p. 611. Simplex

Warwickshire

Eathorpe (Eathorpe) SP 3969. *Ethorpe* 1232
    EPNS WAR, p. 129, SSNEM, p. 125, DEPN, p. 158, CDEPN, p. 206. OE *ēa* 'river'

Princethorpe (Princethorpe) SP 3970. *Prandestorpe* 1221
EPNS *WAR*, pp. 141–2, SSNEM, p. 130, DEPN, p. 374, CDEPN, p. 483. OE pers.n.?
Stoneythorpe Hall (Long Itchington) SP 4062. *Torp* 1199, *Samsonesthowrp* [sic] 1220,
Stonythorp 1309
EPNS *WAR*, pp. 134–5, SSNEM, p. 133 (no. 11). Simplex

Wiltshire
Barstroppe Ford (Purton) SU 1087. *de Barsthrop* 1282
EPNS *WLT*, p. 39. Uncertain
Burderop (Chisledon) SU 1879. *Burithorp* 1249, *Burythrop(e)* 1279
EPNS *WLT*, pp. 281–2. OE *burg* 'stronghold'
Cock-a-troop Cottages (Mildenhall) SU 2069. *Crokerestrope* 1257
EPNS *WLT*, p. 301. OE *croccere* 'potter'
Eastrop (Highworth) SU 2092. *Esthropp in Worthe* 1216–72
EPNS *WLT*, p. 26. OE *ēast* 'east'
Restrop (Purton) SU 0987. *Radestrope* c.1250
EPNS *WLT*, p. 39. Uncertain
Throope Farm & Hill (Bishopstone) SU 0625. *Thrope, Ebblesburnthorpe* 1289
EPNS *WLT*, p. 393. Simplex. Second spelling with place-name Ebbesborne
(Wake)
Thrup (Warminster) ST 8745. *Thrup* 1216–72
EPNS *WLT*, p. 448. Simplex
Thrup Farm (Ramsbury) SU 2771. *de Latrope* 1166, *Thrope* 1478, *Esthorpe juxta
Remmesbury* 1420
EPNS *WLT*, p. 289. Simplex
Westrop (Highworth) SU 1992. *Westrop* 1249
EPNS *WLT*, p. 26. OE *west* 'west'

Worcestershire
Huntingtrap Farm (Dodderhill) SO 6669. *Huntingthrop* 1271
EPNS *WOR*, p. 283. OE pers.n.?
Uppthrop (Bredon) SO 9236. *Uppþrop* 990 (e.11th)
cf. EPNS *WOR*, p. 186 and see above, p. 69, n. 30. OE *upp* 'up, above'
Upthorpe Farm (Alderminster) SP 2348. *Upthrop* 1275
EPNS *WOR*, p. 186 (see above, p. 69, n. 30). OE *upp* 'up, above'

iii. Unassigned

Uppthrop (unlocated). *on Upþrope* 869 (9th/10th)
S 214, and above, pp. 83–4, 145–6. OE *upp* 'up, above'

Bibliography

Abrams, L. and Parsons, D.N., 'Place-names and the history of Scandinavian settlement in England', in J. Hines, A. Lane and M. Redknap (eds), *Land, sea and home*, Society for Medieval Archaeology Monograph 20 (Leeds, 2004), pp. 379–431.

Addington, S., 'Landscape and settlements in south Norfolk', *Norfolk Archaeology*, 38/2 (1982), pp. 97–139.

Aldred, D. and Dyer, C., 'A medieval Cotswold village: Roel, Gloucestershire', *Transactions of the Bristol and Gloucestershire Archaeological Society*, 109 (1991), pp. 139–70.

Allison, K.J., Beresford, M.W. and Hurst, J.G., *The deserted villages of Northamptonshire*, Department of English Local History Occasional Papers 18 (Leicester, 1966).

Anderson, O.S., *The English hundred-names* (Lund, 1934–9), 3 vols.

Armstrong, A.M., Mawer, A., Stenton, F.M. and Dickins, B., *The place-names of Cumberland*, 3 parts, EPNS vols 20–22 (Cambridge, 1950–52).

Arnaud-Lindet, M.-P. (ed.), *Orose: Histoires (contre les païens)*, vol. 1 (Paris, 1990–).

Arnott, W.G., *The place-names of the Deben Valley parishes* (Ipswich, 1946).

Astill, G., 'An archaeological approach to the development of agricultural technologies in medieval England', in G. Astill and J. Langdon (eds), *Medieval farming and technology: the impact of agricultural change in northwest Europe* (Leiden, 1997), pp. 193–224.

Aston, M., 'Rural settlement in Somerset: some preliminary thoughts', in D. Hooke (ed.), *Medieval villages*, Oxford University Committee for Archaeology Monographs 5 (Oxford, 1985), pp. 81–100.

Aston, M. and Gerrard, C., '"Unique, traditional and charming": the Shapwick Project, Somerset', *Antiquaries Journal*, 79 (1999), pp. 1–58.

Ault, W., *Open-field farming in medieval England: a study of English by-laws* (London, 1972).

Avery, B., Findlay, D. and Mackney, D., *Soil map of England and Wales* (Southampton, 1975).

Bailey, K., 'Some observations on Gē, Gau and Go', *JEPNS*, 31 (1998–9), pp. 63–76.

Baker, A. and Butlin, R. (eds), *Studies of field systems in the British Isles* (Cambridge, 1973).

Barney, S.A., Lewis, W.J., Beach, J.A. and Berghof, O. (eds and tr.), *The etymologies of Isidore of Seville* (Cambridge, 2006).

Baron, C., 'A study of the place-names of East Suffolk', MA thesis (Sheffield, 1952).

Beaumont James, T. and Gerrard, C., *Clarendon: landscape of kings* (Macclesfield, 2007).

Benson, L.D. (ed.), *The riverside Chaucer* (1957; Oxford, 3rd edn, 1988).

Bilson, J., 'Weaverthorpe church and its builder', *Archaeologia*, 72 (1921–2), pp. 51–70.

Bishop, M. and Freeman, P., 'Recent work at Osmanthorpe, Nottinghamshire', *Britannia*, 24 (1993), pp. 159–89.

Blair, J., 'Frithuwold's kingdom and the origins of Surrey', in S. Bassett (ed.), *The origins of Anglo-Saxon kingdoms* (Leicester, 1989), pp. 97–107.

Blair, J., *The church in Anglo-Saxon society* (Oxford, 2005).

Bond, C.J., 'Medieval Oxfordshire villages and their topography: a preliminary discussion', in D. Hooke (ed.), *Medieval villages*, Oxford University Committee for Archaeology Monographs 5 (Oxford, 1985), pp. 101–24.

Brewster, T., 'An excavation at Weaverthorpe Manor, East Riding, 1960', *Yorkshire Archaeological Journal*, 44 (1972), pp. 114–33.

Brooks, N.P. and Kelly, S.E., *Charters of Christ Church, Canterbury* (forthcoming).

Brown, T. and Foard, G., 'The Saxon landscape: a regional perspective', in P. Everson and T. Williamson (eds), *The archaeology of landscape* (Manchester, 1998), pp. 67–94.

Brown, V. (ed.), *Eye Priory cartulary and charters*, 2 vols, Suffolk Records Society, 12–13 (1994–6).

Burrow, J.A. and Turville-Petre, T. (eds), *A book of Middle English* (1992; Oxford, 3rd edn, 2005).

Cameron, A. and O'Brien, C., 'The deserted mediaeval village of Thorpe-in-the-Glebe', Nottinghamshire, *Transactions of the Thoroton Society*, 85 (1981), pp. 56–67.

Cameron, K., *The place-names of Derbyshire*, 3 parts, EPNS vols 27–29 (Cambridge, 1959).

Cameron, K., *Scandinavian settlement in the territory of the Five Boroughs: the place-name evidence*, inaugural lecture (Nottingham, 1966).

Cameron, K., 'Scandinavian settlement in the territory of the Five Boroughs: the place-name evidence' in K. Cameron (ed.), *Place-name evidence for the Anglo-Saxon invasion and Scandinavian settlements: eight studies* (Nottingham, 1975), pp. 115–38.

Cameron, K., 'Scandinavian settlement in the territory of the Five Boroughs: the place-name evidence, part II, place-names in Thorp', *Mediaeval Scandinavia*, 3 (1970), pp. 35–49. Cited from reprint in K. Cameron (ed.), *Place-name evidence for the Anglo-Saxon invasion and Scandinavian settlements: eight studies* (Nottingham, 1975), pp. 139–56.

Cameron, K., 'Bynames of location in Lincolnshire subsidy rolls', *Nottingham Medieval Studies*, 32 (1988), pp. 156–64.

Cameron, K., *Dictionary of Lincolnshire place-names* (Nottingham, 1998).

Cameron, K. with Field, J. and Insley, J., *The place-names of Lincolnshire*, 6 parts, EPNS vols 58, 64–65, 66, 71, 73, 77 (Nottingham, 1985–2001).

Campbell, A., *Old English grammar* (Oxford, 1959).

Carroll, J. and Parsons, D.N., *Anglo-Saxon mint-names. Vol. 1: Axbridge–Hythe* (Nottingham, 2007).

Coates, R., *The place-names of Hampshire* (London, 1989).

Coates, R., 'New light on old wics: the progeny of Latin *vicus*', *Nomina*, 22 (1999), pp. 75–116.

Coatsworth, E., *British Academy corpus of Anglo-Saxon stone sculpture, 8. Western Yorkshire* (Oxford, 2008).

Cole, A., '*Ersc*: distribution and use of this Old English place-name', *JEPNS*, 32 (1999–2000), pp. 27–40.

Cole, A., 'The use of *Netel* in place-names', *JEPNS*, 35 (2002–3), pp. 49–58.

Colman, F., *Money talks: reconstructing Old English* (Berlin and New York, 1992).

Cooper, N. and Priest, V., 'Sampling a medieval village in a day: the "Big Dig" investigation of Great Easton, Leicestershire', *MSRG Annual Report*, 18 (2003), pp. 53–6.

Coppack, G., 'Low Caythorpe, East Yorkshire: the manor site', *Yorkshire Archaeological Journal*,

46 (1974), pp. 34–41.

Costen, M.D., 'Some evidence for new settlements and field systems in late Anglo-Saxon Somerset', in L. Abrams and J.P. Carley (eds), *The archaeology and history of Glastonbury Abbey* (Woodbridge, 1991), pp. 39–55.

Cox, B., 'The place-names of Leicestershire and Rutland', PhD thesis (Nottingham, 1971).

Cox, B., 'The place-names of the earliest English records', JEPNS, 8 (1975–6), pp. 12–66 at 65–6.

Cox, B., *The place-names of Rutland*, EPNS vols 67–69 (Nottingham, 1994).

Cox, B., *The place-names of Leicestershire*, 4 parts, EPNS vols 75, 78, 81 (Nottingham, 1998–2009).

Cox, B., *A dictionary of Leicestershire and Rutland place-names*, English Place-Names Society, Popular Series, 5 (2005).

Crick, J., *Charters of St Albans* (Oxford, 2007).

Cullen, P., 'The place-names of the lathes of St Augustine and Shipway, Kent', PhD thesis (University of Sussex, 1997).

Dam, P., Gammeltoft, P., Jakobsen, J.G.G., Knudsen D.N. and Svensson, O. (eds), *Torp: som ortnamn och bebyggelse*, Konferensrapport, Tvärvetenskaplig torp-konferens Malmö, 25–27 April 2007 (Lund, 2009).

Dance, R., *Words derived from Old Norse in early Middle English: studies in the vocabulary of the south-west Midland texts* (Tempe, 2003).

Darby, H.C., *The Domesday geography of eastern England* (Cambridge, 1971).

Darby, H.C., *Domesday England* (Cambridge, 1977).

Darby, H.C. and Campbell, E.M.J. (eds), *The Domesday geography of south-east England* (Cambridge, 1962).

Darby, H.C. and Maxwell, I.S., *The Domesday geography of northern England* (Cambridge, 1962).

Darby, H.C. and Terrett, I.B. (eds), *The Domesday geography of midland England* (Cambridge, 1971).

Dark, P., *The environment of Britain in the first millennium AD* (London, 2000).

Davis, R.H.C. (ed.), *The Kalendar of Abbot Samson of Bury St Edmunds and related documents* (London, 1954).

Davis, R.H.C., 'Alfred and Guthrum's frontier', EHR, 97 (1982), pp. 803–10.

Davison, A., 'The field archaeology of the Mannington and Wolverton estates', *Norfolk Archaeology*, 42/2 (1995), pp. 160–84.

Davison, A., 'Besthorpe', *Norfolk Archaeology*, 45/1 (2006), p. 124.

Draper, S., 'Old English *wīc* and *walh*: Britons and Saxons in post-Roman Wiltshire', *Landscape History*, 24 (2002), pp. 27–44.

Draper, S., *Landscape, settlement and society in Roman and early medieval Wiltshire*, BAR British Series 419 (Oxford, 2006).

Draper, S., 'The significance of Old English *burh* in Anglo-Saxon England', *Anglo-Saxon Studies in Archaeology and History*, 15 (2008), pp. 240–53.

Dumville, D.N., *Wessex and England from Alfred to Edgar* (Woodbridge, 1992).

Dyer, C., 'Place-names and pottery', in O.J. Padel and D.N. Parsons (eds), *A commodity of good names: essays in honour of Margaret Gelling* (Donington, 2008), pp. 44–54.

Dymond, D. (ed.), *The charters of Stanton, Suffolk, c.1215–1678*, Suffolk Record Society 18 (Woodbridge, 2009).

Ekwall, E., 'The Scandinavian element', in A. Mawer and F.M. Stenton (eds), *Introduction to the survey of English place-names*, EPNS I, part 1 (Cambridge, 1924, 2nd edn, 1933), pp. 55–92.

Ekwall, E., *The concise Oxford dictionary of English place-names* (1936; Oxford, 4th edn, 1960).

Ekwall, E., *English place-names in -ing* (1923; Lund, 2nd edn, 1962).

English, J., 'Worths in a landscape context', *Landscape History*, 24 (2002), pp. 45–52.

Everson, P. and Stocker, D., *British Academy corpus of Anglo-Saxon stone sculpture, 5. Lincolnshire* (Oxford, 1999).

Faith, R., *The English peasantry and the growth of lordship* (London, 1999).

Faith, R., 'Worthys and enclosures', *MSRG Annual Report*, 21 (2006), pp. 9–14.

Fellows-Jensen, G., *Scandinavian personal names in Lincolnshire and Yorkshire* (Copenhagen, 1968).

Fellows-Jensen, G., *Scandinavian settlement names in Yorkshire* (Copenhagen, 1972).

Fellows-Jensen, G., *Scandinavian settlement names in the East Midlands* (Copenhagen, 1978).

Fellows-Jensen, G., *Scandinavian settlement names in the North-West* (Copenhagen, 1985).

Fellows-Jensen, G., 'Place-names in -*þorp*: in retrospect and in turmoil', *Nomina*, 15 (1991–2), pp. 35–51.

Fellows-Jensen, G., 'Scandinavian settlement names in East Anglia: some problems', *Nomina*, 22 (1999), pp. 45–60.

Fellows-Jensen, G., 'Torp-navne i Norfolk i sammenligning med torp-navne i andre dele af Danelagen', in P. Gammeltoft and B. Jørgensen (eds), *Nordiske torp-navne* (Uppsala, 2003), pp. 47–59.

Finberg, H.P.R., 'Charltons and Carltons', in H.P.R. Finberg (ed.), *Lucerna* (London, 1964), pp. 144–60.

Foard, G., 'Systematic fieldwalking and the investigation of Saxon settlement in Northamptonshire', *World Archaeology*, 9 (1978), pp. 357–74.

Fox, H., 'Approaches to the adoption of the midland system', in T. Rowley (ed.), *The origins of open-field agriculture* (London, 1981), pp. 64–111.

Frere, S. and St Joseph, J.S., 'The Roman fortress at Longthorpe', *Britannia*, 5 (1974), pp. 1–129.

Gaffney, V. and Tingle, M., *The Maddle Farm Project: an integrated survey of prehistoric and Roman landscapes on the Berkshire Downs*, BAR British Series 200 (Oxford, 1989).

Gammeltoft, P., '"I sauh a tour on a toft, tryelyche i-maket", part two: on place-names in -toft in England', *Nomina*, 26 (2003), pp. 43–63.

Gardiner, M., 'Hythes, small ports, and other landing places in later medieval England', in J. Blair (ed.), *Waterways and canal-building in medieval England* (Oxford, 2007), pp. 85–110.

Gelling, M., based on material collected by D.M. Stenton, *The place-names of Oxfordshire*, 2 parts, EPNS vols 23, 24 (Cambridge, 1953 and 1954).

Gelling, M., *The place-names of Berkshire*, 3 parts, EPNS vols 49–51 (Cambridge, 1973–6).

Gelling, M., 'Some meanings of stōw', in S.M. Pearce, *The early church in Western Britain and Ireland: studies presented to C.A. Ralegh Radford*, BAR British Series 102 (Oxford, 1982), pp. 187–96

Gelling, M., *Signposts to the past: place-names and the history of England* (1978; Chichester, 3rd edn, 1997).

Gelling, M., 'Anglo-Norse place-names on the Yorkshire Wolds', in P. Gammeltoft and B. Jørgensen (eds), *Names through the looking-glass: festschrift in honour of Gillian Fellows-Jensen* (Copenhagen, 2006), pp. 85–93.

Gelling, M. and Cole, A., *The landscape of place-names* (Stamford, 2000).

Gerrard, C. with Aston, M., *The Shapwick Project, Somerset: a rural landscape explored*, Society for Medieval Archaeology Monographs 25 (London, 2007).

Gover, J.E.B., 'Hampshire place-names', unpublished manuscript (1961).

Gover, J.E.B. and Stenton, F.M., *The place-names of Northamptonshire*, EPNS vol. 10 (Cambridge, 1933).

Gover, J.E.B., Mawer, A. and Stenton, F.M., *The place-names of Devon*, 2 parts, EPNS vols 8 and 9 (Cambridge, 1931 and 1932).

Gover, J.E.B., Mawer, A. and Stenton, F.M., with Houghton, F.T.S., *The place-names of Worcestershire*, EPNS vol. 4 (Cambridge, 1927).

Gover, J.E.B., Mawer, A. and Stenton, F.M., with Bonner, A., *The place-names of Surrey*, EPNS vol. 11 (Cambridge, 1934).

Gover, J.E.B., Mawer, A. and Stenton, F.M., with Houghton, F.T.S., *The place-names of Warwickshire*, EPNS vol. 13 (Cambridge, 1936).

Gover, J.E.B., Mawer, A. and Stenton, F.M., *The place-names of Hertfordshire*, EPNS vol. 15 (Cambridge, 1938).

Gover, J.E.B., Mawer, A. and Stenton, F.M., *The place-names of Wiltshire*, EPNS vol. 16 (Cambridge, 1939).

Gover, J.E.B., Mawer, A. and Stenton, F.M., *The place-names of Nottinghamshire*, EPNS vol. 17 (Cambridge, 1940).

Gray, H., *English field systems* (Cambridge, 1915).

Green, B., Rogerson, A. and White, S., *The Anglo-Saxon cemetery at Morning Thorp, Norfolk 1*, East Anglian Archaeology 36 (Gressenhall, 1987).

Gross, C. (ed.), *Select cases from the coroner's rolls, AD 1265–1413*, Selden Society 9 (London, 1896).

Hadley, D., 'Multiple estates and the origins of manorial structure in the northern Danelaw', *Journal of Historical Geography*, 22/1 (1996), pp. 3–15.

Hall, D., 'Late Saxon topography and early medieval estates', in D. Hooke (ed.), *Medieval villages*, Oxford University Committee for Archaeology Monographs 5 (Oxford, 1985), pp. 61–70.

Hall, D., 'The late Saxon countryside: villages and fields', in D. Hooke (ed.), *Anglo-Saxon settlements* (Oxford, 1988), pp. 99–122.

Hall, D., *The open fields of Northamptonshire*, Northamptonshire Record Society 38 (Northampton, 1995).

Hall, D. and Martin, P., 'Brixworth, Northamptonshire: an intensive field survey', *Journal of the British Archaeological Association*, 132 (1979), pp. 1–6.

Harling-Kranck, G., 'Namn på -torp och torpnamn i Finland', in P. Gammeltoft and B. Jørgensen (eds), *Nordiske torp-navne* (Uppsala, 2003), pp. 79–94.

Harper-Bill, C. (ed.), *Blythborough Priory cartulary*, 2 vols, Suffolk Records Society, 2–3 (1980–1).

Haslam, J., 'Market and fortress in England in the reign of Offa', *World Archaeology*, 19/1 (1997), pp. 76–93.

Hayfield, C., *An archaeological survey of the parish of Wharram Percy, East Yorkshire. 1. The evolution of the Roman landscape*, BAR British Series 172 (Oxford, 1987).

Hedemand, L., Dam, P. and Gøgsig Jakobsen, J., 'De danske torp-landsbyers jordbundsforhold', in P. Gammeltoft and B. Jørgensen (eds), *Nordiske torp-navne*

(Uppsala, 2003), pp. 95–108.

Hill, D., 'Unity and diversity: a framework for the study of European towns', in R. Hodges and B. Hobbley (eds), *The rebirth of towns in the west AD 700–1050*, CBA Research Report 68 (London, 1988), pp. 8–15.

Hinton, D., *A smith in Lindsey: the Anglo-Saxon grave at Tattershall Thorpe, Lincolnshire*, Society for Medieval Archaeology Monographs 16 (London, 2000).

Hodges, R., 'The rebirth of towns in the early Middle Ages', in R. Hodges and B. Hobbley (eds), *The rebirth of towns in the west AD 700–1050*, CBA Research Report 68 (London, 1988), pp. 1–7.

Hodges, R., *Dark Age economics: the origins of towns and trade AD 600–1000* (London, 1989).

Holt, R., 'Milling technology in the Middle Ages: the direction of recent research', *Industrial Archaeology Review*, 13/1 (1990), pp. 50–8.

Hooke, D., 'Open-field agriculture: the evidence from pre-Conquest charters of the West Midlands', in T. Rowley (ed.), *The origins of open-field agriculture* (London, 1981), pp. 39–63.

Hooke, D., *The Anglo-Saxon landscape: the kingdom of the Hwicce* (Manchester, 1985).

Hooke, D., 'Early forms of open-field agriculture in England', *Geografiska Annaler*, Series B, 70 (1988), pp. 123–31.

Hooke, D., 'Early medieval estate and settlement patterns: the documentary evidence', in M. Aston, D. Austin and C. Dyer (eds), *Rural settlements of medieval England* (Oxford, 1989), pp. 9–30.

Horovitz, D., *The place-names of Staffordshire* (Brewood, 2005).

Hoskins, W.G., *The making of the English landscape* (London, 1955).

Hoskins, W.G., *Leicestershire: an illustrated essay on the history of the landscape* (London, 1957).

Hough, C., 'Chilton and other place-names from Old English Cild', *JEPNS*, 30 (2003–4), pp. 65–83.

Hurst, J.G., 'The Wharram Research Project: results to 1983', *Medieval Archaeology*, 28 (1984), pp. 77–111.

Insley, J., *Scandinavian personal names in Norfolk* (Uppsala, 1994).

Irvine, S. (ed.), *The Anglo-Saxon Chronicle: a collaborative edition*, 7 MS. E (Cambridge, 2004).

Isidore, *Etymologiarum sive Originum*, ed. W.M. Lindsey, 2 vols (Oxford, 1911).

Jones, G., 'Early territorial organization in England and Wales', *Geografiska Annaler*, 43 (1961), pp. 174–81.

Jones, G., 'Multiple estates and early settlement', in P.H. Sawyer (ed.), *Medieval settlement: continuity and change* (London, 1976), pp. 11–40.

Jones, G., 'Multiple estates perceived', *Journal of Historical Geography*, 11 (1985), pp. 352–62.

Jones, R., 'Signatures in the soil: the use of pottery in manure scatters in the identification of medieval arable farming regimes', *Archaeological Journal*, 161 (2004), pp. 159–88.

Jones, R. and Page, M., *Medieval villages in an English landscape: beginnings and ends* (Macclesfield, 2006).

Kelly, S.E. (ed.), *Charters of Peterborough Abbey* (Oxford, 2009).

Kelly, S.E. (ed.), *The Charters of Chertsey Abbey*, Anglo-Saxon Charters Series (Oxford, forthcoming).

Ker, N.R., *Catalogue of manuscripts containing Anglo-Saxon* (Oxford, 1957).

Keynes, S. and Lapidge, M., *Alfred the Great* (Harmondsworth, 1983).

Kindschi, L., 'The Latin–Old English glossaries in Plantin-Moretus MS 32 and British Museum MS Additional 32,246', PhD dissertation (Stanford University, 1955).

Kitson, P., 'How Anglo-Saxon personal names work', *Nomina*, 25 (2002), pp. 91–131.

Knox, R., 'The Anglo-Saxons in Leicestershire and Rutland', in P. Bowman and P. Liddle (eds), *Leicestershire landscapes*, Leicestershire Museums Archaeological Fieldwork Group Monograph 1 (Leicester, 2004), pp. 95–104.

Kron, G., 'Roman ley-farming', *Journal of Roman Archaeology*, 13 (2000), pp. 277–87.

Lang, J., *British Academy corpus of Anglo-Saxon stone sculpture, 3. York and Eastern Yorkshire* (Oxford, 1991).

Lang, J., *British Academy corpus of Anglo-Saxon stone sculpture, 6. Northern Yorkshire* (Oxford, 2001).

Laur, W., 'Torp-navne i Sydslesvig og sprogskiftet', in P. Gammeltoft and B. Jørgensen (eds), *Nordiske torp-navne* (Uppsala, 2003), pp. 167–76.

Laverton, S., *Shotley Peninsula: the makings of a unique Suffolk region* (Stroud, 2001).

Lendinara, P., *Anglo-Saxon glosses and glossaries* (Aldershot, 1999).

Lepelley, R., *Dictionnaire étymologique des noms de communes de Normandie* (Condé-sur-Noireau, 1993).

Lerche Nielsen, M., 'Sognekriteriets betydning for vurderingen af torp-navnenes alder', in P. Gammeltoft and B. Jørgensen (eds), *Nordiske torp-navne* (Uppsala, 2003), pp. 177–202.

Lewis, C., Mitchell-Fox, P. and Dyer, C., *Village, hamlet and field: changing medieval settlements in central England* (1997; Macclesfield, 2nd edn, 2001).

Lewis, C.T. and Short, C., *A Latin dictionary* (Oxford, 1879).

Lindkvist, H., *Middle-English place-names of Scandinavian origin* (Uppsala, 1912).

Loveluck, C., *Rural settlement, lifestyles and social change in the later first millennium AD at Flixborough, Lincolnshire: Flixborough in its wider context* (Oxford, 2007).

Loveluck, C. and Tys, D., 'Coastal societies, exchange, and identity along the Channel and southern North Sea shores of Europe, AD 600–1000', *Journal of Maritime Archaeology*, 1/2 (2006), pp. 140–69.

Lund, N., 'Thorp-names', in P.H. Sawyer (ed.), *Medieval settlement: continuity and change* (London, 1976), pp. 223–5.

McCarthy, M. and Brooks, C.M., *Medieval pottery in Britain AD 900–1600* (Leicester, 1988).

Maitland, F., *Domesday Book and beyond* (1897; London, repr. 1960).

Martin, E., '"Wheare most inclosures be": the making of the East Anglian landscape', in M. Gardiner and S. Rippon (eds), *Medieval landscapes* (Macclesfield, 2007), pp. 129–36.

Mawer, A., *The chief elements used in English place-names*, EPNS vol. 1, part 2 (Cambridge, 1924).

Mawer, A. and Stenton, F.M., *The place-names of Buckinghamshire*, EPNS vol. 2 (Cambridge, 1925).

Mawer, A. and Stenton, F.M., *The place-names of Bedfordshire and Huntingdonshire*, EPNS vol. 3 (Cambridge, 1926).

Mawer, A. and Stenton, F.M., with Gover, J.E.B., *The place-names of Sussex*, 2 parts, EPNS vols 6 and 7 (Cambridge, 1929 and 1930).

Millett, M., *The Romanization of Britain: an essay in archaeological interpretation* (Cambridge, 1998).

Mills, A.D., *The place-names of Dorset*, 4 parts, EPNS vols 52–3, 59–60 (Nottingham, 1977–89).

Mills, A.D., *Dorset place-names: their origins and meanings* (Newbury, 1990).

Morris, R., *Churches in the landscape* (London, 1989, rev. edn 1997).

North, J.J., *English hammered coinage I* (London, 1994).

Oliphant, R.T., *The Harley Latin–Old English glossary* (The Hague, 1966).

Oosthuizen, S., 'Medieval settlement relocation in west Cambridgeshire: three case-studies', *Landscape History*, 19 (1997), pp. 43–55.

Oosthuizen, S., 'New light on the origins of open-field farming', *Medieval Archaeology*, 49 (2005), pp. 165–93.

Oosthuizen, S., *Landscapes decoded: the origins and development of medieval fields in Cambridgeshire*, Explorations in Local and Regional History 1 (Hatfield, 2006).

Oosthuizen, S., 'The Anglo-Saxon kingdom of Mercia and the origins and distribution of common fields', *Agricultural History Review*, 55/2 (2007), pp. 153–80.

Owen, A.E.B., 'Salt, sea banks and medieval settlement on the Lindsey coast', in N. Field and A. White (eds), *A prospect of Lincolnshire* (Lincoln, 1984).

Owen, D., 'Chapelries and rural settlement: an examination of some of the Kesteven evidence', in P.H. Sawyer (ed.), *Medieval settlement: continuity and change* (London, 1976), pp. 66–71.

Parry, S., *Raunds Area survey: an archaeological study of the landscape of Raunds, Northamptonshire* (Oxford, 2006).

Parsons, D.N., 'How long did the Scandinavian language survive in England? Again', in J. Graham-Campbell, R. Hall, J. Jesch and D.N. Parsons (eds), *Vikings and the Danelaw* (Oxford, 2001), pp. 299–312.

Parsons, D.N., 'Anna, Dot, Thorir…: counting Domesday personal names', *Nomina*, 25 (2001–2), pp. 29–52.

Parsons, D.N., 'Field-name statistics, Norfolk and the Danelaw', in P. Gammeltoft and B. Jørgensen (eds), *Names through the looking-glass: festschrift in honour of Gillian Fellows-Jensen* (Copenhagen, 2006), pp. 165–88.

Parsons, D.N., *Pre-Viking place-names of Northamptonshire* (forthcoming).

Parsons, D.N. and Styles, T, with Hough, C., *The vocabulary of English place-names* (Nottingham, 1997–).

Pestell, T. and Ulmschneider, K. (eds), *Markets in early medieval Europe: trading and productive sites AD 650–850* (Macclesfield, 2003).

Pevsner, N., *The buildings of England: Suffolk* (Harmondsworth, 1961).

Pevsner, N. and Harris, J., *The buildings of England: Lincolnshire* (London, 1995).

Pheifer, J.D., *Old English glosses in the Épinal-Erfurt Glossary* (Oxford, 1974).

Pheifer, J.D., 'Early Anglo-Saxon glossaries and the school of Canterbury', *Anglo-Saxon England*, 16 (1987), pp. 17–44

Pierce, G.O., *The place-names of Dinas Powys hundred* (Cardiff, 1968).

Rackham, O., *The history of the countryside* (London, 1986).

Rahtz, P. and Meeson, R., *An Anglo-Saxon watermill at Tamworth: excavations in the Bolebridge Street area of Tamworth, Staffordshire, in 1971 and 1978* (London, 1992).

RCHME, *An inventory of the historical monuments in the county of Northamptonshire. Vol. 1: archaeological sites in north-east Northamptonshire* (London, 1975).

RCHME, *An inventory of the historical monuments in the county of Northamptonshire. Vol. 3: archaeological sites in north-west Northamptonshire* (London, 1981).

RCHME, *An inventory of the historical monuments in the county of Northamptonshire. Vol. 2: archaeological sites in central Northamptonshire* (London, 1979).

Reaney, P.H., *The place-names of Essex*, EPNS vol. 12 (Cambridge, 1935).

Reaney, P.H., *The place-names of Cambridgeshire and the Isle of Ely*, EPNS vol. 19 (Cambridge, 1943).

Reaney, P.H., *The origin of English surnames* (London, 1967).

Richards, J., *Viking age England* (London, 1991).

Riley, D., *Early landscape from the air: studies of cropmarks in south Yorkshire and north Nottinghamshire* (Sheffield, 1980).

Rippon, S., 'Landscapes in transition: the late Roman and early medieval periods', in D. Hooke (ed.), *Landscape: the richest historical record*, Society for Landscape Studies Supplementary Series 1 (Amesbury, 2000), pp. 47–61.

Rippon, S., *Beyond the village: the diversification of landscape character in southern Britain* (Oxford, 2008).

Roberts, B. and Wrathmell, S., *An atlas of rural settlement in England* (London, 2000).

Roberts, B. and Wrathmell, S., *Region and place: a study of English rural settlement* (London, 2002).

Robertson, A.J. (ed.), *Anglo-Saxon charters* (Cambridge, 1956).

Roffe, D., 'Place-naming in Domesday Book: settlements, estates, and communities', *Nomina*, 14 (1990–91), pp. 47–60.

Rotuli hundredorum, temp. Hen. III & Edw. I in Turr' Lond' et in Curia receptae scaccarij Westm. asservati, vol. 2 (London, 1818).

Russell, E., 'Excavations on the site of the deserted medieval village of Kettleby Thorpe, Lincolnshire', *Journal of the Scunthorpe Museum Society*, 3/2 (1974), pp. 1–40.

Sanderson, G., *Map of the country twenty miles round Mansfield* (1835; Mansfield, repub. 2001).

Sandred, K.I., *English place-names in -stead* (Uppsala, 1963).

Sandred, K.I. and Lindström, B., with Cornford, B. and Rutledge, P., *The place-names of Norfolk*, 3 parts, EPNS vols 61, 72, 79 (Nottingham, 1989–2002).

Sawyer, P., *Anglo-Saxon charters: an annotated list and bibliography* (London, 1968); updated electronic version at <www.esawyer.org.uk>.

Sawyer, P.H. (ed.), *Medieval settlement: continuity and change* (London, 1976).

Sawyer, P.H., *From Roman Britain to Norman England* (London, 1978).

Sawyer, P.H. (ed.), *Charters of Burton Abbey*, Anglo-Saxon Charters, 2 (1979).

Sawyer, P.H., *Anglo-Saxon Lincolnshire* (Lincoln, 1998).

Schneider, J., *Field-names of four Bedfordshire parishes (Tilsworth, Eggington, Hockliffe, Stanbridge)*, English Place-Name Society Field-Name Studies, 3 (1997).

Semple, S., 'Defining the OE *hearg*: a preliminary archaeological and topographical examination of *hearg* place names and their hinterlands', *Early Medieval Europe*, 15/4 (2007), pp. 364–85.

Shaw, M., 'A changing settlement pattern at Warmington, Northants', *MSRG Annual Report*, 8 (1993), pp. 41–8.

Sigmundsson, S., 'Þorp på Island', in P. Gammeltoft and B. Jørgensen (eds), *Nordiske torpnavne* (Uppsala, 2003), pp. 203–9.

Slade, C.F., *The Leicestershire survey c. AD 1130: a new edition*, Department of English Local History Occasional Papers 7 (Leicester, 1956).

Sleath, S. and Ovens, R., 'Martinsthorpe', *Rutland Record*, 14 (1994), pp. 167–74.

Smart, V., *Sylloge of coins of the British Isles 28: cumulative index of volumes 1–20* (London, 1981).

Smith, A.H., *The place-names of the North Riding of Yorkshire*, EPNS vol. 5 (Cambridge, 1928).

Smith, A.H., *The place-names of the East Riding of Yorkshire and York*, EPNS vol. 14 (Cambridge, 1937).

Smith, A.H., *English place-name elements*, 2 vols (Cambridge, 1956).

Smith, A.H., *The place-names of the West Riding of Yorkshire*, 8 parts, EPNS vols 30–37 (Cambridge, 1961–3).

Smith, A.H., *The place-names of Gloucestershire*, 4 parts EPNS vols 38–41 (Cambridge, 1964–5).

Smith, A.H., *The place-names of Westmorland*, 2 parts, EPNS vols 42, 43 (Cambridge, 1967).

Stapleton, T. (ed.) *Chronicon Petroburgense*, Camden Society 47 (London, 1849).

Stocker, D. and Everson, P., 'Five town funerals: decoding diversity in Danelaw stone sculpture', in J. Graham-Campbell, R. Hall, J. Jesch and D.N. Parsons (eds), *Vikings and the Danelaw: select papers from the proceedings of the thirteenth Viking congress* (Oxford, 2001), pp. 223–43.

Stone, E. and Hyde, P. (eds), *Oxfordshire hundred rolls of 1279*, Oxfordshire Record Society Series 46 (Oxford, 1968).

Styles, T., 'Scandinavian elements in English place-names: some semantic problems', in J. Graham-Campbell, R. Hall, J. Jesch and D.N. Parsons (eds), *Vikings and the Danelaw: select papers from the proceedings of the thirteenth Viking congress* (Oxford, 2001), pp. 289–98.

Taylor, C.C, 'Polyfocal settlement and the English village', *Medieval Archaeology*, 21 (1977), pp. 189–93.

Taylor, C.C, *Village and farmstead* (London, 1983).

Taylor, C.C, 'Dispersed settlement in nucleated areas', *Landscape History*, 17 (1995), pp. 27–34.

Taylor, C.C, 'Nucleated settlement: a view from the frontier', *Landscape History*, 24 (2002), pp. 53–71.

Taylor, J., *An atlas of Roman rural settlement in England*, CBA Research Report 151 (York, 2007).

Tennyson, A., *Maud and other poems* (London, 1869).

Thirsk, J., 'The common fields', *Past and Present*, 29 (1964), pp. 3–29.

Thomas, A.G., *The collected poems of Edward Thomas* (Oxford, 1978).

Thomas, E., *Collected poems* (London, 1917).

Thurston, T., 'The knowable, the doable, and the undiscussed: tradition, submission and the "becoming" of rural landscapes in Denmark's Iron Age', *Antiquity*, 73 (1999), pp. 661–71.

Townend, M., *Language and history in Viking age England: linguistic relations between speakers of Old Norse and Old English*, Studies in the Early Middle Ages 6 (Turnhout, 2002).

Trimble, G., 'An Anglo-Saxon settlement at Bishee Barnabee Way, Bowthorpe: excavations, 2001', *Norfolk Archaeology*, 44/3 (2004), pp. 525–35.

Unwin, T., 'Townships and early fields in north Nottinghamshire', *Journal of Historical Geography*, 9/4 (1983), pp. 341–6.

Unwin, T., 'Towards a model of Anglo-Scandinavian rural settlement in England' in D. Hooke (ed.), *Anglo-Saxon settlements* (Oxford, 1988), pp. 77–98.

von Feilitzen, O., *The pre-Conquest personal names of Domesday Book* (Uppsala, 1937).

Wacher, J., 'Excavations at Martinsthorpe, Rutland', *Transactions of the Leicestershire Archaeology and History Society*, 39 (1963–4), pp. 1–19.

Wade-Martins, P., *Excavations in North Elmham Park 1967–1972, vol. 1*, East Anglian Archaeology 9 (Gressenhall, 1980).

Wagner, U., *Studies on English place-names in Thorp* (Basel, 1976).

Wallenberg, J.K., *The place-names of Kent* (Uppsala, 1934).

Watts, V., 'Scandinavian settlement-names in County Durham', *Nomina*, 12 (1988–9), pp. 17–63.

Watts, V., 'Some place-name distributions', JEPNS, 32 (1999–2000), pp. 53–72.

Watts, V., *A dictionary of County Durham place-names*, English Place-Name Society, Popular Series, 3 (2002).

Watts, V., *Cambridge dictionary of English place-names* (Cambridge, 2004).

Watts, V., *The place-names of County Durham*, EPNS vol. 83 (Nottingham, 2007).

Westergaard, W., 'Danish history and Danish historians', *The Journal of Modern History*, 24/2 (1952), pp. 167–80.

Whitelock, D., *The Anglo-Saxon Chronicle: a revised translation* (London, 1961).

Widgren, M., 'Is landscape history possible? Or, how can we study the desertion of farms?', in P. Ucko and R. Layton (eds), *The archaeology and anthropology of landscape: shaping your landscape* (London, 1998), pp. 94–103.

Williamson, T., *Shaping medieval landscapes: settlement, society, environment* (Macclesfield, 2003).

Williamson, T., 'The distribution of "woodland" and "champion" landscapes in medieval England', in M. Gardiner and S. Rippon (eds), *Medieval landscapes* (Macclesfield, 2007), pp. 89–104.

Wilson, R.M., 'English place-name elements', *Review of English Studies*, 9 (1958), pp. 414–24.

Wright, T. and Wülcker, R.P., *Anglo-Saxon and Old English vocabularies*, 2 vols (London, 1884).

Youngs, F.A., *Guide to the local administrative units of England*, 2 vols (London, 1979 and 1991).

Zangemeister, C. (ed.), *Pauli Orosii Historiarum Adversum Paganos Libri VII* (Vienna, 1882).

Index

Individual *thorps* listed in appendix 2 are not indexed here. Pages numbers are given, however, for counties which appear in this handlist.

Thorp – or *throp* in some areas – is a common place-name or part
of a place-name in England. A standard explanation of them is that
unlike *tons*, *bys* and *hams*, *thorps* were small villages attached to more
important places. This new study combines the expertise of linguists
with archaeological evidence, and also examines the names found in
the north and south. It connects the origin of the names with major
changes in the landscape between 850 and 1250.

Thorps, far from lying on the fringes of the settled countryside, were
important because they helped to revolutionise farming methods. Rather than
dismissing them as 'secondary settlements' or dependent hamlets, we need
to think about the characteristics that made them distinctive and therefore
deserving of the name that they were given.

The authors consider the siting of *thorps* and *throps* in relation to the
landscape and to soil types in particular. Amply demonstrating the value of
an interdisciplinary approach to the study of early medieval settlement in
England, the authors are able to draw important conclusions about the changes
in farming that swept the country during this period and by association the
process of village nucleation. By examining both the chronology of place-
names in *thorp* and *throp* and their qualifying elements (notably the presence
or absence of personal names), it appears possible to chart both the speed at
which arable enterprises farmed in severalty converted to communal cultivation
as well as the direction in which the changes spread. There is a sense of real
excitement as many fresh insights are revealed in the course of the book.

Paul Cullen is a Research Associate in the Department of English, Linguistics and
Communication at the University of the West of England, working on the project *Family
Names of the United Kingdom*. He is also editor of the English Place-Name Society's Survey of
Kent and an Honorary Visiting Fellow in the Institute for Name-Studies at the University of
Nottingham.

Richard Jones is a Lecturer in Landscape History in the Centre for English Local History
at the University of Leicester. He is the co-author of *Medieval Villages in an English Landscape:
Beginnings and Ends*, which addresses the relationship between settlements and open-field
farming in the English Midlands, and co-editor of *Deserted Villages Revisited* (University of
Hertfordshire Press, 2010).

David Parsons was, until recently, Director of the Institute for Name-Studies at the
University of Nottingham, and is now Senior Research Fellow at the University of Wales
Centre for Advanced Welsh and Celtic Research. He is Deputy Director of the Survey of
English Place-Names, and the Survey's editor for Suffolk.

Front cover image courtesy of JRC Photography © 2010

ISBN 978-1-902806-82-2

University of Hertfordshire Press